Culture and Customs of Nicaragua

Nicaragua. Cartography by Bookcomp, Inc.

Culture and Customs of Nicaragua

STEVEN F. WHITE
AND ESTHELA CALDERÓN

Culture and Customs of Latin America and the Caribbean
Peter Standish, Series Editor

GREENWOOD PRESS
Westport, Connecticut • London

Library of Congress Cataloging-in-Publication Data

White, Steven F., 1955–
    Culture and customs of Nicaragua / Steven F. White and Esthela Calderón.
      p. cm. — (Culture and customs of Latin America and the Caribbean, ISSN 1521–8856)
    Includes bibliographical references and index.
    ISBN 978–0–313–33994–3 (alk. paper)
  1. Nicaragua—Civilization.   I. Calderon, Esthela, 1970– II. Title.
  F1523.8.W46   2008
  972.85—dc22   2007043154

British Library Cataloguing in Publication Data is available.

Library of Congress Catalog Card Number: 2007043154
ISBN: 978–0–313–33994–3
ISSN: 1521–8856

First published in 2008

Greenwood Press, 88 Post Road West, Westport, CT 06881
An imprint of Greenwood Publishing Group, Inc.
www.greenwood.com

Printed in the United States of America

The paper used in this book complies with the
Permanent Paper Standard issued by the National
Information Standards Organization (Z39.48–1984).

10 9 8 7 6 5 4 3 2 1

Contents

Series Foreword

CULTURE IS A problematic word. In everyday language we tend to use it in at least two senses. On the one hand, we speak of cultured people and places full of culture—uses that imply a knowledge or presence of certain forms of behavior or of artistic expression that are socially prestigious. In this sense, large cities and prosperous people tend to be seen as the most cultured. On the other hand, there is an interpretation of culture that is broader and more anthropological; culture in this broader sense refers to whatever traditions, beliefs, customs, and creative activities characterize a given community—in short, it refers to what makes that community different from others. In this second sense, everyone has culture; indeed, it is impossible to be without culture.

The problems associated with the idea of culture have been exacerbated in recent years by two trends: less respectful use of language and a greater blurring of cultural differences. Nowadays, culture often means little more than behavior, attitude, or atmosphere. We hear about the culture of the boardroom, of the football team, of the marketplace; there are books with titles like *The Culture of War* by Richard Gabriel (1990) or *The Culture of Narcissism* by Christopher Lasch (1979). In fact, as Christopher Clausen points out in an article published in the *American Scholar* (Summer 1996), we have got ourselves into trouble by using the term so sloppily.

People who study culture generally assume that culture (in the anthropological sense) is learned, not genetically determined. Another general assumption made in these days of multiculturalism has been that cultural differences should be respected rather than put under pressure to change. But these assumptions, too, have sometimes proved to be problematic. Multiculturalism is a fine ideal, but in practice it is not always easy to reconcile with the beliefs of the very people who advocate it—for example, is female circumcision an issue of human rights or just a different cultural practice?

The blurring of cultural differences is a process that began with the steamship, increased with radio, and is now racing ahead with the Internet. We are becoming globally homogenized. Since the English-speaking world (and the United States in particular) is the dominant force behind this process of homogenization, it behooves us to make efforts to understand the sensibilities of members of other cultures.

This series of books, a contribution toward that greater understanding, deals with the neighbors of the United States, with people who have just as much right to call themselves Americans. What are the historical, institutional, religious, and artistic features that make up the modern culture of such peoples as the Haitians, the Chileans, the Jamaicans, and the Guatemalans? How are their habits and assumptions different from our own? What can we learn from them? As we familiarize ourselves with the ways of other countries, we come to see our own from a new perspective.

Each volume in the series focuses on a single country. With slight variations to accommodate national differences, each begins by outlining the historical, political, ethnic, geographical, and linguistic context, as well as the religious and social customs, and then proceeds to a discussion of a variety of artistic activities, including the media, cinema, literature, and the visual and performing arts. The authors are all intimately acquainted with the countries concerned; some were born or brought up in them, and each has a professional commitment to enhancing the understanding of the culture in question.

We are inclined to suppose that our ways of thinking and behaving are normal. And so they are . . . for us. We all need to realize that ours is only one culture among many, and that it is hard to establish by any rational criteria that ours as a whole is any better (or worse) than any other. As individual members of our immediate community, we know that we must learn to respect our differences from one another. Respect for differences between cultures is no less vital. This is particularly true of the United States, a nation of immigrants, but one that sometimes seems to be bent on destroying variety at home and, worse still, on having others follow suit. By learning about other people's cultures, we come to understand and respect them; we earn their respect for us; and, not least, we see ourselves in a new light.

Peter Standish
East Carolina University

Preface

A BOOK OF this kind reveals a country's positive and negative qualities, as well as its aspirations. *Culture and Customs of Nicaragua* attempts to give the reader insight into a people whose optimistic and rebellious spirit informs their unique sense of identity. Writing about Nicaragua is a difficult and dangerous task because it is a country composed of dark and painful events that include Spanish colonial rule, U.S. military intervention, the Somoza dictatorship (supported for nearly 50 years by eight successive U.S. presidents), certain aspects of the Sandinista revolution, and corruption and political processes that have produced polarization and misery among the Nicaraguan population. Nicaragua differs from other Central American countries because it has two histories—one before the Sandinista Revolution of 1979 and one after the revolution. It also can be seen as a republic that can be divided into two worlds: one composed of people who live on the Pacific side, who speak Spanish and who are predominantly Catholic, and another on the Caribbean coast, where the majority of the people speak a Creole English and belong to the Moravian Church.

Culture and customs involve more than the history of a country. The chapters in this broad-ranging book contain everything from the music of Nicaragua to the poetic voice of Rubén Darío (1867–1916), a world-class literary figure who renovated the Spanish language and created the influential literary movement called *modernismo*. Internationally recognized painters such as Armando Morales also contribute to a sense of national pride. Dance is another facet of Nicaragua's cultural richness in a variety of forms, from the Afro-Caribbean dances of the Atlantic coast, to the *mazurkas* of northern Nicaragua, to the variety of dance steps associated with the Pacific part of the country. The joyous popular festivals known as *fiestas patronales* are a mixture of elements with both indigenous and Spanish origins.

References to these mestizo (European and Amerindian) characteristics permeate the entire book. Nicaragua's pre-Columbian history includes a wide variety of indigenous groups (Chorotegas, Caribisis, Sutiabas, Nagrándanos, Niquiranos, and Matagalpas, among many others), emigrating south from what is now Mexico, as well as north from South America, and bringing different languages and cultures with them on their long journeys. Indeed, contemporary Nicaraguan Spanish has a rich vocabulary derived from these linguistic sources that predate the arrival of the Spaniards. The indigenous influence that persists to this day can be found in the name of the country. According to one hypothesis, "Nicaragua" comes from the Náhuatl language and means "the journey of the people from Anahuac ends here," referring to an ancient postwar exodus of a defeated indigenous group moving south from Central Mexico. Another theory is that the name corresponds to the name of Nicarao, an early sixteenth-century indigenous leader who maintained a famous dialogue with the Spanish conquistador Gil González, who was astonished by the philosophical sophistication and audacious nature of the Indian cacique's questions. Among other matters related to religion and the cosmos, Nicarao asked Gil González, "Why so much gold for so few men?"

Historical documents from the colonial period clearly demonstrate the persistence of certain characteristics of Nicaraguan culture and customs. These include the sometimes servile adulation of the powerful political figures called *caudillos,* a satirical sarcastic spirit, *machismo,* a culture of prohibition, the violent imposition of ideas despite established laws, the dream of an interoceanic canal, and a fatalism resulting from the harsh realities of extreme poverty and devastating natural disasters.[1]

Included in these pages is a panorama of myths and legends that have been preserved as part of an age-old oral tradition passed on from one generation to the next.

There are also references to Nicaragua's most important cities, as well as to a biologically diverse landscape characterized by volcanoes, mountains, huge lakes, plains, and two bordering oceans. Nicaragua also has a rich architectural heritage of religious and colonial structures that, over the centuries, have been whipped by hurricanes, toppled by earthquakes, and scarred by the fire of pirates and the gunfire of civil wars. Its population of nearly 6 million lives in an area of more than 50,000 square miles, which makes Nicaragua roughly the size of New York state. Much of this area, however, is uninhabited and inaccessible given the harsh geographic conditions and an infrastructure that makes travel by land difficult, especially during the rainy season.

With the exception of the dozen years from 1978–1990 that correspond to the Sandinista revolution and its conflicts with the government of Ronald Reagan, Nicaragua does not figure prominently on the front pages of newspapers or as the lead story on television in the United States. But Nicaragua sometimes emerges in unexpected contexts. For example, during the nineteenth-century gold rush years in the United States, the safest and fastest way to travel between San Francisco and New York was by boat and land through Nicaragua, a journey that Mark Twain describes in his *Travels with Mr. Brown.* In addition, scientists recently have made breakthrough discoveries regarding Darwin's ideas on evolution based on studies of two species of cichlid fish that live in Nicaragua's isolated volcanic crater Lake Apoyo. Mostly, however, Nicaragua's ties with the United States are political, filled with controversy over a long time, beginning with the Monroe Doctrine of 1823.

Much of the information incorporated in these pages was obtained through personal interviews with people who have a deep knowledge and appreciation for Nicaraguan popular culture and an understanding of how it contributes to a collective sense of identity and resistance. In Nicaragua, people believe that reality and myth are often intertwined. This can be seen especially in terms of the mythic heroism of historical figures such as Augusto C. Sandino (1895–1934), who waged a successful guerrilla war in Nicaragua against occupying U.S. Marines.

The book presents an eclectic array of subjects. Some are still considered taboo in Nicaragua, such as AIDS and a gay community that survives in a homophobic society. The topic of women's rights addressed in the chapter on social customs is still not a primary concern in a country where the rules and regulations are made by men and where women traditionally have been under-represented in positions of political authority at the national and local levels. Sports certainly could not remain outside the scope of this project, as Nicaraguans such as Denis Martínez and Alexis Argüello are world-renowned figures in baseball and boxing.

Here, in these pages, is an immense window on Nicaragua's culture and customs. It is hoped that readers will be able to admire the country for what it has been, is, and is yet to become.

NOTE

1. See Nicasio Urbina Guerrero "¿Cómo las voces sostienen las acciones?: textos fundacionales de la nacionalidad nicaragüense," pp. 7–22, Introduction to Orlando Cuadra Downing, ed. *La voz sostenida: antología del pensamiento nicaragüense.* Managua: PAVSA, 2007.

Acknowledgments

THE AUTHORS THANK Estela Chévez Vega, María Manuela Sacasa de Prego, Manuel Calderón, Yolando Padilla de Jirón, Edgardo Buitrago Buitrago, Porfirio García Romano, Clemente Guido, and Wilmor López for their time and for the important contributions they made to enrich the contents of this book.

Chronology

3000 B.C.	The first inhabitants of the area now known as Nicaragua arrive.
A.D. 1064–1168	The Toltecs make their incursions, moving south from the Aztec Empire.
1200–1500	The Ulúa (Chibcha) Indians emigrate north from the region now known as Colombia.
1502	Christopher Columbus reaches Nicaragua.
1512	The Spanish conquistador Gil González discovers the southern part of Nicaragua.
1513	Vasco Núñez de Balboa discovers the Pacific Ocean.
1519	Vasco Núñez de Balboa is decapitated by Pedrarias Dávila. Spanish Court names Gil González Capitán General.
1520	Pedrarias Dávila orders expeditions to Nicaragua under the command of Gil González.
1522	First indigenous uprising against Gil González.
1523	Gil González leaves Nicaragua.
1524	Francisco Hernández de Córdoba arrives in Nicaragua, establishes the cities of Granada and León, and declares Granada the capital of the Province, initiating a nearly 300-year period of colonial rule.

1526	Pedrarias Dávila moves to Nicaragua and has Francisco Hernández de Córdoba executed in the plaza of León. Gil González dies in Avila, Spain.
1527	Pedrarias Dávila is named governor of Nicaragua.
1528	Pedrarias Dávila condemns 18 indigenous leaders to be devoured by dogs.
1579	The infamous English pirate Francis Drake attacks the southern coast of Central America.
1610	As a consequence of the eruption of the Momotombo volcano, León is moved to its current location on land that belonged to the Sutiaba Indians.
1633	England establishes commercial relations with the indigenous population of the Atlantic coast.
1663	Strong tremors raise the bed of the San Juan River, thereby impeding the passage of large ships.
1665	English pirates in alliance with the Miskito Indians sack the city of Granada.
1666	The Spaniards construct a fort at San Carlos.
1685	Pirate attacks destroy Granada and León.
1687	The first king of the Miskito Indians is crowned by the governor of Jamaica.
1698	Buccaneers and Miskito Indians establish the Caribbean settlement of Bragman's Bluff, now known as Puerto Cabezas.
1714	The king of Spain orders the extermination of the Miskito Indians.
1740	The Mosquito Coast (Mosquitia), the area near the Caribbean in northeastern Nicaragua inhabited by the Miskito Indians, is declared a protectorate of England.
1749	The zambo Miskito Indians from the Nicaraguan Caribbean invade Chontales and Matagalpa.
1754	The Miskitos capture and kill the governor of Costa Rica.
1769	Nicaraguan historical heroine Doña Rafaela Herrera defends the Castle of the Immaculate Conception and holds off the English attackers.
1781	The engineer Manuel Galisteo arrives to do the first study on the possibility of constructing an interoceanic canal.

1796   San Juan del Norte is established as a port at the mouth of the San Juan River.

1811   The first revolutionary movements erupt in Central America against Spanish colonial rule.

1821   The process of Nicaraguan independence begins when the captaincy general of Guatemala declares its independence from Spanish rule.

1823   Mexican attempts to control the captaincy general of Guatemala provoke conflicts throughout Central America and lead to five of the United Provinces of Central America (including Nicaragua) to declare their independence from Mexico in July. The expansionist policy of the United States government toward Latin America known as the Monroe Doctrine begins.

1824   Nicaragua is proclaimed a state of the Federal Republic of Central America.

1835   *Telégrafo nicaragüense,* the first newspaper in Nicaragua, is published.

1837   The English engineer John Baily begins detailed studies and surveys the route of the interoceanic canal.

1838   Nicaragua secedes from the Federal Republic of Central America and, through a Constituent Assembly, declares its independence. José Núñez is elected Nicaragua's head of state.

1847   Two new newspapers, *El regenerador nicaragüense* and *El noticioso,* begin to circulate. The first missionaries of the Moravian Church arrive in Mosquitia.

1848   The British take over the port of San Juan del Norte.

1849   The British impose a treaty that grants them control over the Mosquito Coast. The official newspaper *La gaceta* is founded. A civil war between Granada (the Timbucos) and León (the Calandracas) begins. Ephraim George Squier arrives in Nicaragua as the first U.S. representative to visit the country. Cornelius Vanderbilt and the Nicaraguan government sign a treaty that grants Vanderbilt's company the right to construct a canal across the isthmus. A land and water route across Nicaragua enables passengers to travel from the eastern United States to California as the gold rush begins. The treaty with the United States and the contract with Vanderbilt's Accessory Transit Company is approved by the Nicaraguan Congress.

1850   British and U.S. officials sign the Clayton-Bulwer Treaty in which both governments agreed that neither country would have exclusive rights over the canal that was being built.

1854   A new constitution (the third) is promulgated. Complex alliances between liberal and conservative forces with sympathetic governments of neighboring countries weaken Nicaragua.

1855   The civil war continues. Conservative President Fruto Chamorro dies. A group of filibusters from the United States headed by William Walker, a mercenary born in Tennessee, arrives in Nicaragua and seizes Granada with the aid of Nicaraguan liberals.

1856   Walker establishes Patricio Rivas as president of a liberal puppet government while increasing his own political and military strength. Walker makes English the official language of Nicaragua and proceeds with plans to legalize slavery in the country and annex it to the United States as a slave state. An alliance of conservative forces throughout Central America, Vanderbilt, and the British Navy forms to expel the U.S. invaders. Walker retreats from Granada and burns the city to the ground.

1857   The National War culminates in the spring in the southern Nicaraguan town of Rivas. Walker surrenders but is allowed to return to the United States with his troops. Thirty years of Conservative rule in Nicaragua begins.

1858   The Cañas-Jerez Treaty is signed with Costa Rica.

1860   Walker publishes his book, *The War in Nicaragua*. On his fourth attempt to return to Central America, Walker is captured and shot in Trujillo, Honduras.

1867   The poet Rubén Darío is born.

1877   Indigenous communities rebel against the promulgation of the Agrarian Law of President Pedro Joaquín Chamorro Alfaro.

1881   The municipality of Telica in León is seized by indigenous groups protesting the government's expropriation of land. The government sends troops to occupy the indigenous areas called Sutiaba and El Laborío.

1893   The liberal bourgeoisie takes power by means of the repressive military dictatorship of José Santos Zelaya, who remains in power for 16 years. An agreement between Zelaya's government and the British allows Nicaragua to reincorporate the Caribbean coast into its national territory, although the area was to remain physically and culturally separate from western Nicaragua.

1909   The consul of the United States in Bluefields, Thomas Moffat, in conjunction with British interests, provides the political and financial support to undertake an armed rebellion to overthrow Zelaya. On December 1, the United States breaks off relations with Zelaya by means of the infamous "Knox Note" sent by U.S. Secretary of State Philander C. Knox, in which the intervention is announced. Zelaya resigns and goes into exile in New York.

1912   At the request of Conservative President Adolfo Díaz, who hopes to stave off a threat to his government by Liberals Luis Mena and Benjamín Zeledón, U.S. troops land at the port of Corinto and Bluefields and take control of the railroad line to Managua.

1916   The Chamorro-Bryan Treaty, which gives the United States the right to build a canal in Nicaragua that could rival the one opened in Panama two years earlier, is ratified by the U.S. Senate and transforms Nicaragua into a virtual protectorate of the United States. Poet Rubén Darío dies in León.

1925   The occupying force of U.S. Marines temporarily leaves Nicaragua.

1927   As a result of violent conflicts between Liberal and Conservative contenders for political power, the U.S. government sends Henry Stimson, who succeeds in negotiating a peace accord known as the Pact of Espino Negro with Liberal General José María Moncada. Liberal rebel leader Augusto César Sandino does not sign this agreement and forms his Army for the Defense of Nicaraguan Sovereignty, which is based on an isolated mountain refuge in northern Nicaragua called "El Chipote."

1930   Sandino's guerrilla army inflicts serious casualties against the U.S. military forces, who use the most advanced technology of the time, including history's first aerial bombardments of civilian populations (in Ocotal), to try to win the war.

1933   In January, after U.S. troops leave Nicaragua having created in their place a National Guard under the command of Anastasio Somoza García, Sandino agrees to hold meetings with the recently elected government of Juan Bautista Sacasa.

1934   Somoza assassinates Sandino in February and hunts down the remaining members of Sandino's army.

1936   In December, Somoza García is elected president of Nicaragua for the Liberal Party in an election with suspiciously lopsided results and resumes the control of the National Guard that he relinquished temporarily in order to fulfill constitutional requirements as a presidential candidate. This is the beginning of a military dictatorship and family dynasty that lasts for more than 40 years.

1950   Cotton becomes the most important Nicaraguan export. Somoza García signs agreement with Conservative General Emiliano Chamorro Vargas that gives the Conservative elite enough political and economic benefits to ensure the continued power of the Somoza regime. Somoza García is reelected president.

1956   Somoza García, attending a party at the Casa del Obrero in León, is gunned down by the young poet Rigoberto López Pérez. Somoza García's son Luis, as head of the Nicaraguan Congress, becomes president.

1959   National Guard massacres students in León.

1961   Carlos Fonseca founds the Frente Sandinista de Liberación Nacional (FSLN).

1963   The armed struggle against Somoza begins with attacks in Río Coco and Bocay.

            René Schick Gutiérrez wins the presidential elections, but his government is controlled by Luis and Anastasio Somoza Debayle.

1967   Anastasio Somoza Debayle is elected president. FSLN launches an attack in the mountains of Pancasán.

1971   Anastasio Somoza Debayle signs the Kupia-Kumi Pact, which creates a Liberal-Conservative three-person junta under Somoza's control to rule Nicaragua from 1972–1974.

1972   On December 23, an earthquake measuring 6.5 on the Richter scale destroys much of the urban center of the capital city Managua, killing 10,000 people. Somoza's National Guard loots destroyed businesses. Somoza shocks the international community by pocketing much of the foreign aid that arrives for reconstruction efforts.

1974   Somoza is reelected president despite Liberal opposition in his own party, the PLN. Pedro Joaquín Chamorro, director of the opposition newspaper *La Prensa,* forms the Democratic Liberation Union (UDEL in Spanish), which is composed of business and labor groups opposed to the Somoza dictatorship. Somoza increases political repression and censorship of all media. Popular uprisings, especially in the mountains of northern Nicaragua, are more frequent and debilitating to the National Guard. A Sandinista commando captures many high-level Somoza supporters at the home of José María Castillo and receives safe passage to Cuba, a $1 million ransom, and extensive media coverage.

1976	Carlos Fonseca, the leader of the FSLN, dies in combat.
1977	The Somoza dictatorship, supported by eight successive U.S. presidents, weakens. In October, the Group of Twelve, consisting of important Nicaraguan economic and cultural figures, forms an alliance against Somoza.
1978	In January, Pedro Joaquín Chamorro, Director of *La Prensa,* is murdered under mysterious circumstances, which produces widespread demonstrations against the Somoza regime. On January 23, a national strike paralyzes the country. U.S. President Jimmy Carter, citing general human rights violations in Nicaragua, suspends all U.S. military assistance to Nicaragua. In March, business leaders opposed to Somoza form the Nicaraguan Democratic Movement (MDN). In May, the Broad Opposition Front (FAO) forms, uniting against Somoza, the Conservative Party, the UDEL, the Group of Twelve, and the MDN. In August, an FSLN commando led by Edén Pastora seizes the National Palace during a meeting of Congress and takes 2,000 government officials hostage. Somoza grants the Sandinistas' requests for release of prisoners, safe passage out of the country, media coverage of guerrilla demands, and $500,000 ransom. September insurrection occurs in León, Masaya, Estelí, and Chinandega.
1979	In February, the Sandinistas form a broad opposition group, the National Patriotic Front (FPN). In March, the three factions of the Frente Sandinista (Proletarians, Prolonged Popular War, and Third Way) formally unite as a result of Cuban mediation. In June, a five-member provisional Nicaraguan government in exile is formed in Costa Rica that includes Daniel Ortega and Violeta Chamorro (widow of the murdered director of *La Prensa*), two future presidents of Nicaragua. Also in June, ABC correspondent Bill Stewart is summarily shot by Somoza's National Guard. The shocking video footage of his death as a journalist is broadcast around the world. The final offensive of the uprising against Somoza begins. León and other important cities are liberated. Somoza flees Nicaragua with his father's remains, seeking asylum in the United States and then Paraguay. The FSLN army enters Managua and celebrates the triumph of the Nicaraguan people on July 19.
1980	Massive numbers of volunteers initiate a national literacy campaign. Property owned by Somoza and his family, accounting for 20 percent of Nicaragua's arable land, is confiscated by the government. Mines and businesses owned by U.S. interests are expropriated, and 3,500 ex-members of the National Guard seek asylum in Costa Rica. Somoza is killed by an Argentine guerrilla commando in Asunción, Paraguay.

1981   The government institutes an Agrarian Reform Law and distributes land to peasants organized in cooperatives. U.S. President Ronald Reagan cuts off all aid to Nicaragua and gives support to groups called Contras who are based in Honduras and seek to overthrow the Sandinista government.

1982   Creation of the Nicaraguan Democratic Front, based in Honduras, which opposed the Sandinista government. The Sandinistas begin a highly controversial plan to relocate the Miskito Indian population living on traditional lands in northern Nicaragua on the war-torn border with Honduras.

1983   Pope John Paul II visits Nicaragua and enters into an open conflict with the Sandinista government that damages the government's reputation internationally.

1984   In November, Daniel Ortega is elected president with 67 percent of the vote; 75 percent of the country's registered voters cast ballots.

1985   As a result of an intensification of the Contra War, the Nicaraguan government institutes compulsory military service in the Sandinista People's Army (EPS), which increases the army's size to about 80,000 troops, the largest in Central America, as well as the number of deaths of the young drafted soldiers. In April, the U.S. Congress votes to suspend all aid to the Contras. As a way of circumventing this decision, Oliver North orchestrates a plan on behalf of the Reagan administration to sell weapons to the Iranian government and secretly use these funds to support the Contras. Also in April, Ronald Reagan calls for a complete embargo on U.S. trade with Nicaragua.

1986   The International Court of Justice at The Hague rules in favor of Nicaragua, saying that the United States needs to pay Nicaragua for damages incurred during the Contra War financed by the Reagan administration. U.S. military advisor Eugene Hasenfus is shot down in his plane in southern Nicaragua and captured alive by the Sandinista Army.

1987   The Esquipulas II accords are signed by all five Central American republics, creating a basis for peace and national reconciliation in Nicaragua, as well as in Guatemala and El Salvador.

1988   In March, the Sandinista government signs a peace agreement with the Contras, freeing all political prisoners. In October, Hurricane Joan hits the Caribbean coast of Nicaragua, causing $1 billion in damage.

1989	A severe drought has catastrophic effects on Nicaragua's agricultural production. An agreement is signed by the leaders of Central America to facilitate the disarming and reintegration of Contra forces based in Honduras. In September, in preparation for presidential elections to be held in February 1990, 14 political parties unite against the Sandinistas as the National Opposition Union (UNO) nominate Violeta Chamorro as their presidential candidate.
1990	Chamorro, promising peace and an end to compulsory military service, wins a surprise victory in the elections with 55 percent of the popular vote as compared to Daniel Ortega's 41 percent. In May, the Sandinistas, in conjunction with UNO and Contra representatives, sign a formal ceasefire, producing a complete demobilization of the Contra forces a month later.
1991	As president, Violet Chamorro foregoes the indemnity awarded to Nicaragua by the International Court of The Hague after the United States threatens to cut off aid to Nicaragua.
1992	Eruption of the Cerro Negro volcano affects more than 120,000 people.
1993	Tropical Storm Gert causes a national disaster.
1994	Nicaraguan writers José Coronel Urtecho and Edelberto Torres die.
1996	John Paul II makes his second trip to Nicaragua. Arnoldo Alemán, of the Constitutionalist Liberal Party (PLC), is elected president of Nicaragua.
1998	Hurricane Mitch devastates Nicaragua, killing 3,000 people, displacing 20 percent of the country's population, and damaging important parts of Nicaragua's infrastructure.
2000	Poet Rubén Darío is named person of the millennium by the BBC in London.
2001	Enrique Bolaños, of the Conservative Party, in alliance with the PLC, is elected president.
2002	Poet Pablo Antonio Cuadra dies.
2003	Former President Arnoldo Alemán is convicted of corruption and money laundering and sentenced to 20 years in prison.
2004	Two journalists, Carlos Guadamuz in Managua and María José Bravo in Juigalpa, are murdered. José Jirón Terán, the most important disseminator of the work of Rubén Darío, dies in León.
2006	Daniel Ortega wins the presidential elections, and the Sandinistas return to power.

1

Context: Land, People, and History

OFFICIAL NICARAGUA

THE CONFIGURATION OF the Nicaraguan territory is varied and pictur-esque, with numerous volcanoes, lakes, mountains, mesas, plains, lagoons, and valleys. The total area of Nicaragua is more than 50,000 square miles, which makes it the largest country in Central America. It is approximately the same size as the state of New York. Located in the Central American isthmus, Nicaragua links the North and South American continents. To the north of Nicaragua is Honduras, and to the south Costa Rica. To the east lies the Caribbean Ocean, and to the West is the Pacific Ocean. Its geographical coordinates are 13° N, 85° W.

Nicaragua's government is described as a democratic republic. It is a uni-fied, free, sovereign, and independent state that is divided into 15 depart-ments and 2 autonomous regions (on the Caribbean coast). The country has 152 municipalities. Nicaragua's most important cities include the capital Managua, León, Granada, Chinandega, Masaya, Estelí, Jinotega, Bluefields, and Puerto Cabezas. The official currency is the córdoba, which is available in denominations of coins and paper money. The official language of Nicara-gua is Spanish, but in the autonomous regions there is also the official use of English, Miskito, Sumo, and Rama, among other languages.

There is freedom of religion in Nicaragua. The majority (73%) is Catholic, although Evangelicals (15%) are increasing in number. The Moravian Church has a presence on the Atlantic coast, although its members represent only 1.5 percent of the religious affiliations in the country as a whole.

The climate is tropical in the lowland areas, with a rainy season that lasts from May through October and also a six-month dry season from November through April in the Pacific region. The average annual maximum temperature is 95° F and the minimum is 77° F. In the mountainous areas, the rainy season lasts until January. On the Atlantic coast, it rains throughout almost the entire year.

Nicaragua's total population is 5.6 million, of which 54.5 percent live in cities and 45 percent live in rural areas. Nicaragua has an annual growth rate of 2.7 percent (with an average fertility rate of three children per woman), the highest in Latin America whose average annual growth rate is 1.6 percent. The fertility rate among adolescents ages 15–19 is 119 births per 1,000 women. For every 1,000 births, 31 die. The life expectancy for the total population is 70 years. The illiteracy rate is 34.3 percent for adults over the age of 15. Each year, 800,000 children remain outside the classroom. The unemployment rate is 25 percent and 1.6 million people are employed.

The country's principal economic activities are agriculture, cattle, and fishing in the primary sector and mining, industry, and construction in the secondary sector. A third sector that includes government, commerce,

The image of San Marcos carried under a clear sky by traditional devotees who are fulfilling promises they made to the saint. © Wilmor López. Used by permission.

transportation, and banking produces 50 percent of Nicaragua's revenue. One of the main challenges facing the Nicaraguan people is to develop the commercial and social capacity to thrive economically. After Haiti, Nicaragua is the second poorest Latin American country. In Nicaragua, tourism is an important source of income, as well as remittances sent by the substantial number of Nicaraguans living and working outside the country. The latter constitutes more than 25 percent of Nicaragua's GNP, $1 billion in 2005.

Nicaragua has tremendous biodiversity. The conservation of these resources in such a poor country will present many challenges in terms of creating national policies of sustainable development.

The symbols that represent the country are the national flag, which is white and blue with three horizontal stripes of equal size. The blue stripes are on the top and bottom and represent the two oceans that border Nicaragua. In the center, the white stripe represents purity. In the center of the white stripe is the shield, an equilateral triangle containing a series of five volcanoes at the base that evoke the five countries of the Central America isthmus. The rainbow in the shield is a symbol of peace, and the Phrygian cap an emblem of liberty, casting rays of light.

Nicaraguans celebrate their independence from Spain (in 1821) on September 15, which is a national holiday. The national anthem of Nicaragua was written in 1918 by Salomón Ibarra Mayorga (1890–1985). The national bird is the *guardabarranco* the red-backed motmot. The national tree is the *madroño*, lemonwood. The national flower is the *sacuanjoche,* or *flor de mayo,* white frangipani.

Typical food in Nicaragua includes rice, beans, tortillas, and the *nacatamal,* which is dough made from corn filled with pieces of pork and wrapped in banana leaves tied together with the veins of the banana leaves or with twine. The typical Nicaraguan drink is *pinol,* which is made from the flour of toasted corn. The national dance is drawn from a work of theater entitled *El Güegüense, or Macho Ratón,* which was declared patrimony of humanity by UNESCO in 2005.

The mixture of ethnic groups in Nicaragua breaks down as follows: 69 percent *mestizo* (mixed Amerindian and white), 17 percent white, 9 percent black, and 5 percent Amerindian.

Pre-Columbian Indigenous History and Culture

Because of its geographical location in Central America as a kind of continental bridge between North and South America, Nicaragua has always been a crossroads for diverse migrating species including, of course, human beings, representing a wide variety of ethnic groups with different cultures and customs. At the time of the Spanish conquest in the early sixteenth century, the indigenous group with the most marked presence in the area now known as Nicaragua was of Nahuatl origin. Most studies agree that it was this group from the Aztec culture and civilization situated in what is now Mexico that expanded south throughout the isthmus. The descendants of those who migrated from the north established a system of domination that connected the different peoples of the Pacific and the center. The remaining population was pushed to the periphery of the territory, where it coexisted with various ethnic groups and cultures.[1]

It is believed that the Toltecs were the first group to emigrate to Nicaragua, perhaps as early as 3000 B.C. Their last incursions occurred between 1064 and 1168. Afterward, the Ulúa, or Chibcha, Indians emigrated north from what is now Colombia, and more immigrants headed south, including the Chorotega and Nicarao Indians from 1200–1500. A number of ethnic groups came to share a language and worldview, including the Chorotegas (and their subgroups the Nagrándanos and the Dirianes), the Nicaraos, the Mariabios and the Caribisis. Náhuatl became the most commonly spoken language, or *lingua franca*, as a result of the political and economic control of its speakers in the region.

Forms of Indigenous Government

Two systems of government were practiced among the different tribes that inhabited the territory before the Spanish conquest. Some were ruled by a republican form of government, with a council of respected elders elected by the people carrying out civil power. The people also chose a captain for war. The duties imposed on him were very strict. Respect for the authority of the elders was so great that there was no danger of usurpations on behalf of the captain. Furthermore, if the captain did not fulfill his duties or if there were suspicions of treason, he was put to death. This republican form of government was destroyed by the conquistadors, who, in order to better make use of the Indians, divided up the diverse domains among senators, giving them absolute power by breaking up the territories.

Other tribes were ruled by a moderated monarchy. The supreme power was exercised by the caciques called *Teytes* who organized popular assemblies directed by a council of elders called *Monexico*. The cacique proposed to the assembly the measures that were in the best interest of the "nation," and the assembly, after discussing these measures, approved, rejected, or expedited those that were most urgent. This combination of monarchy and democracy among the so-called savage tribes of Nicaragua is similar to the ideas adopted by some contemporary "civilized" European nations. In the monarchical tribes, the cacique was surrounded by princes or lords who formed a kind of courtly nobility. Such was the case of the caciques known as Teocatega, Mistega, Nicaragua, and Nicoya.

INDIGENOUS RELIGIONS

Among the aboriginal inhabitants of Nicaragua, there was a diversity of religions, depending on the ethnic group. In general, they believed in an afterlife and had gods called "teotes," some of whom demanded human sacrifice (like those of the Nicarao Indians) so that there would be rain, food, and good luck during time of war. Other gods were offered flowers, birds, honey, and fruit. But they all had to be invoked and recognized with tributes. Other gods who were worshipped included Quiateot, god of water; Visteot, god of hunger; Mixcoa, god of commerce; Macat, god of the deer hunt; Teoste, god of the rabbit hunt; and Miquetanteot, god of darkness and the underworld, who dragged the *yulio,* or soul, from those whose lack of merit would not privilege them to live after death at the side of Tamagastad, creator of the world and all things. According to their beliefs, Tamagastad and the goddess Cipaltonal were both helped in the creation by the lesser gods Ochomogo, Calchitguegue, and Chicociagat after the destruction caused by a flood. For this reason, the human race descended from them.

In primitive times, Tamagastad and Cipaltonal were believed to have lived on earth as humans, eating the same food of divine origin that their indigenous worshippers ate. While they inhabited this world, it is said that the two gods disseminated the culture that humanity enjoys. Later, they rose into heaven (which is where the sun rises), where they ruled a paradise in which the souls of those who fall in combat enjoy infinite pleasure. These celestial beings joined as a couple were perceived by the Indians to be creator deities, cultural heroes, and gods who rule heaven. The aboriginal inhabitants of Nicaragua considered themselves worthy descendants of these gods and saw themselves reflected in the mythic existence of Tamagastad, using the myth of the wise ruler who made humans to clarify his own existence. If Tamagastad represents an eternal masculine principle of the youthful hero, Cipaltonal embodies the feminine principle of fertility and sexual duality in association with her male counterpart. The goddess's name, Cipaltonal (in the Nahuatl language) joins the terrestrial and the celestial, for it combines the alligator (*cipactli*) with a burning spirit (*tonalli*). Although it may be simplistic to say that these mythic figures offer some understanding of contemporary Nicaraguan character, the magical relationship between the people and their ruler conceived as a caudillo does seem to persist. Tamagastad, after all, is the heroic ruler of a people who emigrated because of wars, disease and hunger, a people who preferred the hardship of beginning a new life in a new land to being the slaves of their enemies.[2]

Commerce of the Indigenous Inhabitants

The exchange of staple products was well organized in Nicaragua and was carried out primarily by women and children. Each village had its own market or *tiangue* controlled by two employees of the Monexico, the Council of Elders. If any man from the village were to enter the *tiangue*, he would be subjected to insults and beatings; however, foreign allies or friends of the tribe were allowed entrance. Money was derived from the Cacao tree called Pek and was denominated in the following way: each *contle* was worth 400 seeds, each *xhiquipil* was worth 200 *contles*, and each *carga* was worth three *xhiquipiles*. In the market, one could buy slaves, gold, vegetables, meat, and other items. It was prohibited by law to buy or sell anything outside the market.

DISCOVERY AND CONQUEST

It is clear, then, that at the time of the conquest, there already existed in Nicaragua a population with its own culture that was subdivided into many different ethnic groups. The main groups were the Náhuatl, Chorotegas, and Sutiabas, who lived along the Pacific coast; the Chontales, Lencas, Panamakas, Cukras, Prinsas, Bawiskas, and Tawiskas, who populated the eastern and central parts of the country; and the Xicates, Sumos, and Miskitos on the Caribbean coast and the southern shore.

On September 12, 1502, Christopher Columbus reached Nicaragua in his search for a possible passage to another sea, but the first documented meeting of a Nicaraguan indigenous leader and a Spanish conquistador did not take place until 1512 in Nicaraocalli (now known as Rivas) between Nicarao and Gil González. The Indian cacique and his tribe were read the Spanish demands in the form of the *Requerimiento*, which simply declared that the lands were conquered for the Spanish King Ferdinand of Castille and León, Queen Juana, and their daughter, who were called "tamers of barbarians." Afterwards, Nicarao and Gil González had a famous dialogue in which the cacique seriously questioned the Spaniards from an economic point of view and held a series of discussions about whether or not slavery was legal, leaving the Spanish adversaries frightened by the Indian leader's intelligence and ability to reason. Nicarao also had other questions regarding, for example, how the wind blew; the general end of the human lineage; the final destination of souls when they leave the bodies where they are imprisoned; when the sun, moon, and stars will cease to shine; the movement, quantity, distance, and effect of the stars; and the causes of warm and cold weather.

Nicarao wanted to know the opinion of the powerful Spanish king about a past cataclysm that had destroyed the entire earth with all its humanity and animals, something the Indian leader had heard from his elders. He then asked if all the Spaniards had come from the sky, to which the interpreter replied affirmatively. Then the cacique asked how they descended. Did they come down in a straight line, spinning, or with an arching movement? To this question there was no answer. He then asked if the earth at some point would roll over on its back. He then asked why so few people wanted so much gold. Although Gil González was an intelligent man and a reader of books translated into Latin, he had not received enough instruction to give sufficient answers. He said that the answers to all those questions could be given only by God. As a way of gaining time in the face of the imminent Spanish domination, Nicarao accepted being baptized together with those who accompanied him. Gil González continued with his mission as conquistador by reading the *Requerimiento* to the Indians and baptizing them.

In another encounter, the cacique Diriangén went to meet the Spaniards with several gifts. He wanted to discover for sure whether these men covered with shiny armor were divine. To find out, he made some young Indian women stand before the conquistadors and ordered them to rub the Spaniards' genitals, thus discovering that they were, in fact, mere mortals. The cacique thought it would be prudent to let three days pass in order to consult with his priests and decide if he would allow himself and his people to be baptized. He employed this strategy to give himself time to prepare for war once he realized that the Spaniards were men and not gods.

When the allotted time ran out, he went to meet the Spaniards not to be baptized but to fight. He returned well armed and proud and struck the place where the Spaniards were encamped with great fervor, keeping it under attack the entire day. When night came, Diriangén returned to his village and gathered his indigenous allies to reinforce the struggle. Frightened by the violence of the indigenous attacks and by the prospect of losing the gold that they had already accumulated, the Spaniards retreated, fleeing toward the sea on other roads. In a similar way, Nicarao, even though he had accepted baptism, did not hesitate to attack Gil González. In both cases, the indigenous actions were astute, for they relied on different approaches to gain time to study the possibilities of successfully defeating the invader.

The men under the command of Gil González returned so happily to Panamá with the wealth of the lands of Nicaragua that Pedrarias Dávila, the governor of that province, suspended the expedition of conquest to Peru and decided to send his lieutenant Francisco Hernández de Córdoba to the recently discovered territories with orders to occupy everything that González had explored.

This time, the welcome that the Indians gave the Spaniards was anything but peaceful. They gave Hernández and his men such untiring resistance that he had to use his sword to cut his way from battle to endless battle. As a result of the technical superiority of his troops, Hernández finally reached the indigenous village of Xalteva, located on the shores of Lake Cocibolca, where he founded the city of Granada. He then moved on to the lands of the Chorotegas of Nagrando, specifically to Imabita, territory of the Maribio Indians on the shores of Lake Xolotlan, where he established the city of León in its first incarnation, destined from its beginnings to serve as the capital of the new Spanish province of Nicaragua.

Later, the Spaniards went to explore the north of the country, moving along part of the Yaré River (now known as the Coco River, which forms the border between Nicaragua and Honduras), where he founded the city of Segovia. For various reasons, this city was never able to become a point of regional importance and was destroyed years later by the Mosco Indians who inhabited the Caribbean part of Nicaragua. Granada and León, however, built the axis on which the future history of Nicaragua would turn.

The adventures of Hernández de Córdoba ended when he returned to León with plans to revolt against Pedrarias Dávila, the governor of Panamá, and take control of the newly conquered region. Instead, Pedrarias Dávila was the victor in this power struggle. He captured Córdoba, put him on trial, and had him decapitated in the central plaza of León, the city that Hernández had established.

Once this bloody episode between the Spaniards had passed, the king named Pedrarias Dávila governor and captain general of the province, making him the first president of Nicaragua in its earliest form. The beginning of his government coincided with several uprisings. Pedrarias decided to terrorize the native inhabitants of Nicaragua. During this time, which the ruler called "a period of organization," there was indigenous resistance for many years throughout the western part of this territory.

SOCIAL HIERARCHY IN COLONIAL NICARAGUA

The province of Nicaragua was created in the sixteenth century under the jurisdiction of the Audience of Guatemala, annexed to the Council of Indias. The governor, who was the highest authority during the seventeenth and eighteenth centuries, lived in León, the capital of the province. Administrative control extended to cover approximately half of what is now the republic of Nicaragua, in other words, the Pacific side and the center of the country.

The ethnically diverse population that lived in that territory consisted of approximately 20,000 inhabitants at the beginning of the seventeenth century and reached possibly 120,000 in 1821, the year that Central America began declaring its independence from Spanish rule. Conquered Indians, Spanish conquistadors, and blacks brought as slaves from Africa at the beginning of the sixteenth century made up this ethnic mixture called *mestizaje*. This era was marked by a social ideology that established a hierarchy, whose criteria of classification were based on skin color. Society was divided into two "republics": the republic of the Indians and the republic of the Spaniards. Each population group had to live in geographically determined areas. There was a social pyramid of the groups that constituted this population. At the top were the Spaniards, or those who pretended to be, whose numerical importance was insignificant, as it never surpassed 5 percent of the total population. In the second place were the *mestizos* supposedly of Indian and Spanish origin. This group, however, had no special privileges, as it did not belong to one group or the other. In third place were the Indians, whose population continued to decline, making up 50 percent of the population in 1821. In fourth place were mulattos, who were descendants of the African slaves and who carried what was called at the time "the stain of servility." Occupying the lowest place in society were the blacks and the slaves who never accounted for more than 5 percent of the total population.

In any case, the group to which one belonged was subject to an overarching reality: all people were vassals of the king of Spain and therefore under his absolute authority. The supreme power was the king, legislator and sole arbiter of justice. In his person was concentrated what are currently called the executive, legislative, and judicial powers. Laws made in Spain applied to all the provinces.

Some of the customary laws of the Indians survived, but only when they did not contradict Spanish laws, for example, the collective ownership of land by indigenous communities. The king, however, named all military, religious, and civilian officials. Power was established based on the legitimacy of the rights acquired at the time of the conquest. There was never any sign in colonial Nicaragua of what today would be called democracy. The king's power came through God, not the people.

Slavery was one of the most crucial themes during the colonial period. In spite of certain legal prohibitions, there was a parallel reality that permitted slavery (including the branding of slaves) to varying degrees. It is also important to mention the *encomiendas* (the concessions of land and inhabitants to conquistadors), which had such a great influence on the subjugation of the indigenous population to the Spanish crown. The *encomiendas* made up a large percentage of the entire production that the Indians accumulated and then had to hand over to the governors named by the king. In many cases, the king gave *encomiendas* to the Catholic Church for the "favor" of instructing the Indians in the Catholic faith, all under royal decree. The Spaniards used the indigenous workforce to exploit the land and to work in the cities. The governor, named by the king, was the maximum authority in Nicaragua for a term of five years. All were Spaniards and very few ever took up long-term residency in Nicaragua.

COLONIAL ECONOMY

The economy of Nicaragua was based on agriculture. The entire province, just as in the pre-Columbian era, grew corn and beans. To this activity was added the practice of keeping cattle, which grew dramatically. The land was abundant and its appropriation and use reflected ancient indigenous practices, as well as Spanish innovations. The Indian people maintained their system of communal property. The exploitation of the gold mines was one of the primary sources of income for the crown, as well as the sale of slaves. The idea of private property was introduced and practiced by the Spaniards, a cultural phenomenon that paved the way for the creation of *latifundios,* extensive tracts of land held by the richest families of the cities. For their part, the *mestizos* and mulattos lived on *tierras realengas* (remnants of royal land), which was the majority of the land, giving way to the creation of the smaller *minifundios.*

The monarchic ideology of the sixteenth century had divided society into two separate groups, each with its clearly demarcated space. The Spaniards lived in the cities, and the Indians lived in villages; each group had its own rights and duties.

The Spaniards held the province's political, administrative, religious, economic, and social power. Each of the local governments was subject to royal power and directed by the Spanish aristocracies. With the passage of time, the ethnically diverse population modified society in such profound ways that the Spaniards were an extreme minority by the end of the eighteenth century.

León, originally founded in 1524 near the indigenous village of Imabite on the shore of Lake Xolotlan, was moved to its current site in 1610 on land occupied by the Sutiaba Indians after an eruption of Momotombo volcano. The move also was precipitated by the need for a place with a large labor force, something that did not exist on the city's original site.

In this area of Nicaragua, the catastrophic decrease in the numbers of the indigenous population can be attributed to a variety of causes: (1) the sale of indigenous slaves to Panama, the Antilles and Peru, almost all of whom died of hunger and thirst on the journey; (2) poor treatment of the Indians who were whipped, lived in chains, eaten by dogs, and forced to carry excessive burdens, all of which were imposed by Pedrarias de Avila; (3) work in the mines, which killed more than 40,000 Indians in less than two years; (4) voluntary sexual abstinence by the indigenous population so that they would not give birth to more slaves for the Spaniards; (5) parricide and abortions; and (6) the destruction of indigenous villages.

Other colonial cities were established in the sixteenth century. Granada was founded near the Indian village of Xalteva in 1524 and has been there ever since. Nueva Segovia, in the north of the territory, was founded in 1543. In seventeenth-century León and Granada, there was a certain decay aggravated by the invasions of pirates in the mid-1600s. Nueva Segovia was almost completely sacked and destroyed by English pirates with the collaboration of the Miskito Indians.

STEPS TOWARD INDEPENDENCE

The descendants of the first Spaniards who were born and lived in Central America (Spanish *criollos,* or Creoles) lost their social hegemony and were replaced by Spaniards from Spain who arrived in the eighteenth century to fulfill their royal duties as functionaries and businessmen. In this way, a new aristocracy was formed by families who built a Nicaraguan oligarchy in the second half of the nineteenth century. Soon, the new aristocracy became the owner of land; cattle farms; plantations of cacao, sugarcane, and indigo; slaves; stores; finished silver; and public jobs. They considered themselves superior to other ethnic groups because they had access to education, even at the university level.

Many of these Creoles grew discontented. They believed they had the right not only to govern the land they inhabited but *not* to be governed by the Spaniards named by the king and sent directly from Spain. The contradictions with regard to political power worsened, for the people who occupied all the highest positions of power were from Spain. The Creoles had access only to minor positions. Even though they shared economic power with the monarchy and enjoyed certain privileges, they always found themselves as subordinates with respect to the people who held power. The imperial bureaucracy that protected the interests of the king bothered them tremendously, especially because they were obliged to share all the wealth they obtained.

There were strong clashes between the two classes of Spaniards in each province, as well as between the provinces (Honduras, Costa Rica, Nicaragua, and El Salvador) and the seat of power in Guatemala, which was the captaincy general and monopolized commerce to benefit its own economic groups. The discontent reached irreconcilable levels between Central America and the Crown, for Spain drew on all the natural resources of Central

America and received all these benefits solely for itself, leaving the provinces with the enormous burden imposed by colonialism.

Although the inhabitants of these areas longed for independence from Spain, the Creoles were divided into two groups. The conservative wing fought for emancipation but wanted to leave the colonial structure intact in order to govern in keeping with the interests of their social class. For this reason, they made a pact in 1821 with the representative of Spain, General Gabino Gaínza, to proclaim independence peacefully. The liberal wing proposed that independence ought to be made violently and with the support of all the middle and lower class urban inhabitants, in other words, in conjunction with the poor. In practice, however, both groups controlled the movement for independence, so that independence meant the taking of power on behalf of their social class.

The eminent members of the "Group of 13" belonged to the conservative wing of those who were fighting for freedom from Spanish rule. As signers of the declaration of independence, they represented the position of the class of large landowners, who exploited the Indians. For this reason, their political stance was considered reactionary, for it planned to conserve independence by maintaining the predominance of their class in society. Nevertheless, the ideology of the upper middle urban class was revolutionary for its time. In keeping with liberal ideas, these people sought to fight for the peasants, redistributing the land and linking the struggle with the armed movement of the people that was occurring at the same time in Mexico.

The group of Creoles seeking independence wanted to structure a constitutional state in the style of North American presidential elections and French liberalism. As a result, an individualistic bourgeois transplanted order was created that did not coincide with Nicaraguan culture, and the neofeudal socioeconomic structure continued without transformations. An order was superimposed in a formal way, but it had no deep roots of its own. All of a sudden, society had moved from a traditional concept of sovereignty identified with the king to a completely new idea of popular sovereignty, which produced dual contradictions between form and reality. These conflicts dating from the nineteenth century have been the primary cause of political instability in Latin America, especially in terms of military *caudillismo* and economic dependency. There was no real political awareness of what was truly and authentically Hispanic American. Instead, the emphasis was on foreign models, negating original Hispanic American values, whether they were indigenous or from Spain.

The declaration of independence itself came from the open town council of September 15, 1821, which was held in Guatemala City. After being discussed at length, it was voted on and passed with some significant gaps and unresolved issues. For example, the document established separation from Spain, but independence for whom? The people were not considered in the adoption of these decisions. In the end, the indigenous and *mestizo* populations simply had a different owner.

POST-INDEPENDENCE

The social structures did not change significantly after independence. Perhaps the most notable change was that the skin color of the general population slowly ceased to be a factor in social stratification, as mulattos, *mestizos,* and the Afro-Caribbean *zambos* ascended the social scale. The struggles of independence and the civil struggles were the vehicle for Indians to abandon their villages and integrate themselves into the life of the new republic. This type of Indian moved to the city, became part of the battles together with the *caudillos,* and even received public positions. But these were Indians who stopped being Indians. Their social position obliged them to leave behind their customs, traditions, and ethnic origin. The government proclamations addressed the equality of the Indians with regard to buying and selling the land that they legitimately owned, but the application of these legal measures only resulted in jeopardizing the Indians, who became victims of unscrupulous businessmen and landowners who stripped the Indians of their land at ridiculously low prices. Many communities disappeared when its members were contracted with a salary to work on haciendas and in the mines. Since independence, the word "Indian" no longer meant belonging to an ethnic group, but rather referred to an individual who continued to live in a "primitive" traditional way in his or her community, marginalized from all "progress." A number of communities of this kind have survived to this day in Nicaragua.

When it initiated its independent life, Nicaragua also began a new series of civil wars for power. In one of them, foreign filibusters that were the armed extension of U.S. expansionism were brought in. *Legitimistas* from Granada and *Democráticos* from León in 1854 found themselves facing a new civil war. The biggest problem, however, was that no one was measuring the consequences of the idea of contracting the services of foreign soldiers. These filibusters came under the command of William Walker, who planned to make Nicaragua a colony to serve the U.S. slave states at that time. This proposal could not be carried out, however, because at the moment Walker declared himself president of Nicaragua and decreed that slavery would be reinstituted in Nicaragua, the people united to unleash a vigorous resistance and annihilate these plans. On September 14, 1856, Central American troops defeated the filibusters in the anti-interventionist civil war at the San Jacinto hacienda. After this long-sought intromission, Nicaragua remained in the sights of the growing power of the United States. Throughout Nicaragua's history, time and time again the North American political presence has made itself felt in Nicaragua.

This expansionist policy has its origin in the Monroe Doctrine, which received its name from President James Monroe's declaration in 1823. It became the new North American government basis on which it formed its foreign policy in relation to the European colonialist powers. The United States, as a close neighbor to the rest of the Americas, did not want the old Spanish colonies of the American continent to fall under the control of European powers. The U.S. government hoped to reserve this zone as the exclusive field of action for the future commercial expansion of its growing industrial and economic power. Monroe's famous declaration that America was for the Americans initially confused Central American political leaders, who thought that the objective and interest of the new power was in protecting Hispanic American sovereignty. But this supposition was soon revealed for what it really was—a plan to control the American continent with no opposition.

Once again, the U.S. military presence was felt in Nicaragua when the government of the United States rejected the foreign policy of Nicaraguan President José Santos Zelaya, who governed from 1893–1909, and who marked an important stage in the history of Nicaragua by erasing many of the elements of Spanish colonial order. The government of Zelaya represented a compromise between the old and the new.

The nationalism of the Zelaya government clashed with the expansionist projects of the U.S. government. Nicaragua developed a policy of friendship with the rest of the countries in Central America with the idea of establishing with them a federated state that, through international solidarity, could oppose the imperialistic plans of the United States.

In October 1909, with the political and financial support of the U.S. Consul in Bluefields, Nicaragua, Thomas Moffat, an armed uprising exploded against Zelaya. The rebellion was apparently directed by Juan José Estrada, but it was manipulated by the conservative leaders Emiliano Chamorro, Adolfo Díaz, and Luis Mena. The troops involved in the uprising were defeated, and, for this reason, Moffat hired the services of two U.S. citizens who were working as dynamite experts in the mines in Honduras to mine the waters of the San Juan River where the Nicaraguan government was sending steamships with reinforcements and supplies. The two saboteurs were captured in the act, judged by a war tribunal, found guilty, condemned to death, and executed.

This event was the pretext for the U.S. government to accelerate its intervention in Nicaragua. On December 1, 1909, the document known as the Knox Note was delivered to the Nicaraguan business relations officer in Washington. In it, Zelaya was accused of being an international threat, of destroying democratic institutions in Nicaragua, and of exercising a pernicious influence over Honduras. It also affirmed that Estrada's movement represented the majority of the people and concluded by threatening military intervention in Nicaragua if Zelaya did not resign as president of the republic in the near future. Zelaya resigned on December 17, handing over control of the government to Dr. José Madriz who was not able to crush the rebel movement, above all because the United States had decided that all remnants of the Zelaya government had to be eliminated. Madriz resigned in 1910, turning over presidential power to a representative of the triumphant "revolution." In 1910, with the help of U.S. soldiers and warships, a government representing the most reactionary conservative positions was imposed. This government never would have been able to sustain itself without the support of the United States, which intervened in the internal affairs of Nicaragua to keep the country in its sphere of influence and maintain its interests throughout the Central American region. U.S. Marines remained as an occupying force in Nicaragua for approximately the next 20 years, producing anti-interventionists such as the young general Benjamín Zeledón, whom the Conservatives captured and killed when he was 33 years old, and, later, the General of Free Men, Augusto C. Sandino, one of Nicaragua's most important historical figures.

THE HEROIC STRUGGLE OF A. C. SANDINO

On May 6, 1926, a revolution led by liberals under the command of General José María Moncada erupted. These liberals felt completely marginalized and excluded from the political affairs of importance, for the conservatives were considered by the U.S. government to be the most trustworthy allies. Augusto C. Sandino, who was born in Niquinohomo in 1895 as the illegitimate son of Gregorio Sandino and Margarita Calderón, emerged in this conflict as a nationalist, anti-imperialist figure. Together with 29 *campesinos,* Sandino joined the struggle against the conservative oligarchy and the foreign military occupation of Nicaragua, forming with them the so-called column from Segovia. At that time, the president was Adolfo Díaz, and, while the armed conflict developed, it was clear to Díaz that he had no possibility of restoring peace without the armed intervention of his defenders from the north. With this goal in mind and at the insistence of the U.S. embassy, in January 1927, Díaz requested "the friendly help of Washington so that it can proceed in re-establishing peace and order in the country." In less than a month, thousands of U.S. Marines disembarked in the port of Corinto on the Pacific Ocean, occupying the vital railroad lines, the ports, and all the major cities of Nicaragua. At the same time, the U.S. military participated with its planes in the battle of Chinandega, leveling the city and leaving it in flames. The "column from Segovia" of General Sandino grew in strength, increasing in size from 29 patriots in the beginning to 800 men on horseback who were well trained and equipped under the red (representing blood) and black (for death) flag that meant fatherland or death. These men managed to accumulate significant military and organizational experience in multiple battles.

For its part, the U.S. Congress pressured President Calvin Coolidge even more to send Henry L. Stimson as a special envoy to Nicaragua with the task of resolving the crisis in Nicaragua, however possible, even if it meant a large-scale military intervention. They were desperate and fearful of the major advances of the Constitutionalist forces. Stimson convinced himself immediately when he arrived that it was preferable to make a deal directly with the military powers of the Liberal party, which, at that time, was in Moncada's hands.

On November 4, 1927, in Tipitapa, Moncada and Stimson held talks beneath a tree called an *Espino Negro* in search of a solution to the armed conflict; they eventually signed a peace agreement. The U.S. emissary offered Moncada two alternatives. One was to sign an armistice with the Conservatives and accept the points of the plan in their entirety, which implied immediate peace allowing Díaz to remain in power until the next elections, disarming of both armies controlled by the Marines (who would pay $10 per rifle and $20 for each machine gun), general amnesty, participation of the Liberals in Díaz's cabinet, organization of a nonpartisan internal military force commanded by U.S. officials, and presidential elections in 1928 held under U.S. supervision. The U.S. Marines under this plan would remain in the country until their presence was no longer necessary when the other points of the plan had been fulfilled. The second alternative was to go to war with the occupying U.S. forces.

Moncada chose the first plan for one main reason: Stimson told him that Moncada's personality was appealing to the U.S. government and that the first option was the only way that Moncada eventually could become president, which was Moncada's most fervent dream.

When Moncada proposed the agreement to his generals, all but one accepted the idea of surrendering to the foreign occupying forces: General Augusto C. Sandino. Sandino arrived at Moncada's barracks when the pact had already been signed and refused to sign it and surrender. While Moncada was preparing to sign the pact, Sandino occupied Común Mountain near the city of Boaco, which constituted an advanced position in relation to the capital, Managua. Moncada had sent representatives there to look for Sandino. Sandino returned to Común Mountain and isolated himself from his men so that they would not see him cry as he reflected bitterly on the destiny that awaited the nation. Then Sandino spoke to his soldiers and told them his proposal to fight the occupying troops if necessary. To do so, he moved his army to the most remote mountains of Jinotega. Some of his men were released from service when they did not show the resolve to make this sacrifice. Sandino, left with 300 men, moved to San Rafael del Norte, establishing his new encampment there in this second phase of his struggle against the oligarchy of the Liberals and the Conservatives as well as the U.S. Marines. In the face of the superior force of the occupying troops, Sandino developed his own style for waging a long-term guerrilla war of resistance that consisted of surprise ambushes and assaulting garrisons in small villages. The primary objective was to cause the greatest number of casualties with the least amount of ammunition, to recover arms and other war supplies, to engage in battles that were not prolonged, and to leave no trace as they gathered their wounded. Sandino had a well-organized intelligence system that informed him about the enemy's movements.

Sandino's name was transformed into a banner, and many Latin Americans recognized his struggle and supported it, creating an international brigade composed of Mexicans, Argentines, Salvadorans, Guatemalans, Dominicans, Venezuelans, Peruvians, Colombians, and Hondurans. Some fought as soldiers and others belonged to the military command structure, which was the case of the Salvadoran Farabundo Martí, the Peruvian Estevan Pavletich, the Dominican Gregorio Urbano Filbert, the Venezuelan Carlos Aponte, and the Guatemalan José María Jirón Ruano.

By 1931, the rebel army was waging its guerrilla war on a national scale. The situation grew worse when, on March 31, an earthquake leveled Managua, affecting the poorest people the most. The U.S. government, well aware of the consistent military offensive developed by Sandino's army (called the Defending Army of National Sovereignty, or E.D.S.N. in Spanish), admitted defeat at the end of 1931 when U.S. President Herbert Hoover publicly announced that the U.S. occupying troops would be withdrawn immediately after the elections of November 1932. On January 1, 1933, Dr. Juan Bautista Sacasa became the next president of Nicaragua. That same day, the Marines left the country, creating the incredible spectacle of how that "crazy little army" (as Nobel-Prize winning Chilean poet Gabriela Mistral called the Sandinista fighters) had triumphed over the world's most powerful nation after seven years of military resistance.

On February 2, 1933, Sandino and some of his followers arrived in Managua and were taken immediately to the presidential residence where President Sacasa and Sandino signed an historic peace agreement. By signing the document, Sandino was eliminating an excuse for the United States to invade

Nicaragua yet again. By standing up to the invading U.S. military forces and forcing them to withdraw, Sandino had acquired great moral authority both in Nicaragua and abroad. For this reason and others, the U.S. government considered Sandino a threat to future American policy in Nicaragua, and made plans to assassinate Sandino. These plans coincided with the political ideals of the local oligarchs in Nicaragua's Liberal and Conservative parties, who were collaborating with Anastasio Somoza García, the new head of the consolidated National Guard who was chosen by the United States to represent the military and political interests of the U.S. government.

On February 20, 1934, Sacasa signed a decree naming the Sandinista general, Horacio Portocarrero, as the presidential military delegate with jurisdiction in the villages of Segovia in northern Nicaragua. With this appointment, Sacasa was seeking a balance in his authority, which was being undermined by Somoza García, who was not at all pleased with the appointment, for he viewed it as an attack on his infinite ambitions for power. Somoza held a meeting on February 21 with several trusted soldiers, and he convinced them of the necessity to liquidate Sandino, something that the U.S. ambassador Arthur Bliss Lane supported.

That very night, as Sandino was leaving the president's house after having dinner with President Sacasa, the car that he was riding in with his father Gregorio, his Minister Salvatierra, and two of his generals Estrada and Umanzor, was intercepted by a National Guard patrol. The Minister and Sandino's father were taken to the jails called El Hormiguero. Sandino and his two generals were taken to the eastern part of Managua and cruelly assassinated with machine guns and rifles. Sandino's body was burned so that there would be no trace of his remains.

THE SOMOZA DICTATORSHIP

In 1936, Somoza became the president of Nicaragua after a military coup against his uncle, Juan Bautista Sacasa. For more than 40 years, the Somoza family dominated Nicaraguan political life and was supported by eight successive U.S. presidents. In the 1950s, the dictatorship would last another 20 years backed by the National Guard and the United States. Nevertheless, among the Nicaraguan people there was a legacy of struggle that would never be lost. The Somoza dictatorship was marked by the constant harassment and cruel persecution of any and all political opponents, who were arrested, often tortured and killed, or sent into exile. At the same time, the Somoza family, as well as its functionaries and supporters, enjoyed a seemingly endless string of luxurious social events and an arrogant lifestyle guaranteed by the dictatorship's absolute hold on power backed by the military.

On September 21, 1956, as Somoza García celebrated his reelection plans in the so-called House of the Worker in the city of León, he was executed by the poet Rigoberto López Pérez, the one who began, in his own words, "the beginning of the end of the dictatorship." The poet was killed immediately, but his action marked a new stage of the struggle against the Somoza regime that continued over the years with other members of the family and a few people outside the family but always under the Somoza family control.

THE SANDINISTA REVOLUTION

In 1961, the Frente Sandinista de Liberación Nacional (FSLN) was founded by Carlos Fonseca Amador, Tomás Borge Martínez, Silvio Mayorga, Colonel Santos López (a survivor of Sandino's army), José Benito Escobar, Germán Pomares, Rigoberto Cruz (Pablo Ubeda), Faustino Ruiz, Francisco Buitrago, and Jorge Navarro. This historical event meant that there was an alternative for the people in the fight to create social change. Many events were undertaken to awaken the political awareness of the people so that they would join the Frente Sandinista with the common goal of overthrowing the dictatorship.

There were other factors that contributed to the success of this endeavor. For example, the Somoza family in the mid- to late 1970s was becoming relatively more isolated in terms of its international relations. This was due in large part to the new U.S. foreign policy proposed by President Jimmy Carter, who was concerned with the defense of human rights. Carter restricted military and economic aid to the government of Nicaragua and pressured for a democratic opening to allow other political sectors in Nicaragua the opportunity to form a different alternative. The assassination on January 10, 1978, of the anti-Somoza journalist Pedro Joaquín Chamorro, who published the opposition newspaper *La Prensa,* closed the door on any attempt to find a peaceful solution and served as a catalyst for the insurrection.

On July 19, 1979, columns of young combatants entered Managua from all points of the country. They were jubilant and convinced that this sacrifice was the beginning of a new Nicaragua that everyone had longed for. Shortly before this important moment in Nicaraguan history, Anastasio Somoza Debayle fled Nicaragua for Miami, carrying his father's ashes and suitcases stuffed with dollars. Although it is true that the FSLN was the core force that directed the struggle, without the unity of all sectors of society, the revolutionary triumph would not have been possible. In this first stage of Sandinista Nicaragua, a Government Junta of National Reconstruction was formed in which the FSLN would replace the dictatorship and represented all parts of Nicaraguan society. There was also a National Directorate comprised of nine

Comandantes of the Revolution as well as the Council of Guerrilla Comandantes. The majority of these people were young men who had abandoned
their studies in school and had accepted the political commitment to rid Nicaragua of the Somoza dictatorship. Now they were faced with the challenge
of organizing the country again and helping it prosper with justice after nearly
50 years of domination by one of Latin America's bloodiest dictatorships.

Everyone gathered that day in the plaza in Managua hoped to become
owners of their own future. The Frente Sandinista attempted to rebuild a
country that had been impoverished for decades and devastated by the war.
The measures taken by the FSLN to reach this goal included confiscating
and expropriating the wealth of Somoza and his extended family (who owned
more than 60% of Nicaragua's arable land and the production of goods and
services); creating the People's Sandinista Army (EPS) and the Sandinista police; nationalizing the mines, the financial and commercial sector, transportation, agriculture, and industry; transforming the national economy in keeping
with the true meaning of the revolution; opening a variety of relations with
the block of socialist countries—Cuba, the Soviet Union, and Communist
Asia; creating the general directorate of state security; and finally, creating
the ministry of the interior. These reconstruction efforts encountered many
challenges. Many business people, who were associated with the dictatorship
and did not agree with the new economic measures, fled the country. There
was a large flight of capital ($580 million in a period of only 18 months) and
an absence of private investment. Many businesses were stripped of funds by
their owners as a way of avoiding appropriation. The aerial bombardment of
Nicaragua by the Somoza regime at the end of the insurrection caused $1.7
billion in damages. All loans made by the Somoza government during its last
months in power did not even enter the Nicaraguan banking system, as they
were deposited directly in foreign accounts. Finally, the government of Ronald Reagan in the 1980s instituted an economic embargo against Nicaragua.

The measures taken by the Sandinista government did not resolve all the
existing problems. In some sectors, there was resentment as a result of certain
arbitrary measures, especially with regard to confiscations and the nationalization of commerce that eliminated the buying and selling between the
producer and the seller; these transactions were now controlled by the government. What one sector of society considered a success of the revolution,
another thought was totally against its interests. The initial government junta
could not sustain itself amidst so many internal conflicts. It dissolved and
each person acted according to his or her beliefs.

Many of the businessmen, former officials of the National Guard, and the
army organized themselves into what was called the counterrevolution (Contras), armed and financed by the U.S. government. Nicaragua's neighboring

country to the north, Honduras, lent its territory so that the new Contra army could begin a campaign of constant armed harassment to attempt to destabilize Nicaragua's new revolution.

The Sandinista government in 1983 initiated a national petition in support of a new law to create compulsory military service. On many occasions, while they were collecting signatures, government officials made speeches that the law would never be put into effect unless the United States decided to intervene in Nicaragua. The law was approved the same year. In 1984, there were national elections, and Daniel Ortega, commander of the revolution and member of the National Directorate, won. It was then that the government began to draft the first young people, making use of that resource backed by a law. The Frente Sandinista was committing the biggest mistake of its government by subjecting 17-year-old boys to unending hardship. Young people fighting and dying in this war meant a continuation of the bloodshed of previous years. It seemed that the young men who were in power in Nicaragua quickly forgot the horror and cruelty of war. The immaturity and arrogance of the Sandinista leaders unleashed one of Nicaragua's most painful conflicts. The country was filled with Cuban and Soviet military instructors. Every day, the streets of Nicaragua vibrated with the sound of military vehicles. The war began again as a result of an intransigent United States that would not let Nicaraguans decide their future on their own and the inability and romantic view of the revolution perpetuated by the National Directorate of the Frente Sandinista.

There were, nevertheless, some significant accomplishments of the revolution. The agrarian reform was created. The national literacy crusade began, as well as adult education programs, free education at all levels, and free health care. Electricity, water, transportation, and basic foodstuffs were subsidized by the government.

There was support for small and middle-size industrial, agricultural, and crafts endeavors. Urban and rural cooperatives were created. In addition, popular cultural centers throughout the country promoted and supported all forms of artistic expression. Prostitution was almost completely eradicated, and child labor was eliminated.

Nevertheless, the debilitating effects of the Contra war had a marked influence on the results of the 1990 Nicaraguan presidential elections in which Daniel Ortega ran against an alliance of political parties known as the National Union of Opposition (UNO), whose candidate was Violeta Chamorro, the widow of journalist Pedro Joaquín Chamorro, who was murdered in 1978 during the Somoza dictatorship. Violeta Chamorro won, and the Frente Sandinista, recognizing its electoral defeat, turned power over to her. Violeta Chamorro faced an important decision at the beginning of her presidency.

A successful 1986 lawsuit brought by the Nicaraguan government against the United States in the International Court of Justice at The Hague ruled in 1990 that the U.S. government should pay more than $17 billion for material damages to the Nicaraguan economy and infrastructure as a result of the low-intensity (i.e., undeclared) war based in Honduras that the United States was financing in order to destabilize or topple the Sandinista government. The United States threatened to cut off hundreds of millions of dollars to Nicaragua if the Nicaraguan government under Chamorro's new leadership did not forgive the legal claim. Chamorro decided to drop the matter, saying that she sought friendly relations with the United States. She believed that pursuing the judgment in the lawsuit that Nicaragua won would perpetuate damaging conflicts with the U.S. government that already had imposed a trade embargo against Nicaragua. Fortunately, during the Chamorro government from 1990–1997, compulsory military service in Nicaragua ended and, within a short period of time, the counter-revolutionaries (Contras) turned in their weapons, believing in many promises made by the government that were never kept.

THE CARIBBEAN COAST OF NICARAGUA

The Caribbean coast and the rain forest of eastern Nicaragua were inhabited by the Miskito, Sumo, and Rama Indians, who were descendants of the Chibcha indigenous group that emigrated north in ancient times from the area that is now Colombia. There are conflicting and as yet unresolved theories about the origins the Caribbean indigenous population in Nicaragua. Some researchers maintain that the ancestors of the Miskitos, Sumos, and Ramas remained in Nicaragua and Costa Rica during the slow migration of the ancient Chibchas from Mexico toward Colombia. Other theories affirm that the indigenous population of the Caribbean coast may have come from Colombia to Costa Rica and Nicaragua by land in about 1000 A.D. or long before. It is also possible that all the indigenous groups of the Caribbean, or Atlantic, coast belong to the Ulúa or Woolva, with the exception of the Ramas who belong to the Chibchas.

Among these multiple tribes, there is a great deal of confusion with regard to the different names of the descendants of the Ulúa. In 1600, the most well-known groups included:

- Yuskos or Yoskos, who arrived on the Yahoska River
- Panamaka on the Coco River
- Bawinka or Tawira, between the Coco, Wawa, and Bambana Rivers

- Prinsu on the Prinzapola River
- Ulúas or ulvas on the Grande, Escondido, Mico, Rama, and Siquia (including the part that is known today as Chontales) Rivers
- Kukra on the Bay of Bluefields, Laguna de Perlas, and Corn Island

The Miskitos are the result of the mixed blood of the Bawinka or Tawira, Europeans (merchants and buccaneers), and blacks from Africa. Sumus was the name that the Miskitos gave to all the other indigenous groups that belonged to the Ulúa family. The Miskito language was the business language, which meant that the other groups learned it along with their own languages, which slowly went extinct. Later, these people became known as Miskitos. The Sumus were recognized as a weak and peaceful indigenous group. In colonial times, the Spaniards spoke of the Caribs when they were referring to the Sumu tribes from the interior of Nicaragua. In fact, the Caribs were groups of Ulúas who inhabited the central part of the country.

For many centuries, the Spanish crown wanted to conquer this extensive zone of Nicaragua but were unable to do so because of the fierce resistance of the Miskitos. Furthermore, the Miskitos made alliances with French buccaneers and English pirates to sack the cities located in the Pacific zone of the country.

This Miskito nation, including the Sumus and Ramas, who belonged directly to the Chibcha family, had their first contact with the English by means of the merchants from Old Providence Island in the Caribbean, which was settled around 1629 by English Puritans fleeing religious persecution in their country. This encounter was far less traumatic than the one that occurred between the Spaniards and the indigenous groups of the Pacific, because it was characterized by more subtle forms of oppression and opportunism. The buccaneers took advantage of the great navigational skill of the Miskitos and Sumus, letting the Indians take them in boats across the dangerous currents of the Coco and San Juan Rivers and attacking the communities in the interior of Nicaragua, teaching the Indians their deadly profession. With this initiation, it was relatively easy for England to recruit hundreds of Miskitos and Sumus as cannon fodder in their repeated wars against Spain.

The exploitation of the great forests of the Atlantic coast began when the English established plantations of sugarcane and indigo and cattle ranches in Laguna de Perlas and Bluefields. The Miskitos and Sumus were also enlisted to hunt down runaway slaves and return them to their English owners. The worst abuse was the way they were used to capture their indigenous brothers in Nicaragua and Costa Rica and to sell them as slaves to the English in Jamaica. The most important factor that explains this friendship between the Miskitos and the English was the inhumane treatment of the Indians by the Spaniards. The Miskitos considered the province of Nicaragua governed by the Spaniards as a powerful enemy that surrounded them, waiting for a chance to steal their freedom and independence and subject them to the same enslavement as the other Indians of Central America.

Commercially, the Miskitos exchanged turtle shells and canoes for iron tools, nets, machetes and, eventually, firearms to defend themselves from the Spanish conquest. The English also introduced the Indians to the vice of drinking rum, even though the Miskitos had their traditional drink called *Mishla,* which was made from corn or pineapple or yucca that the women chewed to facilitate the fermentation process.

Many English merchants came alone and took indigenous wives. In a short time, the contribution of European blood was evident among the coastal Indians. Blacks also contributed to the ethnic mix; in 1641, there was a shipwreck of a vessel carrying African slaves who were rescued by the members of the Tawihka tribe with whom they intermarried.

The word *Miskito* is spelled many different ways: Mísquito, Mosquito, Mósquito, Mískitu, and Musguito. The word might have its origin in the Spanish expression *indios mixtos* (mixed Indians), referring to the genetic contributions of the Indians and blacks. There is also the possibility that the name comes from the English word musket, for these were the only Indians who had firearms.

The ancestors of the Miskitos did not live under a monarchy like the other seminomadic groups. Instead, they lived in egalitarian communities and had experienced leaders who were skilled at leading hunting expeditions. In the small communities, the parents and grandparents organized the lives of the families with the need for a king or a strong cacique. Even today in the larger Miskito communities, the authority of the leader depends a great deal on the support received from the elders or patriarchs of the area. In 1687, Old Man was crowned the first Miskito king. The final war between the English and the Spaniards ended with a compromise defined by the Treaty of Versailles on September 3, 1783. England recognized the sovereignty of Spain over the Caribbean coast of Nicaragua, and the Spaniards gave the English British Honduras (now known as Belize) with all its important lumber resources. They also promised to treat humanely the Zambos, Miskitos, Sumus, and other indigenous groups.

In spite of so much death and indigenous bloodshed, Spain, in the end, took possession of the Miskito Indian lands. When all the states that formed the captaincy general of Guatemala achieved their independence from Spain in 1821, England took advantage of the situation to adjudicate once again the protection of the Mosquitia kingdom. In 1894, Nicaragua incorporated the Mosquitia reservation and the name of the department of Zelaya in honor of the Nicaraguan president at that time, José Santos Zelaya.

If one studies Nicaraguan history, it is readily apparent that the inhabitants of the Atlantic coast were a part of the national territory that opposed the Spanish conquest that was occurring in the Pacific zone. For the Miskitos of the Caribbean side of Nicaragua, the western part of Nicaragua was filled with cruel enemies who had subjugated the Indians to torture and forced labor. The Miskitos, whose indigenous communities were colonized by the English, forged alliances with the English as a means of protecting themselves against the Spanish invaders. The Miskitos lived with the other tribes of caribisis, mulattoes (a mixture of Indians and blacks), sumus, and ramas, always maintaining a cultural hegemony over these different ethnic groups.

During the Somoza dictatorship (1936–1979), this zone, with its virgin tracts of land, fought against the presence of the multinational corporations engaged in mining, logging, and fishing operations. All the tribes worked for these companies but without changing their traditional daily ways of life that were structured around hunting, fishing, and gathering. Some clandestine revolutionaries of the Frente Sandinista were supported in the Caribbean zone by Indians who gave them food and shelter. The revolution finally triumphed in 1979 in the Pacific, or western, part of Nicaragua. When the revolutionaries subsequently attempted to integrate the indigenous population in the revolutionary process, they did not take into account the advice they received from the guerrillas, who had learned to live with the Indians during the armed struggle against the dictatorship.

The force of the revolution in the late 1970s erupted in that isolated zone in the Atlantic part of the country, toppling the relative tranquility in the relations between the Indians and the mixed race upper class members who lived on huge cattle ranches. After the revolution in 1979, when the Sandinistas nationalized the North American companies that were operating on the Caribbean coast, the social structure that had once predominated changed and relative tranquility no longer made sense. The Sandinistas, in their fervor to create more social equality, wanted to redeem their Miskito brothers, lost, they thought, in the immense forested world of the Caribbean coast. It was the moment for all the country's poor to achieve a new political awareness. But the Miskitos were not so inclined. They had been living in their traditional way for centuries. Thus the solidarity that the Sandinistas offered was interpreted as interventionist. The new invaders were people who came from the Pacific zone, the same place inhabited by their old enemies the Spaniards. The Sandinistas were viewed as a new generation that would exterminate the Indians. The Miskitos' reactions, although easily understood today, were interpreted by the Sandinistas as against the revolution that proclaimed that the Indians were free and would never again be slaves. The great literacy crusade in that zone taught the Pacific coast participants that not everyone in Nicaragua spoke Spanish and that a second campaign was necessary to incorporate the linguistic diversity of the region, an attitude that kept people from thinking that the new revolution was simply a new colonization.

The differences between the regions grew more and more difficult to contain. The Miskito Indians had their own history, roots, culture, and language. To incorporate the indigenous groups into the new world of the revolution, a group was created called MISURASATA, which means "Miskitos, Sumus, Ramas and Sandinistas United"; it was also called "A Single Heart." Once this unity was achieved, the hope was that the differences and internal conflicts would diminish and not become an unmanageable social and political problem. The new government began to feel even greater pressure when the indigenous communities requested that the government give them the right to approximately 17,500 square miles, 38 percent of the national territory of Nicaragua. The indigenous groups also requested political autonomy of the region. The revolutionary government perceived this request as detrimental to the revolution.

The problem of incorporating these different groups was political rather than racial. In 1981, the ethnic leaders who belonged to the recently created MISURASATA group were arrested. The government dissolved the organization, decreeing that it was an attack on national sovereignty, and created the Institute of the Atlantic coast, governed from the Pacific zone. This undermined the trust of the indigenous groups, causing them to move across Nicaragua's northern border to Honduras amidst bloody confrontations. At the same time, in Honduras, the counter-revolution was born and the new government in Nicaragua had suffered its first attacks and resulting casualties. Because of these attacks and to avoid the flight of the Indians into Honduras, the Sandinista government ordered the removal and resettling of Miskito indigenous communities who lived along the Coco River to places 60 kilometers from the river toward the interior of Nicaragua. It is important to mention that the communities on the banks of the Coco River, which forms the border between Nicaragua and Honduras, do not recognize the frontier between the two countries; they consider themselves one large indigenous community separated by opposite riverbanks. They consider the Coco River their home, their traditional land, the place where their ancestors are buried.

To avoid the problem of the Indians' attachment to their land, the villages and crops were burned, the cattle and domestic animals killed, and the churches turned into storage facilities. In all, 300 Indians were declared counter-revolutionaries and were jailed, although they were later released. In spite of everything that the Sandinista government invested to keep the Indians in their new settlement areas, they refused to live in that sort of captivity where they were mixed together with no attention to their aboriginal social structures. In other words, the government did not recognize the importance of their clans, which is a characteristic of indigenous families and political groups as well. In the reservations, the people were in a state of agitation. As a result of the military offensive organized by the contras (counter-revolutionaries) called "Red Christmas," there was a huge increase in the number of indigenous people who fled the settlements. Besides the nearly complete lack of tact on the part of the new authorities attempting to achieve coastal integration with the rest of the country, another important factor was that the Indians believed the highly exaggerated anti-Sandinista propaganda that was circulated by the Contras.

In 1985, after experimenting with different programs, all of which were disastrous, the Sandinista government tried to create reconciliation in the area. On the Atlantic coast, the main problem was with the indigenous communities, even though a large part of the population took advantage of the programs in education and health that the central government was developing in that part of the country. Many of these people were fervent participants in the bilingual education project that was carried out later.

The Miskitos were an example of resistance in spite of all the political manipulation. For the revolution, solving the so-called Indian problem was a major challenge. The Sandinistas had to learn that those inhospitable territories already had their own laws and communitarian structures, which were even more efficient, in many ways, than the social structures of the Pacific.

The indigenous population of Nicaragua's Caribbean coast succeeded in achieving its goal of greater political independence, though it remains the country's most impoverished and marginalized group. Currently, the Atlantic coast is divided into two autonomous regions: the Autonomous Region of the North Atlantic (RAAN) and the Autonomous Region of the South Atlantic (RAAS). The two regions have an extension of approximately 23,700 square miles, which accounts for 51 percent of Nicaragua's total territory.

Almost the entire Atlantic coast population is multilingual. The majority speaks English, Creole, and Spanish in addition to the indigenous languages Miskito, Sumo, and Rama. The economy's strength is primarily related to the sea and the lobster, shrimp, fish, and turtle industry, although agricultural products and cattle are also important. Three mines (Siuna, Bonanza, and Rosita) that produce gold and silver are also located in this region.

For many years, communication with this part of Nicaragua was possible only by land, but now there are roads, although some stretches are often impassible because of deep ruts and mud, especially during the rainy season. The geographic location, in addition to the region's poverty, make Nicaragua's Caribbean coast vulnerable to natural disasters, as exemplified by Hurricane Felix, which ravaged the city of Puerto Cabezas in September, 2007, leaving many dead and homeless among the Miskito population. Under more normal

Destruction from Hurricane Felix on Nicaragua's Atlantic coast, September 2007. © Wilmor López. Used by permission.

weather conditions, boats also make travel possible on the Escondido River between the port of El Rama and Bluefields. This mode of travel is comfortable and visitors are usually quite impressed by the diverse flora and fauna.

By air and by water, one can visit the exotic Corn Island, located 83 km. northeast of Bluefields. The island is 13 sq. km. with a population of 10,000. In the eighteenth century, the first English settlers established themselves on the island after the signing of the Treaty of Versailles and the Convention of London, by means of which England recognized Spanish sovereignty over the Miskito territory and its adjacent islands. On August 27, 1841, Colonel Alexander McDonald, superintendent of the Republic of British Honduras, arrived on Corn Island to declare the freedom of the slaves in the name of Queen Victoria of England and the Miskito King Roberto Carlos Federico. This freedom is celebrated every year as the Crab Soup Festival.

THE *CAUDILLO* AS A FIGURE OF NICARAGUAN POLITICAL LIFE

The most recent governments in Nicaragua, under the banner of democracy, have subjected the country to massive corruption and malfeasance with regard to the public treasury and the goods of the state.

An important concept in the understanding of Nicaraguan culture and politics is *el caudillismo,* which is the support for a *caudillo,* or political strongman. *El caudillismo* is the dark shadow that has been passed on to Nicaragua throughout its history and may even have a parallel in the pre-Columbian indigenous rulers called *caciques.* It was established as the surest way to survive politically in a country where polarization spreads its effects and foreign intervention is constant. It represents the permanence of populist politics as an answer to the poorest, most vulnerable members of society, who are most in need of specific social programs of the so-called democratic governments.

Living examples of *caudillismo* that always have characterized homegrown Nicaraguan politics are Arnoldo Alemán (president of Nicaragua from 1996–2001) and Daniel Ortega (Nicaraguan president, 1985–1990, reelected in 2006). Both are politicians who are rejected by many but acclaimed by an even greater number of supporters. The fundamental difference between *el caudillismo* and democratic governments is its efficiency for solving immediate problems such as health, education, and unemployment more quickly as opposed to democratic governments where these factors are often not necessarily a top priority but rather a concern for future consideration.

Alemán was accused of acts of corruption while he was president and sentenced to jail, but his government created schools and health centers throughout the entire country. People worry less about whether he stole or not, preferring to recognize the accomplishments in health and education. Daniel Ortega, without needing to be in the executive seat, has known how to take advantage of the friendly support offered to him by the governments of Spain, Cuba, Venezuela, and Brazil in order to maintain a program of scholarships and specialized medical treatment for the people with the fewest resources available to them in Nicaragua. The first policies enacted by Ortega after he was reelected included making health and education free and increasing support for cultural activities.

Nicaraguan citizens, whether they live in urban or rural areas, are used to their *caudillos* and believe as part of the collective unconscious: "all politicians are thieves, but Alemán and Ortega remember the poor when they are in power or not in power, so what difference does it make to me if they stole?" The people of Nicaragua are always uncomfortable when there is outside interference in their internal affairs. If people were not happy that the Sandinistas copied a Cuban socialist model, they also do not accept the blessings, condemnations, and blackmail from the U.S. embassy that went beyond all limits in the recent 2006 electoral campaign, which Daniel Ortega Saavedra won. The people on that occasion took as a threat to their voting independence the desperation of the U.S. ambassador Paul Trivelli when he took sides by supporting the rightist candidate Eduardo Montealegre of the

Liberal Nicaraguan Alliance (ALN) and attacked both Daniel Ortega and Arnoldo Alemán (a candidate that the United States preferred in previous years). In fact, this U.S. interference helped worsen the deep divisions in Nicaragua's political right as it attempted to challenge Ortega's frontrunner status during the months before the election. In short, both Ortega and Alemán might be considered the most recent manifestations of the *caudillo* in Nicaragua.

NOTES

1. The authors use two main sources to compile much of the factual information in this chapter. See Tomás Ayón. *Historia de Nicaragua.* Vol. 1. León, Nicaragua: Banco Nicaragüense, 1993 and José Monterrey. *Apuntes básicos para el estudio general de Nicaragua.* León, Nicaragua: UNAN—León, 1989.

2. See Eduardo Zepeda-Henríquez. *Mitología nicaragüense.* Managua: Academia de Geografía de Historia de Nicaragua, 2003.

2

Religion and Religious Celebrations

DURING THE COLONIAL period and up to the twentieth century, Nicaragua was a predominantly Catholic country. Until relatively recently, it would have been difficult to imagine the growth of other religions and sects in the country. New surveys, however, have demonstrated marked changes in Nicaraguan religious practices.

In general, the history of Nicaragua has been written from a conservative ideological perspective reflecting the influence of the Catholic Church. This influence was present in colonial times, of course, but also during the period of independence, as well as during the modern era of the Nicaraguan church, which coincided with the reforms of the Second Ecumenical Council of the Vatican (1962–1965). This period also includes the decade of the Sandinista government in Nicaragua throughout the 1980s.[1]

Beginning with the revolution in 1979, Nicaraguan Catholicism experienced many conflicts. For the first time in Latin America there was strong support on behalf of certain sectors of the Catholic Church from within the insurrectional struggle against the Somoza dictatorship. In the late 1970s and continuing into the 1980s, Christian communities and young people who belonged to Christian groups became more politically active. Faith moved thousands of Nicaraguans in a spontaneous way to see the links between Catholicism and Marxist thought in a religious movement known as liberation theology. Those in this movement committed themselves to the revolutionary struggle at great personal sacrifice. Many were imprisoned and

The image of Santo Domingo is carried through the outlying hills of Managua (where it remains for 10 days) each year on August 1. © Wilmor López. Used by permission.

tortured. Many lost their lives as a result of their religious and political beliefs. For this reason, at the moment of the Sandinista triumph, there was a marked presence of Catholics in the new government cabinet, including, for example, Father Miguel D'Escoto, minister of foreign relations, Father Ernesto Cardenal, minister of culture, as well as officials such as the Jesuit priest Fernando Cardenal, who served as minister of education, and Edgard Parrales, who was the minister of social welfare and, later, the representative of the Nicaraguan government at the Organization of American States. In addition, there were numerous priests and nuns who provided their technical services to the government and popular organizations.[2]

   This conflict inevitably led to a split between the Catholic bishops and the authorities of the Nicaraguan government (for political, not religious, reasons) that resulted in a divided Church. One interesting aspect of this period was the development of the religious practices of the Nicaraguan people in which the celebrations of Mass, processions, and public acts demonstrated a union between religion and politics. An example of this was the "Prophetic Fast" of Father Miguel D'Escoto for 40 days in June and July 1983. This fast enabled him to meditate on the sanction imposed on him by the Vatican, which prohibited government officials from celebrating mass, a prohibition that also affected Ernesto and Fernando Cardenal, both ordained priests.

The Catholic bishops felt that the Frente Sandinista exercised a kind of absolute control over different sectors in Nicaraguan society composed of young people, workers, and students. They believed that the Sandinistas constituted a totalitarian government. As proof, they cited the closing of the Catholic radio station and the denial of entry of some bishops in Nicaragua in 1986.

When Pope John Paul II visited Nicaragua in March 1983, many Nicaraguans were mourning the deaths of 17 young civilians working on a literacy campaign, who were murdered by armed anti-Sandinista groups. The massive number of Catholics gathered in the July 19 Plaza in Managua requested that the Pope offer a prayer for these victims. This produced a strange and lamentable episode: His Holiness asked that people refrain from shouting their impassioned plea. He wanted a more respectful silence, something that was hard for the assembled people to understand. Politics and religion might not be sufficient to explain what happened next: thousands of faithful Catholics began to boo their undisputed leader, who could not establish the communication that his followers had hoped he would achieve. Commentaries included: "The Pope did not know what was going on there," "He came from a very different reality," and "The Pope was poorly advised."

In another incident that was not appreciated by most Nicaraguans, the Pope, disembarking from his plane in Nicaragua, publicly admonished Father Ernesto Cardenal, the minister of culture of the Sandinista government. Father Cardenal, kneeling on the tarmac, kissed the hand of the Pope as a sign of respect. The Pope energetically chastised Cardenal by wagging his index finger over Cardenal's head, a photograph of which circulated in newspapers around the globe. Currently in Nicaragua, the conflicts between the divided Church have diminished considerably. This is perhaps due to a greater tolerance on the part of the more traditional Church, as the miserable social conditions that produced the divisions have not improved.

The official Catholic Church, which has been lax in recognizing and alleviating the severe social problems in Nicaragua, justifies its stance by preferring to meet the spiritual, rather than material, needs of its followers. The same situation that produced the emergence of liberation theology can be linked to the recent proliferation of the numerous conservative Evangelical Protestant groups that demonstrate greater efficacy in resolving the physical needs of their followers. These Protestant groups (many of which are based in the United States and have translated names that sound strange to Nicaraguan ears) have complete freedom to coexist in Nicaragua, which has a constitutional guarantee that protects all forms of religious practices and prevents religious discrimination.

A poll conducted in 1995 indicates that more than 90 percent of the Nicaraguan population belongs to groups with a Christian affiliation: 72.9 percent are Catholic, 15.5 percent belong to Evangelical churches, 1.5 percent is part of the Moravian Church, and 1.9 percent are associated with other churches or religious groups (including Mormons, Amish, Mennonites, and Jehovah's Witnesses). Of those interviewed, 8.5 percent said they belonged to no religious group or were atheists.[3]

In 2003, in a poll that did not include respondents from Nicaragua's Atlantic coast, there was a clear indication of the rapid growth of Evangelical groups in Nicaragua, whose followers seem to be formerly practicing Catholics. According to this poll, 70.5 percent of the population is Catholic, 16.1 percent are members of Evangelical churches, 3.2 percent belong to other groups, and 9.8 percent have no religious affiliation. The quantity of people in non-Christian groups in Nicaragua is smaller, but it is also clear that there is an increase in the number of citizens who are associated with non-Catholic groups. Nicaragua does have minority religious groups, including a Jewish community of 50 people, and approximately 200 Muslims who are primarily foreign immigrants from Iran, Libya, and Palestine who arrived in Nicaragua in the 1980s.[4]

The government of Nicaragua has no official religion, although the Catholic Church has maintained a close relationship with all Nicaraguan governments, with the exception of the Sandinistas in the 1980s. Leaders of the Catholic Church historically have held frequent meetings with high-ranking government officials, and there has been speculation that government funds have been used to support expenses related to the Church, especially in terms of the costs of monuments, religious symbols, and activities. Even so, the predominance of the Catholic Church does not have a negative effect with regard to the ability of other groups to practice their religions freely. Some current religious groups, such as the Evangelicals, have their own political parties. Christian Path, for example, has three representatives in Nicaragua's National Assembly. With the return to power of the Sandinistas in 2006, the relationship between this political party and the Catholic Church has moved beyond the divisions of the 1980s. During the electoral campaign, Daniel Ortega actively sought the support of Evangelical (as well as Catholic) voters, expressing a conservative stand on certain social issues such as abortion.[5] Cardinal Miguel Obando y Bravo, former opponent of the Sandinistas, is now the coordinator of the newly created Council of Reconciliation.

FESTIVALS OF PATRON SAINTS

Each village, region, and municipality, as well as Nicaragua in its entirety, celebrates festivals in commemoration of a patron saint. In Nicaragua, there

Don Juan Moraga, a devotee of Santo Domingo, has been a traditional carrier of the saint for more than 40 years. © Wilmor López. Used by permission.

is a calendar that lists the celebrations and their locations. Every one of these celebrations is linked to a particular saint (see Appendix).

La Purísima, or La Gritería

La Purísima is the most popular celebration of the Nicaraguan people. It is dedicated to the Immaculate Conception of Mary, who is the patron saint of Nicaragua. Each December 7, the streets fill with people who move among the many altars that the majority of the houses have made in honor of the mother of Jesus. Although it is true that the cult to Mary had its beginning during the years of the conquest, the most resplendent, spontaneous, and joyous festival in Nicaragua is the popular *Gritería,* which was first held on December 7, 1857. On that date, Monsignor Gordiano Carranza, the parish priest of the San Felipe Church in León, sent out the first *grito,* or cry (hence the name *gritería,* which is synonymous with La Purísima), "Who is the source of so much joy?," to which the masses of people loudly replied "Mary!" The question has deep and sublime roots in the popular consciousness. The story of such devotion and the influence in the life of Nicaraguans permeates newspapers, chronicles, and studies about the religious, historical, and even folkloric aspects that surround this date.

The origin of the celebration of the Immaculate Conception of Mary dates from 1390 when King John I of Aragon fomented the cult to Mary in Spain and issued a decree that mandated the celebration of the festival of the Conception of the Virgin and imposed a punishment of exile against those who were opposed to this idea. In 1476, Pope Sixto IV (1414–1484), a Franciscan, imposed the festival on the diocese of Rome, still under the name of the Conception of the Immaculate Woman, not the Immaculate Conception, but the object of the celebration was the sanctification of Mary and not the fact that she had conceived. In 1661, Pope Alexander VII declared that the festival celebrated the immunity of Mary from all stain from the moment that her soul was created and infused in her body, in other words, from the time she was conceived by her mother. In 1708, Pope Clement VI imposed the celebration of the Immaculate Conception throughout the Western world as a precept. In 1761, King Charles III declared the Immaculate Conception the patron saint of Spain and the New World, which resulted in the establishing of the cult on the American continent. Finally, another Franciscan, Pope Pius IX, had the honor of promulgating (on December 8, 1845) that the blessed Virgin Mary was preserved immune from all stain of original sin at the moment of her conception by the singular grace of God.[6]

The first image of the Virgin to arrive in Nicaragua was in 1562 and was brought by the brother of Saint Teresa of Avila. It is worshiped in the National Sanctuary of El Viejo, Chinandega, but León is considered the land of the Purísimas, because it is in the San Francisco Church where the Franciscan monks initiated the celebration of the novenas (nine days of public devotion to achieve special graces) in honor of the Immaculate Conception of Mary. So many people attended that there was not enough room in the temple for all of them, and the priests asked families to do the celebrations at home. For this reason, the novenas and the estampas of the Virgin were given as gifts.[7] The novenas begin each year in the second half of November. In homes, schools, and institutions, there are prayers and songs to the Virgin for nine days.

In people's homes, this is normally done at night and lasts for about an hour. Family members and neighbors are invited, and, at the end, sweets and candies (called gorras) are given away. The last day of the novena, the host of the house, "throws the house out the window." This is a Nicaraguan way of saying that the homemade altar with the image of the Virgin (which passersby can see) and the homemade sweets (passed out freely to all) are excellent. Many of the altars to the Purísima are made even more interesting by groups of musicians that accompany the choirs and voices of the singers, presenting the traditional religious music.

The traditional gorra is handed out in packets, little sacks or small baskets made of palm leaves, cardboard, or paper, filled with typical sweets that have names in Spanish such as *nisperitos, suspiros, piñonates, cajetas, pan de rosa, lecheburras,* and the obligatory *gofios.* A jelly made from a kind of fruit called *nancites* is also prepared, as well as squash in honey, bananas, sugarcane, and sweetened lemons. The traditional drink is called *chicha* and is made from corn. There is also a drink made from cocoa and ground calabash seeds. Other items that contribute to the prayers and are part of the *gorra* packet include whistles, rattles, maracas, *chischiles, chicharras,* masks, hats and neck-laces made from *pajillas,* corn of different colors, and beautiful white seeds called tears of Saint Peter. Everything is made by families throughout the year during their free time.

The night of December 7, in other words, the night before the day conse-crated to the Catholic Church to the Conception of Mary, all the activities in Nicaragua are devoted to the celebration that has been prepared for in so many ways. Houses are painted, people are commissioned to do the cloth back-grounds for the altars, sweets are made, and exquisite altars are built, some of which are true works of art that represent the various landscapes of Nicaragua with skies, seas, valleys, fountains, waterfalls, lakes, and volcanoes. The most typical and natural altars are made in the rural areas and adorned with flowers from the *madroño* and *sardinillo* trees and cut flowers such as *pastoras, jalacates, pañal de niño, palmeras, chagüite,* basil, lilies, *disciplinas,* Jupiter, San Diego, and gladiolus. A fireworks display signals that the altar is finished. Then, at midnight, a carefully planned family dinner is served. It is similar to the one served on Christmas Eve and includes stuffed chicken and *nacatamales* (dough made from corn, filled with pieces of pork and wrapped in banana leaves).

At 6:00 P.M., the peeling of bells from all the churches in the city, accom-panied by fireworks, announces the beginning of the great festival to Mary called *La Gritería.* The people, filled with great enthusiasm, spill into the streets and go from house to house, where there are altars, and shout, "Who is the source of so much joy?" "The conception of Mary!" The owners of the houses pass out the *gorras* while the visitors admire the altar and sing to the Virgin. When they leave, the people shout "Long live the Virgin!," the reply to which is "May she live forever!" People hold out bags to receive the *gorra.* In the first celebrations, people hoping to receive gifts would hold out their hats, the Spanish word for which, literally, is *gorras.* That is how the packet of gifts itself came to be called a *gorra.*

This cry, given for the first time in León, originated the most genuine tradition of the Nicaraguan people, and spontaneously became the symbol of this festival celebrated from Granada in the west to Chontales in the east, and from Nueva Segovia in the north to the San Juan River in the south. On December 7, Nicaragua is united in a single cry: "¿Quién causa tanta alegría?"

At midnight, there are explosions of gunpowder that close the celebration of the night. The next day, December 8, at noon, there are more explosions and again at 6:00 P.M., which is the farewell. Many Nicaraguan poets such as Alfonso Cortés, Manolo Cuadra, José María Carmona, Azarías H. Pallais, Joaquín Sacasa, Alí Vanegas, Juan de Dios Vanegas, Cornelio Sosa, Fernando Silva, Sergio Darce, Antenor Sandino Hernández, Mariana Sansón Argüello, Silvia Díaz, Enma Fonseca, Octavio Robleto, Guillermo Gómez Brenes, Tino López Guerra, and Marcial Ríos Jérez have praised the Virgin in their poems and this national celebration with 150 years of tradition. Each December 7, there is also a contest for the best altar. The contestants need to sign up beforehand so that their altars can be evaluated by the jury on the night of La Gritería.

La Gigantona

Some of the most colorful images associated with the December celebrations, including, of course, La Purísima, are the *gigantonas,* giant female figures, dancing through the streets and accompanied by the sound of drums, reminding onlookers that the month of greatest joy is at hand. The *gigantonas* are enormous dolls made of wood, cardboard, and twine. Their rather severe faces look as if they were wearing heavy makeup. From their earlobes hang gaudy earrings. And they also wear showy necklaces. Their hair is long, either loose or in braids. Their arms are filled with sawdust. Some have a hollow head and their eyes are lit by candles placed inside.[8]

These *Damitas,* or Little Ladies, as they are called, begin making noise in November and are always surrounded by many children. Between 7 and 10 P.M., they move through the city streets followed by their cortege: the dwarfs, the street singers, the *pepe chineado,* and the bigheaded dwarf. The general composition of these dances are the band of drummers, some with snare drums and others with bass drums; the lamps; one or two *muñecos*; and the old men, pages, and dancers who dance and recite poetry every so often. The *gigantona* is accompanied by lamps made of wood, lined on the top with colored streamers and holding a lit candle inside. The happy children run from their houses and join the cortege of the *Damitas.* Each barrio in León has its own *gigantona:* San Felipe, Laborio, Sutiaba, La Ermita de Dolores, Guadalupe, Zaragoza, El Coyolar, and San Juan. Since the mid-1950s, the municipality of León has organized a *gigantona* contest each December 8, in which the following aspects are judged: dance, costumes, originality, rhyming couplets and their content, recitation, and the music. Initially, the contests were held in the central park in front of the cathedral, but because of the great numbers of people who competed and the many *gigantonas,* the contest was moved to the Metropolitan Baseball Stadium. There are prizes for first, second, and third place and all the competitors need to follow the rules

The *gigantona* is a figure from the popular culture of León associated with the December celebration of La Purísima. © Wilmor López. Used by permission.

established by the organizers. The recitation of poetry is varied. First, there is the traditional verse, which is frequently fragments from ballads, songs, or very old poetry that is still preserved in the oral tradition of Nicaraguan popular culture. The street poets recite their verse, couplets, and *bombas* each time that the music of the drums stops and the *Damita* and those who accompany her stop dancing. The poetry can be dedicated to the *gigantona* or to any member of the public.

Here is an example of a traditional poem in translation:

I am a wanderer passing through life,
Half wanderer, half troubadour.
Just as the April flowers bloom,

I go on my steed down the green path
And the jungle shudders with the sound of my song
And leaves the sweetness of honey on lips.

The *coplas* are anonymous poems full of life and mischief, which are dear to the people's hearts.

How beautiful the water flows
In the two washing tubs.
Don't let that old lady
Come between us in our love.

The *bomba* is based on fast improvisation, naughty humor and things that are going on at that very moment in the street.

The girls nowadays
Are really marvelous.
They go out at night with their colors
And come in at dawn yellow.
Yesterday, I went by your house
And you were eating a rooster
And your teeth were making more noise
Than the teeth of a horse.

La Purísima or Conchita of Granada

The other city that venerates the Immaculate Conception of Mary with great fervor is the city of Granada, also called La Gran Sultana (The Great Sultaness). Around this venerated image are woven several stories that differ in small details describing its apparition and a box on the waters of Lake Nicaragua. According to the chronicles, in 1752, some women who were washing clothes on the shore of the lake saw a wooden box floating toward them on the waters of the lake. When they tried to bring it ashore, it moved farther away in the lake. The fascinated washerwomen told the monks of the San Francisco convent about the strange apparition. They asked the monks if they could do some of their exorcisms to invoke what surely had come from the devil. The monks went out from the convent prepared with hyssop and holy water and their cord of St. Francis tied tightly around their waists. When they reached the place, they found the floating box, which allowed itself to be secured by the monks with the cords. Then they gently dragged the box ashore. When they opened it, the monks and washerwomen were astonished by an image of the Virgin, delicately carved in wood, with a baby Jesus in her arms and the moon at her feet. No one has ever been able to explain the presence of the image on the coast of Granada. It is possible that it came from some shipwreck and that the currents dragged it down the San Juan River to the lake where the wind blew it to Granada's shore.[9]

The other version of the story, one that is accepted and disseminated by the Church and also historians, tells that the Virgin did not arrive miraculously but rather that it came from El Castillo on the San Juan River because the people from Granada went there to celebrate La Purísima. In one of the many pirate attacks on this place, the Spaniards, to save the object they most treasured, put the image in a box and the box on a boat, heading toward Granada. When it arrived on the coast of the lake, the box fell into the water and, floating there, it surprised the washerwomen, for they believed it was an enchanted box and went to find the Franciscan monks.

La Conchita, celebrated by the people of Granada, receives tributes from all the barrios of the city from November 28 through December 7. In the cathedral of Granada during the ceremony that signals the beginning of the festivities of La Purísima, the image is lowered in the early hours of the night of November 28. The members of the Benemérito Corps of Firefighters lower the Virgin onto her altar and throughout the whole city one can hear the sirens of the fire engines. La Conchita is situated on her platform and is carried on the shoulders of men around the cathedral. The next day, she begins her visits to the altars in the different barrios.

THE ENRAMADAS IN GRANADA

The arrangement of each altar made of branches (called an *enramada*) is very precise and takes a great deal of time to prepare. Generally, the barrio keeps certain things secret, such as how their specific altar and cart will be decorated because the Virgin returns each night to the cathedral in a cart that is designed, arranged, and adorned by the people who live in the barrio. The *enramada* is covered with coconut palms, but it does not always have a roof made of branches. The whole neighborhood is in the streets or at home, working happily on gluing the crepe paper to the *banderolas,* hanging decorations, carrying branches, and so forth. As a group, they lift the *enramada* in honor of their Patron Saint. Nine *enramadas* are prepared, one for each day that the Virgin visits. The altars are always highly original. On December 7, just as in the rest of the country, there are lines of people in the streets, visiting altars house by house.

CELEBRATIONS OF LA PURÍSIMA IN OTHER PARTS OF THE COUNTRY

In Masaya, people carry the Virgin in a procession in the morning from the Magdalena church to the nine barrios (one per day) of the indigenous part of the city called Monimbó and in the afternoon return in carts to the same church where the image is received with songs called *cánticos* and *sones* performed by musicians called *chicheros*. On December 7 at 5 P.M., a happy, colorful parade of women from Monimbó in indigenous costumes comes down to the church from all parts of the department carrying baskets with offerings to the Virgin Mary, including fruit, flowers, and all kinds of sweets.

In Managua, the capital, people from different parts of the country come together, producing a mixture of customs particular to each group in the celebration of the Virgin Mary. During the 1980s, a different kind of stamp was imposed on the celebrations in the capital. They were organized all along Bolívar Avenue. Each business sponsor built its altar, and, on December 7, a multitude of people visited the many altars and received the customary *gorra*. Families also made their altars and *griterías* in the houses of the different barrios.

Jinotega, "the City of Mist," adds a special touch to the celebration with its traditional, delicious drink called *"agua Loja,"* which is exclusively from this part of the country. The drink is made from toasted and broken corn that is fermented with *dulce de rapadura* and lots of ginger. The secret to the unique taste is that the corn is fermented in clay pots. The result is a strong taste and a transparent yellow color. The people from Jinotega also show their religious fervor by building beautiful altars and passing out abundant amounts of *gorras*.

On December 7, in Matagalpa, known as "The Pearl of the North," the people awaken the Virgin with mariachis and sing songs to her called *mañanitas*. The city is famous for having celebrations filled with lots of music. In all the homes, the last day of the *novena* is accompanied by musicians, and *novenas* are accompanied by entire bands of musicians throughout the nine days. Many people grab their guitars and sing from altar to altar, receiving the traditional *gorra*.

On the Caribbean coast, the celebrations do not differ greatly from the ones on the Pacific side of Nicaragua. The altars are constructed in keeping with the landscape of that area and are always made with great devotion. In some parts of the Caribbean, there are songs recorded in Miskito, one of the indigenous languages spoken there.

La Purísima is a celebration of identity. In any country where there is a person from Nicaragua, there will be singing to the Immaculate Conception of Mary in December. It is a celebration that unmistakably identifies a Catholic religious presence rooted in popular mestizo traditions.

NOTES

1. Edgar Zúñiga. *Historia eclesiástica de Nicaragua.* Managua: Hispamer, 1996, pp. xvi–xvii.

2. Teófilo Cabestrero. *Ministros de Dios.* Managua: Ministerio de Cultura, 1983, pp. 9–10.

3. Informe internacional sobre la libertad de culto 2005. Distribuido por la Oficina de Democracia, Derechos Humanos y del Trabajo. Available at: http://spanish.nicaragua.usembassy.gov/rfr-nic-2005.html.

4. Informe internacional sobre la libertad de culto 2005.

5. Sara Miller Llana. "Evangelicals Flex Growing Clout in Nicaragua's Election," *Christian Science Monitor* (November 2, 2006): 1, 5.

6. Enma Fonseca C. *La purísima en Nicaragua* (2nd revised edition). Managua: Impresiones y Troqueles, 2004, pp. 80–90.

7. Personal interview with Estela Chévez Vega, faithful devotee of the celebrations of La Purísima, November 2006, León, Nicaragua.

8. This section was based on a personal interview with Dr. Edgardo Buitrago Buitrago, historian and director of the Rubén Darío Museum Archive, León, Nicaragua, November, 2006.

9. This section was based on Enma Fonseca C.'s *La purísima en Nicaragua* (1st edition). Managua: Impresiones y Troqueles, 1998, pp. 22–33.

3

Social Customs

THE SOCIAL CUSTOMS of a country are an excellent way of understanding traditions and change and how they coexist. Nicaragua is no exception. What people eat and how they celebrate their culinary arts, nontraditional approaches to healing as a result of deficiencies in the Nicaraguan healthcare system, how Nicaraguan families are structured, gender roles in a sexist society, rites of passage, the educational system, as well as the sports Nicaraguans play, all provide fascinating insights into Nicaraguan culture.

FOOD

Whenever one studies the history of any people in the world, nutrition is an essential topic. As might be expected, ancient indigenous customs had a deep and lasting influence on current cultural practices. It is often said that the indigenous population of the Americas did not make an important contribution in terms of the domestic transformation of plants and animals. Because this process is so difficult, it required a prolonged amount of time for the aboriginal groups to achieve a control over this part of their customary way of living. It is almost certain that a grain of corn consumed now by people in Latin America, especially in Mesoamerica where nutrition is based on that ancestral and divine grain, has greater nutritional benefits than the corn in the era before its domestication. Furthermore, the different ways of preparing food developed in tandem with the process of controlling plants and animals. Diverse texture and flavors were invented, and in this way, too, different tribes created marked nutritional preferences even though they used the same fruits and grains. They also used similar methods of preparing food by cooking, grinding, and soaking. To these three techniques should be added the process of fermentation to obtain ceremonial drinks. Corn was definitely the spinal column of life in the New World. The Europeans immediately believed that corn was a variation of wheat and classified as such, linking it to the Christian religious symbolism associated with the word *bread*.[1] The scientific name for corn (what the indigenous groups called *maíz*) is *Zea mays*. It is originally from the Americas and, in current economic terms, represents the third largest global crop after wheat and rice.[2]

Corn has been a transformative economic and social force throughout Mesoamerica. A product of trade and a generator of wealth, corn also has been a resource that has helped define a cultural and culinary identity, especially in Nicaragua. In addition, corn is also thought to possess magicoreligious qualities; in ancient times it was used in sacred rites in honor of Xilonem, "Goddess of the Tender Corn." What corn and everything derived from it represent for the campesino and the Nicaraguan farmer is similar to what it meant for the country's indigenous population long ago: food and a unique

Street vendors preparing a variety of fried foods, which are popular in Nicaragua, a country renowned for its traditional culinary arts. © Wilmor López. Used by permission.

way of preparing it, work and life itself, as well as a religion. It was a gift from the gods that the Indians bequeathed to their descendants.[3]

Nicaraguan indigenous groups served all their food cooked and spiced with hot chilis (*Capsicum solanoidea*), achiote (*Bixa orellana*), and different herbs to create a pleasing taste. Instead of bread made from wheat, they ate *cazabe* or bread made from yucca (*Manihot esulenta*) as well as corn tortillas, which are eaten today on a daily basis in Nicaragua.[4] Nicaragua has its own unique traditions created with ingredients from Nicaragua and elsewhere, although the diet of Nicaraguans is part of a collective culture based on corn.

In terms of meat, pork is a part of many native and popular foods such as the *nacatamal, chancho con yuca* (cooked yucca, fried or seasoned pork, and salad), *vigorón* (cooked yucca, fried pork rinds, and salad), *moronga* or *morcilla* (black pudding made from pig's blood prepared with spices and hot chiles served with tortillas or yucca), and creole-style sausage. There are a wide variety of foods made from pork. There are still small slaughterhouses for the pork in homes where the *nacatamales* are prepared and sold. These houses are clean and meet the standards of the health department; clandestine slaughterhouses do not follow the required health procedures to avoid contamination.

Beef is also frequently consumed. It is often prepared as *carne de baho* (strips of dried and salted meat cooked together with ripe and green bananas, yucca, peppers, and onions, which is later wrapped and served in banana leaves. There are numerous meals that feature meat. The list of soups includes concentrated broths and *mondongos* made with a hefty piece of cow's stomach. This is the specialty of *mondonguerías,* which are very popular places to eat. People in Nicaragua praise the masculine benefits of *mondongo* soup. There is also the succulent soup with a broth from rib bones and the following vegetables: green plums, *quequisque* or *malanga lila* (*Xanthosoma violaceum*), *ayotes* (*Curcurbita maxium*), *chayotes* (*Sechium edole*), yucca, *elotes* (ripe corn), *chilotes* (baby corn), cabbage, and others. All the seasonings have cilantro and *hierbabuena.* Nicaraguans are proud of their culinary culture. Other equally delicious soups that are served at any table regardless of social class are made with beans, fish, crab, shellfish, and *gallina india* (a special kind of hen that the Indians catch near lakes, swamps, rivers, and ponds) served with meatballs.[5]

Each Nicaraguan soup has a distinctive touch that would never be confused with those of another country even if the soups were made with the same or similar ingredients. After three centuries of original experiments, Nicaraguan cooking has evolved without losing its unique tastes.

Each part of the cow has its place on the menu. The best meat, such as *lomos, contralomos,* and *lomos de aguja,* is often grilled on a woodstove. Other cuts are chopped and used to make meals called *salpicones.* Tongue is used in sauce; the brains and marrow in broth that is fried with eggs; liver is fried or served in sauce. Udders are used to prepare sauces, and bull's testicles are served in soup or fried. Delicious little cakes are prepared with chopped meat, potatoes, and carrots or spiced and wrapped in egg or vegetable. All the food is pleasing to the eye in terms of the combinations of colors.

Another excellent soup (used by the Catholic Church as a penance during Lent) is cheese or *cuajada* soup. It is made of fried cakes of cornmeal wrapped in cheese, egg, salt, and *achiote*. The cakes are dropped gently in a soup made with plums, green mangoes, yucca, green bananas, and potatoes. Occasionally, dried sardines are added. Another typical meal during Lent is rice with salted and dried fish. Because it is forbidden to eat meat on Fridays during Lent, these meals are preferred on Nicaraguan tables.

The *almíbares,* or sweets, are made of seasonal fruit during Lent. Especially important is *cusnaca,* a dish whose origin dates from colonial times. To make it, *guaturco* variety plums are cooked with sugar, cinnamon, and milk.

The preferred game meat is venison. In the colonial period, the wives of the hunters would sell the venison haunches in the market or from house to house. They also sold well-cooked pigeons early in the morning; people would eat them for breakfast seasoned with lemon and salt.

The Indians also transmitted to contemporary times their taste for reptiles. Unlike their ancestors, however, Nicaraguans (except for certain regional tribes) do not incorporate caterpillars, worms, and insects in their diets. The maguey worms that are so popular in Mexican cooking are a good example of this eating habit in contemporary times. It is likely that the Nicaraguan indigenous groups stopped eating this kind of food, as it was no doubt repugnant to the Creoles and mestizos during the colonial period. They then invented different styles of cooking that were more in keeping with Nicaraguan colonial taste preferences. Lizards called iguanas and *garrobos* are still commonly eaten in Nicaragua. It is not unusual to see these lizards being sold for food by peasant hunters on the side of the road throughout Nicaragua's western side.

On the Atlantic coast, the preferred dish is sea turtle in all its possible forms: eggs, flippers, intestines, and meat. Hunters slit the throats of the sea turtles, and those who have witnessed this event say that the turtles stare at their executioners and cry. Despite all attempts to ban the killing of sea turtles, hunters ignore the laws.

Coconut milk is the main ingredient in Caribbean Creole cooking, a preference that is more mestizo than indigenous. This food shows the influence of Afro-Caribbean cuisine, especially from Jamaica. Other foods from this part of Nicaragua include *rondón, guabul,* and soups made from a wide variety of shellfish.

Fish from Nicaragua's Pacific side will never rival meat in popularity because the eating habits acquired during the colonial period have barely changed. Seafood has never been as important a part of the Nicaraguan diet as chicken, beef, and pork because the most important cities were established on the shores of rivers and lakes, not on the ocean.

The corn tortilla is the most important part of the Nicaraguan diet. It serves as a plate on which food as served, as a spoon when little pieces are torn off, and as something to eat by itself. Bread made from wheat never managed to displace the corn tortilla. In spite of the presence of bakeries, corn has proudly kept its legendary place of importance. The widest use of corn is for the dough that is made by mixing washed and ground corn with ash or lime (not the fruit). Corn also invaded the Nicaraguan recipes for sweets in the confectionery business throughout the country and beyond its borders. In the western part of the country, the so-called things from the oven include *rosquillas, quesadillas, empanaditas, perrerreques,* and *hojaldras.* With corn, Nicaraguans make unique stews, *encurtidos,* salads, and cakes. Each of the departments in Nicaragua is proud of the specific type of food that is produced there from corn. Citizens from Somoto, Rivas, La Paz Centro, Estela, and Matagalpa are famous for producing and eating large quantities of *rosquillas,* for example.

The other staple of the daily Nicaraguan diet is the bean, or *frijol.* It is especially common to eat the frijol (*Phaseolus vulgaris*) at breakfast or dinner as *gallo pinto,* a mixture of rice and red beans. It is often served with *cuajada* (cheese), sausage, and tortilla.

Drinks that accompany food include a wide variety derived from corn such as *pinol, tiste, pinolillo, chicha, chingue, tibio, horchata, posol,* as well as all the natural juices from a tremendous range of fruits. Nicaragua is also well known for the coffee that grows in the mountainous cooler regions in the north and south of the country.

This is why, when Nicaraguans eat, they never fail to imagine everything that food means in terms of how it has nourished successive generations up to the present day. To understand the food of a people is to know something much more profound than the limits of its national boundaries. To know this is to get closer to a country's beliefs and strategies for survival.[6] Nicaragua's culinary magic is a profound reflection of its origins.

Two Important Nonreligious Festivals

Matagalpa's Corn Fair Celebration

The corn fair celebration in Matagalpa at the end of August is the most important homage in Nicaragua to this grain that constitutes the country's nutritional base and has pre-Columbian origins.[7] The Matagalpa Indians organized festivals and *tiangues,* or markets, at the time of the corn harvest, a celebration that lasted even after the arrival of the Spaniards. Over time, the event was given the name *Feria del Maíz.* The indigenous people were expert archers and had a ritualistic war game called *mazorca,* or corn cob. The ear of corn was thrown into the air and a group of Indians shot arrows at it until it did not have a single remaining grain of corn on the cob before it hit the ground.

In the 1980s, as a result of the war in the northern regions of Nicaragua, especially in the department of Matagalpa, only one *Feria del Maíz* could be organized. In the 1990s, the government of Matagalpa revived the local traditions and cultural values by resurrecting the *Feria del Maíz* as a way of highlighting the region's poetry, music, dance, and the selection of a corn queen, as well as to promote corn's culinary diversity. The festival takes place near the Morazán central park and Matagalpa's cathedral. Throughout the day, there are festivals of local peasant music with groups from the rural zones of Jinotega, Chontales, and Estelí in addition to the municipalities of Diriamba, San Ramón, and El Tuma-La Dalia, all of which are areas that provide a vision of corn's sacred importance to the people of northern Nicaragua.

The selection of the corn queen is a popular contest with many preliminary competitions during the three days of the festival. During the 2006 celebration, there were 60 competitors from different rural communities in the department of Matagalpa. These women presented themselves in typical costumes of the region and demonstrated their knowledge of the region's sociocultural, historical, and economic identity in relation to corn. The festival normally occurs from August 26–28. Representatives of the different commercial sectors, in conjunction with municipal authorities, constitute the organizing committee of the corn festival. The indigenous community of the Matagalpa also participates in the activities, still maintaining some of the traditions of their ancestors such as the election of their formal authorities, among them a council of elders, the cacique, and the mayors with their traditional symbols of power. The indigenous people sell a wide variety of traditional food, drink, and alcoholic beverages made from corn.

The Crab Soup Festival on Corn Island

Each August 27, Corn Island shines with popular celebrations. It begins with a traditional parade of boats adorned with flowers, fishing nets, and shells that serve as a place for the young people to represent a variety of important moments in local history.[8] Some floats depict pirates; others treat slavery on the cotton and sugarcane plantations. Many of the participants wear articles worn by their ancestors, for example an apron made of banana leaves. Other floats show scenes of the few moments when the slaves were able to relax around bonfires or on the beach, where men and women danced to the rhythm of improvised percussion instruments. Each float expresses these scenes with ingenuity and creativity. The route proceeds through the island on Aladaña Street and eventually reaches the airport runway. On some occasions, the sailing vessels from the bay join the parade, pretending to be the pirate ships sailing through Caribbean waters.

The spirit of the festival seeks to unite the community, preserve its identity, and find solutions to community problems. This is an effort that is increasingly popular with villagers. The Festival of Crab Soup is spontaneous. The people in the village get together in thatched restaurants where there is soca, reggae, or calypso music for dancing. The dance is begun beneath a leafy breadfruit tree. The number of villagers who participate in the festival increase every year, so the organizers have changed the scene and celebrate games and contests in a big open area near the historic breadfruit tree. At some point, between songs and dances, the people gather around a greased pole to celebrate whoever can reach the top. The participants try (the majority fail), pressing together their feet, hands, and knees to conquer the pole and reach the prizes that hang from the very top.

The beribboned pole is another dance associated with this festival. The fun begins when the dance group starts to braid the ribbons attached to the top of the tree trunk. It ends when, showing off their skill, the dancers gracefully undo the braids, which finally hang free, amidst the applause of all those watching.

In a circle of stones next to an adjoining stone that the slaves built to delimit the property of the European masters, lie some buried slaves. There are no crosses or names, only the memory of their descendants.

With this festival, the men and women of Corn Island commemorate their cultural heritage and their ancestors' dream of freedom. According to local tradition, with the unexpected news of liberty received in the nineteenth century, dozens of men and women celebrated their freedom with crab soup. From that time on, this holiday is the most important one for the island dwellers, and they have celebrated it every year since 1851.

MEDICINAL PLANTS

From ancient times, before the arrival of the Spaniards in the region now known as Nicaragua, the different indigenous groups used plants for medicinal and commercial purposes, as they had a clear mastery of the properties of the plants and used them daily to improve the quality of their life.[9]

The healers were the physicians of their tribes. They constantly investigated and experimented with the different plant families. For centuries, plants, fruits, and vegetables have constituted the fundamental bastion of Nicaraguan well-being. Thanks to plants, numerous diseases have been cured and the knowledge of ancient civilizations has survived.

Perhaps the two plants that occupied the most privileged place in both medicine and commerce were *cacao* and tobacco. The fruit of *cacao* was said to have energy-giving properties. Tobacco, in ancient times, was thought to liberate people from evil spirits. The healer claimed that many difficult illnesses were caused by the interference of evil sprits that were the product of a curse thrown by one person at another. The healer would chew the tobacco leaves especially selected according to the circumstances and swirl them in his mouth with an alcoholic beverage made from corn or sugarcane. Bit by bit, he would spit mouthfuls over the sick person. In this way, the evil spirits were beaten back and extracted from the body. Tobacco was also used by the healers in cigarettes whose smoke was blown on the sick person so that he or she could find the path to wellness and, through that same path, expel all evil.

In Nicaragua, there have been several studies of medicinal plants; the most important study was undertaken in the nineteenth century by León's Alejandro Valle-Candia (1870–1961), the first Nicaraguan botanist and a topographical engineer. Important research on medicinal plants can be attributed to him. In addition to his work in botany Valle-Candia was also a philologist. This work gave a new legitimacy to many everyday words, showing the influence of indigenous languages from the Sutiaba, Matagalpa, Náhuatl, Chorotega, and Mískito.

The contemporary precursor of natural medicine in Nicaragua was Dr. Alejandro Dávila Bolaños (1922–1979). For the majority of his life, he lived in the northern city of Estelí where he dedicated himself completely to botanical research and to caring for the poorest members of Nicaraguan society. In addition to being the author of a book on pre-Columbian indigenous medicine, he also studied the indigenous origins of geographical place names in Nicaragua, as well as the etymology of native words for Nicaragua's flora and fauna. During Holy Week in Estelí in 1979, there were armed conflicts between the National Guard of the Somoza dictatorship and the revolutionary forces of the Sandinista Front, with whom Dr. Dávila Bolaños collaborated by taking care of the wounded in the hospital along with his colleague Dr. Eduardo Selva. The National Guard entered the hospital's operating room where Dávila Bolaños was conducting surgery, removed him and others, and executed them. They then burned his body.[10]

During the 1980s, greater attention was given to recognizing the work of healers, midwives, and others who worked with herbs and practiced traditional forms of medicine. It was at this time that two natural medicine companies, Snaya and Cecalli, were established in Estelí.

Some of the most important recent contributions are the studies by Alejandro Floripe and Vilma Altamirano, who worked in the municipalities of Río Blanco and Paiwas in the hopes of rescuing popular medicine in the poorest and most abandoned communities in the country. The result of this investigation on the Caribbean coast is the book *Plantas que curan* (Plants that cure).[11] Many people in Nicaragua used to think that knowledge of plants was something for grandmothers, peasants, strange people, and even witches. But now, throughout the world, people have turned to natural solutions to medical problems, producing a tremendous proliferation of alternative medicine. In Nicaragua, these options have been introduced into higher education as a professional line of study. For example, since the 1990s, the Nicaraguan Popular University (UPONIC) has been offering this field through its Faculty of Naturo-Orthopathic General Medicine coordinated by Dr. Rosa Alonso Caracas. There also has been a notable increase in the practice of natural medicine in Nicaragua in recent years.

Another institutional contribution is the garden of medicinal plants located at the Finca El Ojoche that belongs to León's National Autonomous University (UNAN) as of 2001. Its goal is to facilitate educational projects at the primary and secondary school level as well as for students of biology, agroecology, medicine, and pharmaceutical studies.[12]

There are enormous economic difficulties in Nicaragua. It is a country devastated by unemployment, a complete lack of healthcare and nutrition programs, and nearly nonexistent medical supplies in hospitals. Nicaragua's poor have had to seek urgent health solutions through more traditional means—plants.

Research has shown that natural medicine is the most efficient alternative for the population. The treatment that the patient receives is different and the results are astonishing. In Nicaragua, it is not at all uncommon to go into the courtyard of any home and find a wide array of live plants that are used as remedies. Many households have tried-and-true ways of preparing specific herbs, bark, flowers, and fruit with precise indications for usage to cure a range of maladies including asthma, gastritis, coughing, obesity, indigestion, diarrhea, inflammation, postpartum pain, headaches, skin allergies, and parasites. Some of the plants that are used, such as papaya and squash (for their seeds), would be more well known to an English-speaking reader. Others, such as *golondrina, catapanza,* and *jiñocuago,* would be much less familiar to people who live outside the region.[13]

THE HEALTHCARE SYSTEM IN NICARAGUA

The coverage of people's needs by the Nicaraguan healthcare system is more complicated than the rest of the country's social policies, as there is an obvious discrepancy between what the law dictates and the coverage that actually exists. Although there is a legal disposition that describes the rights of the population with regard to medical attention, the sad reality is that effective application of this law is insufficient to resolve the problem of providing citizens adequate and timely access to the healthcare system. There is a great deal of inequality in terms of who receives medical attention in Nicaragua. This is determined not only by a person's sociocultural and geographic origin, but also by a person's level of income. In general, the urban poor have greater access to healthcare than those who live in rural zones (including Nicaragua's indigenous population), where poverty is more extreme and there are fewer healthcare centers for preventive and emergency medical attention. In Nicaragua, the cost of medicinal drugs affects urban poor perhaps to a greater extent, for the rural poor make greater use of natural medicines extracted directly from plants in keeping with traditional knowledge.[14] Other sectors of the general population adversely affected by a healthcare system in Nicaragua that rarely takes them into account are elderly people, those who are physically impaired, and adolescents who do not receive adequate coverage.

In Nicaragua, more than 50 percent of the cost of medicinal drugs is paid by families and not by the government, employers, or insurance companies. This is a real and daily tragedy in a country where 80 percent of the population lives on less than $2 a day and 43 percent lives on less than $1 a day. Despite this level of poverty, the people still are responsible for paying the cost of medicinal drugs out of their own pockets. The problem no longer affects only the unemployed; today people who work under precarious conditions in the informal sector are also negatively affected.

Furthermore, from 1990–2006, under a neoliberal economic system of three successive governments in Nicaragua, there has been a consistent reduction in the healthcare budget and in social programs. This has had an enormous effect on the healthcare workers themselves because the wage scale in Nicaragua is much less than the rest of Central America. For example, in Honduras, a doctor on average earns $18,000 per year. In Nicaragua, a doctor with the same qualifications earns $6,000 per year. Nurses in Honduras earn $6,000 per year. In Nicaragua, the annual salary is less than $1,200.[15]

Government corruption has had a negative impact on Nicaragua's healthcare system. For example, the government of Enrique Bolaños of the Liberal party siphoned off $200 million that was designated for the healthcare system, education, and other expenses related to social programs and could have

benefited the poorest sectors of Nicaragua's population. The illicit enrich-
ment of former President Arnoldo Alemán is inseparable from the corruption
on the part of bankers and businessmen who protected this illegal behavior
during his entire presidency.

AIDS in Nicaragua

The first case of AIDS in Nicaragua was diagnosed in 1987. From 1987 to
2000, there have been 533 official cases reported. The country has the lowest
rate of infections in Central America, which has led to the belief that AIDS is
not a serious problem. In Nicaragua, there certainly has not been the kind of
serious vigilance of the epidemic that exists in other countries.[16]

Nevertheless, the epidemic is expanding in Nicaragua. In 2000, there were
2.2 cases per 100,000 inhabitants. That figure has risen to 7 cases per year per
100,000 inhabitants. The popular belief that AIDS is a disease that primarily
affects homosexuals is gradually being replaced with the truth: national studies have shown that AIDS is an epidemic that affects women primarily as a
result of the promiscuity of married men.[17]

FAMILY LIFE

The family in Nicaragua is organized around social principles such as formal matrimony and informal relationships called *uniones de hecho*. Families
supposedly have a patriarchal style, but, as a result of the irresponsibility of
many fathers, the majority of families are matriarchal. It is the mother who
sustains the home, especially in the case of poor families. In middle- and
upper-class families, divorces produce scandals regardless of the cause, and
it is women who are the most severely affected in the eyes of society. In the
case of wealthy couples, it is the custom to hide any matrimonial difficulties
as a way of maintaining the image of the perfect indissoluble marriage, a
situation that also affects women more negatively than men. Men, because
of the rampant sexism in Nicaraguan society, have other sexual relationships,
which may be public or hidden. Separation is something that the woman
defines when she decides that she can no longer tolerate infidelities, abuse,
or humiliation.

Family unity is most clearly reflected among siblings. Family reunions are
celebrated at different times of the year, especially during Holy Week, Mother's Day, Christmas, New Year's Eve, and birthdays. It is also common for
families to gather to celebrate marriages, baptisms, First Communions, confirmations, graduations, and in times of sorrow when a family member dies.

From an early age, children are taught to respect and obey their elders even
when they do not belong to the same family. Family meetings are common

when there is a problem to resolve. This means that many individual matters compete with those of the entire family. The extended family exercises a great deal of influence over the lives and decisions of each individual. It is not uncommon for parents, aunts, uncles, and cousins to live together or in nearby houses. No matter how old a person is, parents are still influential. Family decisions (especially the mother's) are respected. Traditional Nicaraguan families depend on mutual help. The Nicaraguan family might be compared to a cart that everyone pulls together. If a person in the family is dating someone, the relationship is not taken seriously until the boy or girl is formally presented to the family.

As in other countries in the Hispanic world, a person has two last names. The first is the name of the father's family. The second is the name of the mother's. Normally, it is the father's name that is used as a person's last name. Thus a person named Alberto Romero Ríos would be known as Mr. Alberto Romero. Families are identified by both last names. In this case, it would be the Romero-Ríos family. As a formal courtesy, the terms *señor, señora*, and *señorita* are used as a sign of respect, especially if the person is older or from a higher social category. The forms *don* and *doña* can also be used with the person's first name to indicate special respect, familiarity, and affection, for example, Doña Josefina and Don José.

The celebration of the 15th birthday is a special event, especially for girls, as it is a ceremony that means that the person is ready for the next stage of her life in the passage from adolescence to young adulthood. It is a ceremony that all girls in Nicaragua dream about. The predominant color of the ceremony is pink. The girl celebrating her birthday often selects 12 accompanying women with their respective gentlemen in addition to a principal gentleman with whom the girl will have the first dance at a party. The party is held after a religious ceremony where a priest explains the importance of the event and the next stage of life to the girl. In many rural areas, the girl is waiting for her 15th birthday to run away with her boyfriend. In the celebrations of the 15th birthday, all the people who are invited bring gifts. There is a procession from the house to the church. The girl (*quinceañera*) wears a beautiful, long pink dress and a tiara and holds a bouquet of flowers; she is accompanied by the 12 women and men. After the religious ceremony, the participants go to the reception. The *quinceañera* toasts her guests and drinks her first glass of champagne, wine, or fruit punch. The music begins and she dances with her father and brother. The second song is reserved for the principal gentleman. The event is attended by the entire family.

Young men do not participate in this kind of elaborate ceremony. The celebration for them usually consists of receiving a substantial gift and having dinner with family and a party with friends of both sexes.

The birthday celebrations for children under the age of seven include the breaking of a piñata, which in Nicaragua are ceramic vessels covered with colored paper. Nowadays, piñatas represent some cartoon figure preferred by children. It is believed that the origin of the piñata is pre-Columbian, as suggested by the use of certain ceramic vessels. The clay container, later covered with colored paper, represents the merging of indigenous and Spanish customs. Also, it is important to point out that piñatas are important in Mexico, which reaffirms the theory about their origin.

After the age of eight, children at birthday parties enjoy eating ice cream and playing games such as pin the tail on the donkey. The person who wins gets a surprise, which is often a small amount of cash. Adults, too, often celebrate their birthdays in a similar fashion as a way of remembering days that will never return.

Legal age is 18 for women and 21 for men, although at 16, with a national identity card, young people can exercise their right to vote. Nicaraguans generally get married before they turn 30. If a woman is over 30 and has not married, people say with scorn that the train has left her behind. Women usually marry between the ages of 18 and 25. Men and women are often the same age when they marry, or the man may be older. It is uncommon for a woman to be older than the man she marries. After marriage, the woman can continue to use her father's last name followed by the word *de* and then her new husband's last name. For example, La señora María Luisa Mendoza de Salinas, or, simply, la señora de Salinas.

When one meets someone for the first time in Nicaragua, it is customary to shake hands and say, "Hola. Mucho gusto. Soy Adriana Palacios" (for example). Between men the greeting is a warm handshake. Close friends join the handshake with a couple of pats on the back with the left hand. Between women, the most common greeting is a kiss on the cheek. The expressions of personal admiration among Nicaraguans are more valued than praise regarding material possessions. Nicaraguan families are considered hospitable, honest, empathetic, hardworking, and happy.

LEISURE TIME

Leisure time among young people and adults is usually spent in groups. Young people go to see a movie, play in the parks, participate in school-organized sports, attend concerts, and belong to dance, theater, literary, music, and singing groups. On Friday and Saturday nights, with the permission of their parents, young people go to dance clubs and drink beer. Adults generally gather on the weekends at friends' houses.

Many regions in Nicaragua are close to the beach. In these cases, people often spend the weekends with family and friends at some beautiful place that has a good restaurant to eat seafood and sit in the sun. Other people prefer to spend time at a family farm or travel to more distant places of interest in the country. During the baseball season, people young and old go to the stadiums to see a game. In the rural areas, men often go to cockfights. Bull riding events are attended by both men and women.

There are an almost infinite number of cyber cafes in Nicaragua with Internet access that serve as a meeting place for many students who enjoy playing games, doing research, chatting, and navigating the Web. This is a relatively new phenomenon that high school and university students have made very popular.

NICARAGUAN WOMEN IN A SEXIST SOCIETY

It is difficult enough to be born a woman, but it is even more challenging to be a woman in Nicaragua where sexism is still common and produces terrible effects. The daily domestic violence that is reported in the newspapers, radio, and television would seem to indicate that even though Nicaragua is a country where women have played an important role in revolutionary struggles that have produced deep social transformations, sexual equality and respect are a mere illusion for the majority of Nicaraguan women.

With the triumph of the Sandinista revolution in 1979, the women who held positions of authority during the insurrection had high expectations of continuing in leadership positions in the new government. The majority of the positions given to women were less important than those of soldiers in the armed forces. This was less true, however, in the structure of the new police force. In 1984, for example, the Sandinista guerrilla Doris Tijerino was promoted to chief of police, becoming the first woman in Nicaraguan history to occupy that position. In addition, Dora María Téllez was named minister of health. Many other women created divisions of interest in that new period of Nicaraguan history. On the one hand, there were the women who fought hard for the Sandinista cause and felt it was their right to obtain a dignified space in the government based on their intellectual, organizational, and administrative qualifications. On the other hand, there were many women who belonged to upper class families who had lost their exclusive positions of power as a result of the revolution and dedicated themselves to establishing intimate relationships with the young male revolutionary commanders so that they could continue enjoying the privileges that come with power.

A new machismo blossomed in the middle of that revolutionary attempt to create social and sexual equality. The feminism that emerged was nothing more than the feminine liberation to have many different sexual partners. Certain women poets, for example, published books of erotic poetry, and the literary success of these opportunistic women writers was celebrated in official luxurious parties. These authors, who were often from well-to-do families displaced by the 1979 revolution, lined up to take advantage of the Sandinista's access to power and privilege. Other women, seeking an honest place and not a bed, were dismissed by males in power as being resentful. The division of labor based on gender was once again in place, and women were destined to carry out tasks that were servile, classified as second-class citizens, just as society was structured in colonial times. During the 1990s, after the Sandinistas lost the elections, the situation for women was even worse. Although women in the 1980s who fought for their place in society did not achieve the equality they longed for, they did learn to struggle, to protest, and to act in solidarity with other women. The government of Violeta Chamorro, Nicaragua's first woman president, created great expectations among Nicaraguan women. Unfortunately, the dream of strengthening the representation of women in public office was not fulfilled. The government was, in reality, directed by Violeta Chamorro's son-in-law, Antonio Lacayo. It is important to mention that the family in power during this government was one of the most historically conservative and patriarchal families in Nicaragua. For this reason, there was a new resurgence of cruel sexist ideas regarding the natural virtues of women such as being polite, needing protection, and being perfect mothers and submissive wives, who should be willing to put up with everything. This tone did not change much with the subsequent governments of the Liberal Party under the leadership of Arnoldo Alemán and Enrique Bolaños. Gradually, there was an increase in violence against women who fought for their rights. And these women came from all social classes, from the rural farmer working her small plot of land to professional urban women.

As a way of pointing out the difficulties for women in terms of being named to ministerial positions in Nicaragua under recent governments, it is important to consider the following statistics.[18] Although the first woman was appointed to a high-ranking position in 1955, it was not until 1974 that Prof. María Elena Porras was named minister of education during the government of Anastasio Somoza Debayle. Between 1979 and 1981, during the first years of the Sandinista government, three women were appointed to ministerial positions, which gave women a 12 percent representation. This figure dropped to 11 percent (2 women) when Daniel Ortega formed a new government after winning the elections in 1984. In 1990, Violeta Chamorro, despite being Nicaragua's first woman president, did not appoint *any* women to ministerial positions. Similar appointments under the Alemán government (1997–2001) gave women 7 percent representation and, later,

13 percent. Under the Bolaños government (2002–2006), there was an interesting phenomenon. The number of women in cabinet positions increased significantly, although in secondary positions as vice-ministers. In all, 50 percent of the vice-ministers were women and 17 percent of the ministers were women during the presidency of Bolaños, Nicaragua's oldest president in recent decades. With the recent electoral victory of the Sandinistas in 2006, Daniel Ortega named five women to important cabinet positions, which resulted in 40 percent representation of women, the highest percentage in Nicaraguan history. Additional appointments bring the total to 50 percent, a figure that fulfills one of Ortega's campaign promises.

Compared with previous governments in Nicaragua, the new Sandinista government clearly demonstrates new ways of incorporating women in official activities, beginning with the First Lady, Rosario Murillo, who has assumed her role as secretary of communication and citizenship, with a level of power and decision-making authority that has never before existed for a First Lady in Nicaragua (whose role, traditionally, has been merely decorative). This has created a great deal of controversy and concern, especially among the most conservative sectors of Nicaraguan society. In this new context, women are struggling for their place in society not simply because they are women and deserve a right to be represented, but because they have demonstrated that they have the ability to do all kinds of work at every level. An example of this is the naming of Aminta Granera as the chief of police. The biggest challenge in Nicaragua currently is to carry out deep changes in terms of human rights, as it is clear that there has been a daily increase in the number of men who abuse their wives and daughters.

Nicaragua is currently one of the few nations in the region that does not have a law that truly protects the rights of women. There is a Nicaraguan Women's Institute, but it does not have a ministerial rank of importance, a fact that makes it far less effective than it might be. It is obvious that in Nicaragua there has been no real progress in terms of legislation to defend women's rights.[19] Furthermore, 60 percent of Nicaraguan families are headed by women.

The task to create social change in this area is not easy because existing Nicaraguan laws are designed to protect men. There are thousands of cases of single mothers who have never received the child support to which they are entitled. Opportunities for women have been *decreasing*. Any woman who has been able develop herself professionally and contribute to the development of Nicaragua has done so with great personal struggle, ignoring what the more traditional members of Nicaraguan society might think. These women have earned the respect of their communities, demonstrating that when women trust their abilities, they do not have to depend on the government for work.

In addition, even if they do receive a job, many women often have to put up with sexual harassment from their male superiors at work. Even now, in the twenty-first century, with the new Nicaraguan law that bans abortion even when a woman's life is threatened, the National Assembly, which is dominated by men, wants to turn women into the image of what women are for the Catholic Church: beings whose sole function is procreation.

Despite all the limitations in Nicaragua, there is a great deal of participation by women in the business world in terms of professional development. This means that women have assumed active roles. Nevertheless, to achieve this success, women have had to engage in superhuman efforts and have been obliged to learn how to divide their time between family and work. Other differences between the opportunities for work between men and women are the salaries and age discrimination. In Nicaragua, it is generally assumed that women over age 40 are too old to be members of the workforce. Even when women have an excellent resume and evident abilities, this kind of discrimination exists. What is needed, perhaps, is a greater emphasis on the decentralization of government in order to increase the representation of women in positions of authority at the local level, for example, as mayors.[20] For this reason, the struggle to achieve equal rights and representation in the workplace needs to be connected with the issues of equal pay and age discrimination.

THE GAY COMMUNITY IN NICARAGUA

With regard to homosexuality, Nicaragua is a country of contradictions. On the one hand, there are laws prohibiting homosexuality, lesbianism, and bisexuality as punishable crimes. On the other, in 2007 the Nicaraguan government launched a two-month campaign against homophobia, with the secondary goal of promoting condom use in sexual relations, as well as encouraging acceptance in families with sons and daughters who have different sexual preferences. But this will be an arduous process. In Nicaragua, there are educational institutions, especially religious ones, where boys and girls with overt traits of homosexuality are not allowed to matriculate or are expelled. As in other countries, Nicaragua has created prototypical sectors of the workforce where homosexuals are allowed to participate as hair stylists, cooks, waiters, and choreographers. In Nicaragua, homosexuals are regularly made fun of and rejected by a large part of the population, particularly among men. Even so, and amidst this hostile environment that marginalizes them, homosexuals have managed to create cultural spaces in poetry, dance, and film. In 2003, poet Hector Avellán, winner of the first prize in the Juegos Florales poetry competition, broke the silence about homosexuality in Nicaragua, openly declaring he was gay. In the city of León, the Ballet Nueva Compañía, directed by Ernesto Lanzas, is a professional, highly praised group of dancers, all of whom are openly gay. In 2007, a pioneering short film directed by Bolívar González called "Historia de amor con un final anunciado" (Love Story with a Foretold Ending) was shown in Nicaraguan theaters. Produced by ANCI and Mirarte Films, with performances by Eneizel Díaz and Hector Avellán, the film contains love scenes between men and generated controversy by showing a male couple who dared to walk through the village where they lived, holding hands. Gays in Nicaragua have begun to fight actively for their rights in a society that is fiercely homophobic.

CLOTHING IN NICARAGUA

Nicaragua is a country with a tropical climate, with average temperatures between 28° C (84° F) and 22° C (72° F) in the higher elevations. The cities with the highest temperatures, up to 35° C (95° F) in April and May, are Managua, León, and Chinandega. Nicaraguans wear different kinds of clothing depending on the occasion, but it is always clean. The use of blue jeans for both men and women of all ages is normal, accompanied by T-shirts, blouses, or light clothing, but it is important to remember that residents in the cooler areas in the northern part of the country wear jackets in the late afternoon and evening. More formal clothing is used for theater events, receptions, *quinceañera* celebrations, and weddings. For these occasions, men wear coats and ties and women wear elegant dresses and high heels. Clothing worn by people on the Atlantic coast of Nicaragua is different. It is normal for people to wear shorts and sleeveless T-shirts. Sometimes the men don't wear shirts and the women wear less clothing because the population lives close to the sea.

In recent years, Nicaragua has gained a place in the Central American market with its designs for men's and women's high fashion. Current talented designers include Aura Rayo, Rosibel de Chévez, Emperatriz Urroz, Damaris Núñez, Keria Ramírez, Neptalí Matute, Juan de la Torre, Fernando Fuentes, Shantall Lacayo, Kely Molina, Bárbara Pozo, Fátima Sandino, Kelvin Dávila, and Vicente Castellón. Their designs have been used by Nicaragua's First Ladies and by Nicaraguan representatives in competitions such as Miss Universe and Mr. Continente del Mundo, in which, for the 2005 contest, Nicaragua won first prize in the fantasy costume entitled "The Golden Crab" (see Chapter 4) by the young designer Juan de la Torre.

EDUCATION

Education in Nicaragua is divided into four levels. *Pre-escolar* (kindergarten) is the beginning of the educational system for children from 4–5 years old with up to three years of study. Primary is the continuation for which the average age is 6–9 years old, with six years of study, from first to sixth grade. *Secundaria* or *bachillerato* (high school) is usually started by children from 10–12 years old upon finishing the primary level and consists of five years of study. During this period there are also options to study the *bachillerato* accompanied by a technical course of study that includes auto mechanics, woodworking, electrical work, graphic design, computer programming, etc. The average age for beginning studies at the university level is 17 and is part of a process of becoming a professional, for example an engineer or doctor.

Public investment in education is insufficient. It barely covers 40 percent of the need for the system to function as it should. There is a notorious imbalance between resources for rural and urban educational initiatives. In the urban zones, there is an increasing deterioration in coverage. In the rural zones, the problem is one of significant exclusion. The principal factor that has contributed to the steady decrease in the number of children registering for the primary level is the expense that this entails for families at the beginning of the academic year in terms of the purchase of uniforms, books, and the payment of tuition. Since the government of Violeta Chamorro in 1990, education in Nicaragua is no longer free. This has caused a tremendous hardship for Nicaraguan families who also became unemployed under the Chamorro government, creating even further erosion in the number of children attending school. In 1996, the government of Arnoldo Alemán built a large number of primary schools, but the unemployment problem persisted. Furthermore, Alemán's program of *autonomías escolares* (private schools partially supported by the government) created quotas of "voluntary payments" of tuition that increased each month. Nevertheless, parents could see no improvement in the quality of education and came to believe that the increase in tuition was being used for corrupt purposes unrelated to education. This practice continued under the Bolaños government.[21]

The first presidential decree of the government of Daniel Ortega after assuming the presidency in 2007 was to make education free, which once again opened the educational possibilities for thousands of children and young adults from the poorest families in Nicaragua. Furthermore, the latest literacy campaign called Yo Sí Puedo (Yes, I Can) is being strengthened. The program, which began in 2006 in various places throughout the country under the leadership of Sandinista mayors with the support of the Venezuelan government, benefited rural and urban Nicaraguans who were unable to finish their primary school education during the last 16 years.

Some official sources cite a low level of unemployment in Nicaragua. For example, according to one source, in 2003, more than 165,000 people were without work in Nicaragua, and each subsequent year, 80,000 more were unemployed, with a million people underemployed or in small rural businesses with a low level of production as a result of a lack of financing.[22] These figures are misleading. More than 52 percent of the Nicaraguan population is in the informal sector, people who sell fruit or clothing and water at stoplights and other places. A more accurate unemployment figure for Nicaragua would be 37 percent. It is important to remember that official figures do not include the 20 percent of the Nicaraguan population that is living and working outside Nicaragua (especially in Costa Rica and the United States). Nicaragua has the region's lowest minimum wage: 37 cents per hour. This figure translates into approximately $852 per year. The lowest market wage is 67 cents per hour.

Nicaragua's gravest problem is social inequality. This is the result of a lack of educational opportunities and a faulty distribution of wealth that has produced even more poverty and unemployment. In terms of education in Nicaragua, studies have shown that 33 percent of the population over the age of 15 is illiterate, and half of these are women. A total of 71 percent of Nicaraguans categorize themselves as poor. In Nicaragua, 10 percent of the wealthiest people control 46 percent of the total wealth. The top 1 percent of the richest Nicaraguans receive 18.4 percent of the total income. This social inequality is most evident in the capital city Managua. The middle class, constituted by a new group of educated professionals that began to emerge in the 1980s, has been displaced to the point that it is difficult to know with certainty if it even exists any longer, given the current high levels of unemployment among these people.

Forced emigration for economic reasons also has a devastating effect on the ability of many Nicaraguans to receive an education in their country of origin. Like other Latin Americans, Nicaraguans have been disillusioned with the government institutions and weak administrations in urgent need of reform. Many disenchanted Nicaraguans have preferred to leave their country in search of employment, in the belief that in Nicaragua, at least in the near future, they will not have sufficient opportunities. During the harvest seasons, an estimated 105,000 Nicaraguans emigrate to Costa Rica and Honduras each year. For some, emigration is permanent and, in the short term, they do not return to Nicaragua. At least 200 Nicaraguans cross the border into Costa Rica on a daily basis, although they remain connected to their families by sending money to them, and never lose interest in their country. Another place Nicaraguans dream about is the United States. Approximately 178,000 per year risk everything in a desperate attempt (that takes them across many dangerous Mesoamerican borders) to improve their lives in the United States.

Nicaraguans possess great talents that they sometimes do not take full advantage of. But, often, it is the government that fails to provide opportunities to the people that would allow them to reach their potential more fully. Nicaraguans are hospitable, outgoing, and determined to test their luck outside their country. Nicaragua is a complex country, and it is almost impossible to determine progress in a place where advances occur much less quickly than they should. Nicaragua cannot necessarily provide short-term solutions to its problems because, in many ways, contemporary Nicaraguan society is premodern, with modern institutions and laws coexisting with postmodern urban landscapes as a result of the effects of the globalization of communication and international aid. But these visions of the ultra-new are quite superficial and do not reflect the deeper realities of Nicaragua.

SPORTS

Baseball, the King of Sports in Nicaragua

Unlike in most Latin American countries, soccer is *not* the most important sport in Nicaragua. Three things provoke impassioned interest in Nicaraguan men: baseball, politics, and women, in that order! Baseball is without a doubt the king of sports in Nicaragua. This sport, originally from the United States, was introduced into Nicaragua during the last decade of the nineteenth century, despite the widely held belief that Nicaraguan baseball was the result of the first U.S. military intervention in 1912.[23] Although it is true that the Marines occupying Nicaragua popularized the sport among the general population, baseball actually was brought to Nicaragua in 1891 by young Nicaraguans from wealthy families who spent time studying in New York. Another theory holds that Nicaraguan baseball originated in the English-speaking Caribbean city of Bluefields in 1890, when it was still a British protectorate. According to this story, Albert Addlesburg, a U.S. businessman, taught Nicaraguans how to play the game and imported equipment from the United States. At any rate, it did not take long for baseball to become a Nicaraguan obsession. The first league was organized on the Pacific side of the country in 1915 and consisted of a series of friendly games. The first teams, however, were established earlier, in 1904, in Granada and Masaya. The Bóer team in Managua was formed by the U.S. Ambassador to Nicaragua Carter Donaldson, also in 1904. In 1910, the Titan team from Chinandega was established. A special regional series of games was held in Costa Rica in 1925 in which Nicaragua beat Costa Rica and defeated the Coco Solo team, which was the champion of the military bases of the United States in Panama's Canal Zone.

On November 20, 1948, the first National Baseball Stadium was inaugurated. In 1956, the first professional baseball league in Nicaragua was born, although there was no winner that year because the Nicaraguan dictator Anastasio Somoza García was killed in León by Rigoberto López Pérez. After the revolution in 1979, the National Baseball Stadium was named after Rigoberto López Pérez in memory of his heroism and sacrifice. During the government of Violeta Chamorro in the early 1990s, however, the stadium was renamed to recognize the tremendous accomplishments of Nicaragua's Denis Martínez. Martínez was the first Nicaraguan to play major league baseball in the United States, signing with the Baltimore Orioles in 1976. He was also the first Latino to pitch a perfect game, which occurred in 1991 when Martínez, playing for the Montreal Expos, defeated the Los Angeles Dodgers. Other Nicaraguans who played U.S. major league baseball include Antonio Chévez, Al Williams, David Green, Porfirio Altamirano, Marvin Bernard, Vicente Padilla, Oswaldo Mairena, and Devern Hansack. Some of the best hitters in Nicaragua's national league, all of whom had more than 1,000 hits, include Ariel Delgado, Nemesio Porras, Ernesto López, Julio Medina, Pablo Juárez, Freddy García, Arnoldo Muñoz, Alvaro Muñoz, Marlon Abea, and Genaro Llanes. Three of Nicaragua's most successful baseball managers are Noel Aréas (León), Julio Sánchez (Managua), and Omar Cisneros (Managua).

During the 1980s, interest in baseball grew enormously, resulting in 12 teams competing in a national league. From 1970–2007, León's first division team, having won 10 championships, held the best league record.

Beginning in 2004, the professional Nicaraguan baseball league filled stadiums with fans supporting their favorite teams and enabled Nicaraguans to get to know the star international players from Cuba, the United States, Puerto Rico, Venezuela, the Dominican Republic, and Panama. These players are hired to play with a Nicaraguan team, generally for a whole season, which in Nicaragua is October through February.

Boxing

The second most popular sport in Nicaragua is boxing. Alexis Argüello, "The Explosive Flaco (Skinny Guy)," was born on April 19, 1952, and became the most respected figure in world boxing for ten years in three different divisions: featherweight, super featherweight, and lightweight, never losing any of his belts.[24] In 1974, he knocked out the Mexican Rubén Olivares in a championship match. He also defeated the Puerto Rican Alfredo Escalera in 1978 and Jim Watt from Scotland in 1981. When Argüello attempted to win in a fourth division, Aaron Pryor from the United States kept him from reaching this goal. Argüello retired with 82 wins, 62 by knockouts, and only 8 losses. He is currently the vice-mayor of Managua for the Frente Sandinista party. He has been active promoting sports and donating his own resources for building sports facilities. In 2001, the Association of Sports Writers in Nicaragua named Alexis Argüello "Athlete of the Twentieth Century." He is also a member of the Hall of Fame of World Boxing. Nicaragua also has produced five other world champions in boxing: Eddie Gazo (1977), Rosendo Alvarez (1995), Adonis Rivas (1999), Ricardo Mayorga (2001), and Luis Pérez (2002).

NOTES

1. Tomás Ayón. *Historia de Nicaragua,* vol. 1. Managua: Banco Nicaragüense, 1993, p. 46.

2. José Coronel Urtecho. *Elogio de la cocina nicaragüense.* San José, Costa Rica: EDUCA, 1977, pp. 123–129.

3. Ibid.

4. Ibid.

5. Ibid.

6. Sophie D. Coe. *Las primeras cocinas de América.* Mexico City: Fondo de Cultura Económica, 2004, p. 349.

7. Luis Eduardo Martínez M. "La Feria del Maíz." *La Prensa* (Revista), August 28, 2002, p. 10B.

8. Vilma Duarte. "Vamos a la sopa del cangrejo" in *Almanaque escuela para todos.* Managua: n.p., 2004, pp. 52–54.

9. Tomás Ayón. *Historia de Nicaragua.* vol. I, chapter III (Cultura intelectual, artes, industria, comercio y agricultura). Managua: Banco Nicaragüense, 1993, pp. 49–52.

10. "Alejandro Dávila Bolaños," *El Nuevo Diario* (in Spanish). Available at: archivo.elnuevodiario.com.ni/1999/noviembre/27-noviembre-1999/cultural/cultural6.html.

11. *El Nuevo Diario* (in Spanish). Available at: archivo.elnuevodiario.com.ni/1999/febrero/14-febrero-1999/cultural/.

12. *Educación para la conservación de las plantas medicinales.* Managua: TRAMIL, 2001.

13. Oswaldo Pérez Ramírez. *Naturaleza y salud: naturismo centroamericano.* Managua: n.p. 2006, pp. 8–12.

14. CONPES. *Acción ciudadana para el próximo quinquenio.* Managua: CONPES, 2007, pp. 31–32.

15. "El fracaso neoliberal en Nicaragua, según Oscar René Vargas," *La Gente* (in Spanish). Available at: www.radiolaprimerisima.com/noticias/2835.

16. *El Nuevo Diario* (in Spanish). Available at: archivo.elnuevodiario.com.ni/2000/diciembre/01-diciembre-2000/nacional.

17. CONPES. *Acción ciudadana para el próximo quinquenio.* Managua: CONPES, 2007, p. 33.

18. Personal interview with historian Clemente Guido, former Director General of the Nicaraguan Institute of Culture, June 18, 2007.

19. Fundación DEMUCA. "Estudios sobre la aplicación de políticas públicas de género en los gobiernos de Centroamérica y República Dominicana." San José, Costa Rica: DEMUCA, 2006, p. 96.

20. Rebecca Centeno. "Preguntas pendientes a la descentralización: ¿Está conduciendo hacia la igualdad de género?" *Encuentro* 76 (2007): pp. 82–83.

21. CONPES. *Acción ciudadana para el próximo quinquenio 2007–2011, propuestas y sugerencias para fortalecer la democracia y el desarrollo en Nicaragua.* Managua: CONPES, 2007, pp. 28–29.

22. Personal interview with Manuel Calderón, Executive Director of the Association of Municipalities of León (ADMUL), June 2007.

23. See Jorge Eduardo Arellano. "¿Por qué el béisbol es nuestro deporte rey?" *Lengua* (Revista de la Academia Nicaragüense de la Lengua) 28 (February 2004): pp. 141–144.

24. Boxeo Hispanoamericano (in Spanish). Available at: www.kusuco.com/torna gua/boxeo.htm

4

Folklore and Legends

THE NICARAGUAN ORAL tradition manifests itself abundantly in stories about ghostly beings that inhabit the night searching for people who stay out too late on lonely roads and streets so that they can carry them off to the depths of hell. The majority of these tales are thought to have had their origin in colonial times, and they became an efficient means for transmitting the idea that a person turned into a ghost if, during the person's lifetime, the person committed some crime, sold his or her soul to the devil, did not give money as a legacy but instead selfishly kept it buried in ceramic pots, made an important promise but died without keeping it, or was murdered.

Riches were always condemned by the poor community and it was believed (perhaps as a way of resigning oneself to one's misfortune) that when a rich person died, the person wandered among the living, frightening them. The rich person never knew eternal rest until, somehow, the person's wealth was distributed. No doubt, because of these strongly held beliefs, the people created their own ways of talking about them, choosing the oral form as the mechanism most within their reach. It should be remembered that as high as the illiteracy rates are today, they were much higher during the colonial period. In this atmosphere, many legends and stories were born that were especially appreciated by children. These tales are also a way of teaching Nicaraguan history in a fantastic and mysterious way.

All the cities have their legends. Sometimes they are about similar events and characters, which is the case of the *cadejos,* one bad, the other good. But each community adapted the story in keeping with its own way of life. In addition, many of these legends have been a source of inspiration for songwriters who have set these stories to music. This is the case of contemporary Nicaraguan singer Frank Torres, who has turned stories about La Mokuana, La Gigantona, and Pepé Cabezón into pop music. It is an ancestral custom (more deeply rooted in the rural areas) to sit in a circle around a storyteller (a man or a woman with great skill in keeping the attention of a mostly young audience). Some storytellers try to scare their audience. It is also a form of educating, for each story has a moral about obedience, fear, honesty, making fun of someone, as well as the Indians' sorrow and the denunciation of their abuse. This custom was transmitted to urban areas by means of the Indian women who came to take care of domestic tasks in the homes of the Creoles and Spaniards. Normally, the indigenous woman would tell the stories to the Creole children, who, in turn, would tell them to their own children. These stories are the equivalent of the Grimm fairy tales from Europe.

All of the legends mentioned here are very popular and are widely told by the people in Nicaragua even today. As a rich source of Nicaraguan legends, the city of León often appears in these stories. Not surprisingly, perhaps, the Colonel Arrechavala Museum of Myths and Legends is located in León and directed by Carmen Toruño, the most important researcher of these legends and the characters who populate them. There are too many tales to treat in a book of this kind, but some of the other legendary spirits and characters are known by the following names in Spanish: La Mokuana, La Cegua, La Negra Camila, El Viejo del Monte, Tomá tu teta, La Chancha Bruja, Chico Largo, and others.

THE BAD *CADEJO*

The bad *cadejo* refers to a black animal, similar in appearance to a dog, that appears at night before people who have stayed up too late and who are drunk, irresponsible, and have spent all their money partying. People say that when the dawn arrives and many of these drinkers are still out on the town, the bad *cadejo* appears before them with its red ghostly eyes and follows them, growling, until they go home.

THE GOOD *CADEJO*

The good *cadejo* also resembles a dog but it is white with gentle eyes and serves as a guardian for the people who work late or have some mishap that keeps them out after dark. This animal accompanies them so that they reach their homes safely and no one does them any harm.

THE NAHUA CART

The Nahua cart is a sad, brutal story that refers to life in colonial times. The cart that appears at midnight is made of human bones and is drawn by the skeletons of two oxen. The cart is filled with the skeletons of Indians who cry in the darkness about their cruel fate as slaves. The lament and the sound of the creaking bones announce the cruelty that they had to endure.

THE HEADLESS PRIEST

The headless priest tells a story from colonial times in the city of old León about a priest named Fray Antonio Valdivieso, who defended the Indians from the cruelty of the Spaniards. The Contreras brothers, who held land granted to them by the Spanish crown, were upset by the priest. They accused him of conspiring against the crown and had him decapitated. From that moment on, the repression of the Indians grew worse, and the indigenous people invoked Fray Valdivieso so that he could continue to protect them. Later, when a group of Indians was about to be thrown to hungry dogs as a punishment, the headless body of the monk appeared, defending the unfortunate Indians. From that moment on, the fear that the priest would appear grew and the inhumane treatment diminished.

Another version of the same story tells of a priest who defended the Indians and was decapitated by a single blow of a machete in the atrium of the church. The head rolled and rolled until it reached a lake, and, in punishment for such a sacrilegious act, many misfortunes befell the city, one of them being that when the head fell into the lake, an immense wave rose up and submerged the city. According to this version of the tale, this is why old León had to be moved to a different location. The headless priest wears a robe and black shoes. From his neck dangles a rosary and from his waist a cord from which a bell hangs and rings as he walks, looking for Spaniards who abuse the Indians.

THE GOLDEN CRAB

The Golden Crab (El Punche de Oro) is a legend in the indigenous community of Sutiaba in León, where it is said that there is a great buried treasure that consists of the riches of the Indian leaders who died without telling the Spaniards where it was located. The Golden Crab is the spirit of this treasure and, twice a year, like a brilliant apparition with jeweled eyes, it emerges from the Pacific Ocean on the beach at Poneloya. From there, it traverses the road from the coast to the church of the indigenous people of

Sutiaba, where it pays homage to the sun when it enters the church. The Golden Crab also moves through the nocturnal streets and parks of the city, expertly avoiding the hands of the people who seek to catch it and thus break its spell and become the owners of the buried treasure, which, it is believed, is buried under the church where the Indians worship. It is said that whoever the Golden Crab passes becomes paralyzed and unable to speak for several days. The legend is said to have been born in colonial times after the Spaniards hanged the indigenous leader Adiac from a giant Tamarind tree that can still be seen today. It is easy to imagine the appeal of this legend, which can be interpreted as being linked to the rich indigenous identity itself and how it resists and persists over time in different historical contexts.

THE WEEPING WOMAN

The Weeping Woman (La Llorona) tells the story of a beautiful *mestiza* maiden. She fell in love with a Spaniard who took advantage of the girl's innocence. One day, as she was bathing in the river, he approached her and then raped her. The girl got pregnant, but the Spaniard denied that the child was his. She was thrown out of her house and wandered through the countryside until it was time for her to give birth. The only place she could find was a riverbank. When the baby was born, the mother was so tired that she fell asleep. The river rose and carried off the baby in the current. When the mother awoke and could not find her child, she began to run along the river, crying and frantically searching for her baby.

THE GOLDEN ALLIGATOR

The Golden Alligator is a legend from the city of Juigalpa in the Department of Chontales. It is said that many years ago a French nobleman named Francisco de Valdis arrived in Chontales. He was fascinated with the landscape that surrounded the hacienda Hato Grande, which was located not very far from Juigalpa. He fell in love with a beautiful young girl named Chepita Vital. A few months later, they married and later had a baby girl who was baptized with the name Juana María. Don Francisco fell ill one day and decided to travel to Guatemala for medical treatment. Before he left, he told the hacienda administrators to take care of the hacienda and his family. Time went by, but Don Francisco did not return. Finally, the family heard that he had died before arriving in Guatemala. Doña Chepita later died, having buried her will in a place where no one could find it. Juana María grew up and became a young lady. She was not aware that the administrator named Fermín Ferrari had stolen all the goods that belonged to her. Don Fermín was evil and ambitious and decided to drive Juan María mad by making her believe that there was a ghost that lived on the hacienda. He told her such horrible stories that she soon died of fear. Juana María was buried in the mountain of Hato Grande on the shore of a lake, where, from that time on, an enormous golden alligator began to appear. The people in the village believe that it is the sorrowful soul of Juana María, seeking her fortune. It is also said that Don Fermín was devoured by this alligator one day when he went to bathe in the cool waters of the lake.

CORONEL ARRECHAVALA

Colonel Arrechavala is the main character of a legend about a ghost that haunts the streets of the Laborio section of León. Colonel Arrechavala was so wealthy and owned so much property that people say he lost track of what he had. He never shared any of these riches with anyone and died with no inheritor. This is why he has been seen many times riding a black stallion whose iron-shod hooves echo through the streets, carrying the colonel to the mountain who searches in vain for his wealth so that he can give it away and lay his soul to rest.

OMETEPE

Another geographical focal point for Nicaraguan legends is the island of Ometepe, which is composed of two volcanoes called Concepción and Maderas that jut from Lake Nicaragua and can be reached by ferry from Rivas/San Jorge and Granada. According to legend, the Náhuatl Indians were searching for a promised land that an Indian priest, or *alfaquí*, saw in his dreams. That prophesied place was Ometepe, and it is a privileged site for legends that the aboriginal groups developed during their stay there. The first indigenous name for the Concepción volcano (which came into being in the Quaternary period and the Cenozoic Era and is now 1,610 meters tall) was Choncoteciguatepe, which means "brother of the moon." The Chorotega and Nicaragua Indians later called it Mestliltepe, which means "mountain that bleeds."

The other volcano, Maderas, was known by the aboriginal population as Coatlán, "the place where the sun lives." According to a legend, one morning, as fog covered the volcano's crater and dozens of deer and other wild animals were drinking water from the shore of the lake, the animals retreated into the jungle landscape so that a mysterious sphere rising from Coatlán Lake could pass. As it did, its brilliance could be seen from anywhere on the island. The next day, a group of brave farmers climbed to the top of Maderas to investigate what had happened, but they did not find any sign that could identify the strange luminous object that had come from deep inside the volcano. This gave birth to the idea that the island is a place where luminous objects and shooting stars find a place to rest before they move on. Everything is an enigma in Ometepe. The origin of its inhabitants, their strange petroglyphs, and the subterranean world of myths and shamans are still largely unknown. There is something about the island that provokes dreams about distant paradises and magical prophecies.

The Hunter from Krin Krin

On the Atlantic (or Caribbean) coast, the Miskito indigenous community has many important legends that concern ecology and the need to take care of the environment. The legend called The Hunter from Krin Krin tells the story of Barnak, the best deer hunter in Krin Krin, a community on the Coco River. He always went hunting alone, and when the game was abundant, he went down to the village to get people to help him carry the load of deer. The people in the village secretly commented that Barnak had a special magnetic ball that attracted the deer. They said that Barnak found the magnetic ball in the stomach of the first deer that he killed. In the mountains, all Barnak had to do was wait. The deer appeared, one after the other, and with his deadly arrows, he hunted as many as he wanted. One day, Barnak did what he always did—he took his dugout canoe and crossed to the other side of the river to hunt animals. The afternoon came, then the evening, and no one had any news from the hunter. The next day, the villagers found his canoe where he had left it on the bank of the river. A group of men prepared their bows and arrows and went to look for him. They searched everywhere, and after a long time, they found two deer pierced by arrows and, next to the deer, Barnak's bow and arrows. The men decided to return to the village and give the news to their brothers that Barnak had disappeared.

But this is what really happened to the hunter. The first deer that Barnak killed was really big, but the hunter wanted more meat to fulfill his commitments, because the meat was not only for eating but for selling as well. So Barnak waited a while and then another deer appeared, which he cut down with a single arrow. At that moment, as if by magic, the sides of the mountains opened up and two strange beings appeared who were naked and hairy and had giant hands and feet and ugly eyes that popped out. The beings seemed able to vomit fire and there was lightning in their gaze. The two beings approached Barnak and leaned over the two dead deer, looking at their ears and their hooves. Turning toward the hunter, they said, "These deer belong to us. You are the one who is killing all these deer. Now you're coming with us." Barnak was petrified with fear. He could not even open his mouth. He was pale and he dropped his bow and arrows.

From the mountains, a giant wild boar trotted over to them. They all got on. After going up hills and mountains, and crossing rivers and valleys, they reached a well-known hill called Asang Busna, an inaccessible place where these beings lived. In fact, the place was full of these beings. One of the kidnappers said, "Brothers, this is Barnak, the one who is responsible for the disappearance of so many deer. Let us judge him amongst ourselves." They all agreed, and, one by one, they approached and pointed at him, many of them threatening him and condemning him to death. But the majority said that they could not kill the hunter, even though the hunter was an animal who killed when he was not hungry. They all knew that the dead deer were not just for his food, but also meat that he would sell.

Day after day, Barnak was in captivity, tied up with barbed wire in a truly lamentable state. Meanwhile, the Sukia Indians sang about the legendary Barnak and assured everyone that one day he would return. Time passed, and, because they could not agree about whether to kill Barnak, the Indians mounted Barnak again on the great wild boar that carried him to Tilba, a place that resembles a big bowl full of black water in which, every day, any vessel that nature itself did not protect was swallowed by the dark waters. Then they put Barnak on a boat and traveled down the Coco River, always in the protective custody of the guardian-demons. After three days, they reached the capital of the guardian-demons for a final verdict. In that place were all the evil people serving their punishment and dragging thick chains. On the fifth day, the chief of the guardian-demons said, "A moon and a half has passed since this man was captured. He has had enough punishment. Take him back to where they found him. It is time to give him his freedom. But before you let him go, take away the magnetic ball he carries so that he can never hunt deer again anywhere. That will be his worst punishment." The next day, some fishermen found Barnak with his clothes ripped to shreds and unable to speak. Everyone recognized him and took him to the Sukia Angú (healer) who cared for him for seven days in his home. He gave Barnak medicine and, when Barnak could speak, the healer let him go back to his community. Barnak went back to his home but never hunted deer again. This is why one has to take care of the flora and fauna: at any given time, the guardian-demons could appear on their wild boar and carry off anyone who doesn't respect nature.

$$5$$

Literature

RUBÉN DARÍO

ALTHOUGH NICARAGUA IS a small country with scarce resources for education and a relatively high illiteracy rate, literature is a defining element of Nicaraguan culture, as well as a high point of national pride primarily because of the monumental presence of internationally renowned poet Rubén Darío (1867–1916). If Simón Bolívar was the historical figure most readily associated with Hispanic America's *political* independence from Spain, a strong case can be made that Rubén Darío was the impetus for the region's cultural freedom from Spain. This may sound like an exaggeration, but before Darío's innovative *modernista* prosody, poets from Spain in the nineteenth century had been unable to revitalize Spanish in the exciting ways that French, German, and English Romantic poets had been able to do in their languages. Darío's major works include *Azul . . .* (1888), *Prosas profanas y otros poemas* (1896 and 1901), *Los raros* (1896), *Cantos de vida y esperanza, los cisnes y otros poemas* (1905), *El canto errante* (1907), *El viaje a Nicaragua e intermezzo tropical* (1908), *El poema del otoño y otros poemas* (1910), and *Canto a la Argentina y otros poemas* (1914).

How did Darío succeed (although not without controversy) in transforming the Spanish language? Darío sought new musical patterns and symmetries in the French poetry of Victor Hugo and the contagious rhythmic power of U.S. poet Walt Whitman. Darío's idea was not to imitate these models from Europe and the United States in a servile way, but rather to adapt them and

Marble statue of Nicaragua's great poet Rubén Darío (1867–1916) in Managua's Central Park. © Wilmor López. Used by permission.

see them flourish in a new Hispanic American context. Darío did more than assimilate this "foreign" literature of his time in Spanish. He also enriched his language by incorporating many words of indigenous origin from ancient civilizations that remained current in Nicaragua. Underlying the spoken Spanish in many Hispanic American countries is an indigenous linguistic heritage that Darío and the writers who followed him studied carefully to understand their country's interethnic layers and violent cultural conflicts.[1]

In the case of Nicaragua, the Spaniards who arrived in the sixteenth century encountered an enormous diversity of native languages. At that time, the most important indigenous group of original inhabitants of the area, who spoke Mangue or Chorotega, had been displaced by the later Nahuatl-speaking immigrants, moving south from what is now Mexico. In addition to this Aztec influence, there was also a presence, although to a lesser degree, of Mayan culture. Darío provided a voice for these cultural influences to enter the world of Hispanic literature for the first time. It is important to remember that Darío's first trip to Spain was in 1892, the year that Spain was celebrating the 400th anniversary of Columbus's arrival in the New World. At that time, despite Hispanic America's relatively recent political independence from Spain, Hispanic America was still considered by the cultural elite of Spain to be an extension, an appendage, of the colonial motherland. When Darío composed his poem to the volcano Momotombo in his native Nicaragua, it was a geographical rebellion against Spain, an assertion of identity that carried with it the indigenous toponymical power of place-names. And this particular place in Darío's poem is a mountain that, according to indigenous myths, is inhabited by the fire of God.[2]

Part of Darío's difficulty in being accepted as an immensely talented writer was precisely his origin. Some Spanish writers scorned Darío for being part Indian. They imagined feathers protruding from beneath his elegant European hat. Darío countered this racist thinking by asserting his *mestizo* identity with pride. It is true that Darío might have done more in his work to denounce the miserable social conditions of the indigenous population of his own country (something that is easy to see nearly a century after Darío's death), but he did recognize the Indian as a source of literary originality and audacity, worthy of inclusion in poems such as "Caupolicán" and "Tutecotzimí."

For Nicaraguans, Darío is an important *geographical* event. Even though he did not spend much time actually living in Nicaragua, preferring Europe and large Europeanized South American capitals such as Buenos Aires, Darío, as a hyperinternational national figure (like Augusto C. Sandino), was the antidote to the isolation and humiliation that Nicaraguans felt, living in their own small, invaded, and scorned country. Rubén Darío put Nicaragua on the map forever.

Nicaraguans construct their cultural identity to a great extent by means of a deep and abiding love of Darío's work. The pride and prestige associated with Darío have positive and negative aspects. On the one hand, there is a tendency to talk about Darío with many rhetorical flourishes, exalting the poet in highly superficial ways. On the other hand, Darío's poetry is memorized competitively by schoolchildren throughout the country, professionally recited in a moving (although sometimes bombastic) way at innumerable literary events, and is such an important part of Nicaraguan culture that even the three-time world-champion Nicaraguan boxer Alexis Argüello can recite Darío's poetry at public occasions. It is impossible to imagine a similar phenomenon in the United States.

Darío is a poet of contradictory, nuanced identities, something that his partisans tend to overlook, depending on which way the political winds are blowing. To understand Nicaragua's cultural identity more fully, it is important to read Darío's poetry and seek out these conflicting truths. For example, one can read his critique of the United States as a future invader of Nicaragua in "To Roosevelt" together with "Saluting the Eagle," in which Darío praises the work ethic and entrepreneurial spirit of Nicaragua's great neighbor to the north. Darío wrote escapist poems, celebrating journeys to exotic lands inhabited by mythological creatures but also deeply metaphysical poetry that expresses existential anguish.[3] There are thousands of books and academic articles on this controversial figure, and it is hard to do Darío justice in a study of this kind. But, ultimately, there is something in Darío for everyone, even those who use his writing as a negative point of departure. In terms of the history of Latin American literature, it is impossible to understand the writing of major twentieth-century literary figures from Spain and Hispanic America such as Federico García Lorca, Pablo Neruda, César Vallejo, Jorge Luis Borges, and Gastón Baquero without thinking about them as rebellious sons of Rubén Darío. The same is also true of the young Nicaraguan *vanguardista* writers in the late 1920s and 1930s: they made a name for themselves by attacking Darío's poetics, but they came to regard him over their long lives with deep reverence and respect, although sometimes as a beloved enemy who casts a very long shadow. One can go back to Darío's vast production of poetry, short stories, novels, essays, chronicles, and letters again and again; and there will always be something new to console, shock, and stimulate the psyche.

INDIGENOUS ANTECEDENTS

Nicaraguan literature might have begun officially with the monumental presence of Darío in the nineteenth century, but there are indigenous and outside (non-Nicaraguan) antecedents that provide many insights into Nicaraguan culture and customs during the pre-Columbian and colonial periods. Unfortunately, little remains of the indigenous songs and codices from the area now known as Nicaragua, which were destroyed in public bonfires at the time of the conquest. Researchers have been able to speculate about the remnants of an indigenous Nicaraguan past. Certainly, these elements persist as part of a vigorous oral tradition and, more basically, as the etymology of everyday words and place-names in both urban and rural areas in Nicaragua. Because of the cultural affinities throughout Mesoamerica, however, some Nicaraguan writers (especially Pablo Antonio Cuadra [1912–2002] and Ernesto Cardenal [b. 1925]) have been able to benefit from the work of researchers such as Angel María Garibay K. from Mexico, where the Aztec indigenous past has been reconstructed more fully. A shared culture also depends on a similar flora and fauna that know no national boundaries and are the source of myths and human language itself. In this sense, Nicaraguan writers also have found literary sustenance in works such as the *Popol vuh,* a cornerstone of the Mayan civilization. Pablo Antonio Cuadra, for example, takes a myth about the calabash tree from the *Popol vuh* to create a contemporary story of heroism and sacrifice based on the life and death of his friend Pedro Joaquín Chamorro.[4]

CHRONICLERS AND TRAVELERS

Nicaragua's cultural past also has been described by Spanish *cronistas* (chroniclers) at the time of the conquest and knowledgeable travelers from the nineteenth century. The oldest of these sources is by Pedro Mártir de Anglería and dates from the early sixteenth century. Perhaps the most comprehensive of these chronicles, in that it includes observations about the natural world of Nicaragua as well as the culture and customs of the aboriginal population, is *Historia general y natural de las Indias* (1526) by Gonzalo Fernández de Oviedo y Valdés. The great defender of indigenous rights, Bartolomé de las Casas, also refers to Nicaragua in his writings. Orlando W. Roberts, Ephraim George Squier, Julius Fröbel, Pablo Levy, Thomas Belt, and Carl Bovallius are all travelers from the nineteenth century who wrote with great insight about Nicaragua's geography, people, and indigenous past. These works, as well as sophisticated archaeological studies on ceramics, such as Samuel K. Lothrop's *Pottery of Costa Rica and Nicaragua* (1926), also have enabled contemporary Nicaraguan writers not only to understand their past more fully but also to incorporate it in their own poetry in innovative ways, which is exactly what Pablo Antonio Cuadra was able to do in *El jaguar y la luna* (1959).

POST-*MODERNISTAS*: AZARÍAS H. PALLAIS, ALFONSO CORTÉS, AND SALOMÓN DE LA SELVA

Reading the poetry of the three great post-*modernista* writers, Azarías H. Pallais (1885–1954), Alfonso Cortés (1893–1969), and Salomón de la Selva (1893–1959) also provides a variety of insights into Nicaraguan culture and customs. Pallais was known as a rebellious priest in a frayed black cassock who always sided with the poor in his poetry (guided by the teachings of the Gospel) and in his religious work in León and Corinto.[5] His books include *A la sombra del agua* (1917), *Espumas y estrellas* (1918), *Caminos* (1921), *Bello tono menor* (1928), *Epístola católica a Rafael Arévalo Martínez* (1947), and *Piraterías* (1951).

Alfonso Cortés is a metaphysical poet concerned with the relativity of time and the preeminence of space from his perspective as an individual trapped by mental illness and a lack of intimate human contact, someone who was literally restrained in chains in his home (the same house where Rubén Darío had lived) and often forbidden to write on the recommendation of physicians who did not have an adequate understanding of how to treat schizophrenia in the first decades of the twentieth century in León. Cortés's work is extremely uneven, but his best poems (such as "Yo," "La gran plegaria," "Pasos," and

"La canción del espacio"), with all their enigmatic beauty, delve deeper into the mysteries of the cosmos than the verse of Darío, or García Sarmiento, as Cortés chose to call his more well-known compatriot.[6] Cortés's most accomplished poetry is included in *Poesías* (1931), *Tardes de oro* (1934), and *Poemas eleusinos* (1935).

Salomón de la Selva's *Tropical Town and Other Poems* (1918) appeared in English in the United States, where the poet had been living since 1906. At the time of the publication of this first book, de la Selva was publishing poetry in major U.S. magazines such as *Harper's*, corresponding with important literary figures of the time such as Edna St. Vincent Millay, and teaching at Williams College. But when he had written his second book, *El soldado desconocido* (1922), a testimonial work about his experiences as a soldier in World War I, the poet had made the decision to abandon the English language and write exclusively in Spanish. His books, which draw on a deep knowledge of Greco-Roman myth and history (occasionally mixed with themes from the Aztec world), include *Evocación de Horacio* (1949), *La ilustre familia* (1954), *Canto a la independencia nacional de México* (1956), *Evocación de Píndaro* (1957), and *Acolmixtli Netzahualcóyotl* (1958).

THE VANGUARD MOVEMENT

The writers associated with Nicaragua's *Movimiento de Vanguardia* were talented, precocious iconoclasts, who wanted to burst onto the literary scene of the early 1930s from their city of Granada by breaking some of the windows of the establishment and letting in some fresh air with their irreverent humor and innovative ideas. Their name, the *vanguardistas,* is a word that belongs to the vocabulary of war. What were they fighting against? They challenged the bad taste and upper class values espoused by people of their own social extraction and they loathed the mediocre imitators of Rubén Darío. Their rebellion was nationalistic and quite conservative (they initially supported Somoza in Nicaragua and Franco in Spain), unlike the more politically progressive vanguard movements in other Latin American countries championed by writers who were a little older than the Nicaraguans. The most important *vanguardistas* in Nicaragua, who would sometimes conspire and laugh in the steeple of La Merced church in Granada, were José Coronel Urtecho (1906–1994), Pablo Antonio Cuadra (1912–2002), and Joaquín Pasos (1914–1947). Other members included Luis Alberto Cabrales (1901–1974), Octavio Rocha (1910–1986), Alberto Ordóñez Argüello (1913–1991), Luis Downing Urtecho (1913–1983), and the caricaturist Joaquín Zavala Urtecho (1911–1971). Coronel, given his age and the fact that he was a brilliant, utterly convincing conversationalist, was the leader of the group, and tended to order around the younger members of the group by giving them things to read and assigning projects. Some of this material that eventually renovated Nicaragua's cultural life was new poetry from the United States and France that the *vanguardistas* translated and assimilated in their own work. In 1927, Coronel was 21 when he returned to Nicaragua from San Francisco, which coincided with Luis Alberto Cabrales's return from Paris with the latest literary novelties from a time when all the rules were being broken in Europe by cubists, creationists, and futurists; and Ezra Pound was making U.S. poetry new by means of his quirky, but effective, translations of Sextus Propertius and classical Chinese poetry. In addition, the *vanguardistas* did extensive research on Nicaraguan popular culture. All this was a potent recipe for literary renovation. The *vanguardistas* successfully broke the isolation that has kept many literary movements in small countries strictly provincial.

José Coronel Urtecho's poetry (and some translations of U.S. poetry that he made into his own poetic manifestoes) is collected in a volume with a curious title taken from the Greek of Homer's *Odyssey: Pol-la d'ananta katanta paranta* (1970 and 1993). His *Paneles del infierno* (1981) is a long poem that takes its rhetorical point of departure in support of the Sandinista revolution from the opening poem of Edgar Lee Masters's *Spoon River Anthology.* Coronel is always interesting to read, whether it is his reflection on Nicaraguan history *Reflexiones sobre la historia de Nicaragua de la colonia a la independencia* (1962–1967), an essay praising Nicaraguan food, an often humorous meditation on life in the United States and also Mark Twain's trip to Nicaragua in *Rápido tránsito (al ritmo de Norteamérica)* (1953), the satirical verbal fireworks of the early play *La chinfonía burguesa,* or the classic narrative poem "Pequeña biografía de mi mujer" about his wife María Kautz of German extraction, who ran the farm just across the Nicaraguan border in Costa Rica on the Río Medio Queso, where she and Coronel lived for decades and raised their family.

If one wanted an intensive course in Nicaraguan culture and customs and could choose only one writer, that author would have to be Pablo Antonio Cuadra. In essential booklength essays such as *El nicaragüense* and studies of folklore in *Muestrario del folklore nicaragüense,* Cuadra explores the Nicaraguan perspective on their *mestizo* world with unfailing clarity and depth. It is difficult to imagine a writer who has done more to describe the geographical and biological landscape of a country in as comprehensive a way as Cuadra does in world-class collections of poems such as *Poemas nicaragüenses* (first published in 1934, but revised extensively throughout the poet's life for subsequent editions); *El jaguar y la luna* (1959); *Cantos de Cifar* (1971), a striking series of narrative poems about the people who navigate the dangerous Homeric waters of Lake Nicaragua; *Siete árboles contra el atardecer* (1980), a book in which seven different species of Nicaraguan trees are repositories for a country's myths, history, and collective memory; and *La ronda del año* (written between 1984–1986), a series of 12 poems that correspond to a year's natural cycle in Nicaragua. Through publications such as the five issues of *Cuadernos del Taller San Lucas* (1942–1944 and 1951), to the literary journal *El Pez y la Serpiente,* published for decades beginning in the late 1950s, to his work as the editor of *La Prensa Literaria,* Cuadra has revealed his country's visible and invisible landscapes, as well as the mindscapes of a people who have suffered the tragic blows of history in the form of wars, natural disasters, and the grinding poverty of everyday life.

It is a shame that the poetry of Joaquín Pasos, who died prematurely in 1947 and who barely had a chance to travel beyond the borders of his country except in his imagination, is so unknown outside Nicaragua. His collected poetry *Poemas de un joven* (1962) was published by Ernesto Cardenal in Mexico. Pasos's long apocalyptic poem "Canto de guerra de las cosas," which he wrote at the end of his life, is perhaps the most important overlooked masterpiece in twentieth-century Latin American poetry.

GENERATION OF THE 1940s

If the *vanguardistas* had a bellicose, conflictive attitude toward the writers of previous generations (something that manifested itself most clearly in Coronel's early "Oda a Rubén Darío"), the three most important post-*vanguardista* writers had more of an active mentoring relationship with their literary predecessors. Ernesto Mejía Sánchez (1923–1985), Carlos Martínez Rivas (1924–1998), and Ernesto Cardenal (b. 1925) contribute in different ways to a definition of a generational poetics.

Mejía Sánchez was a brilliant academic who received his education in Mexico and is widely recognized as the most gifted researcher of Rubén Darío's poetry. His own verse is collected in the anthology *Recolección al mediodía* (first published in 1972, but revised and augmented in 1980 and 1985). One of his pioneering contributions as a writer is the work he did on *prosemas,* brief prose poems.

Carlos Martínez Rivas is the author of perhaps the single most influential book of poetry in Nicaraguan literature for several generations, *La insurrección solitaria,* first published in Mexico in a limited edition in 1953 after his formative years in Madrid and Paris in the late 1940s, where he met Octavio Paz and Julio Cortázar. He achieved his perfection as a writer at a very early age and spent the rest of his life working on a second book, doubting his abilities to produce literature at the same impossibly high level (although a poem such as "Dos murales U.S.A." might have been enough to convince him, at least temporarily, that he still had talent). His prodigious memory was a powerful showstopper when, at social gatherings, he recited the poems of others and occasionally his own poetry, especially "La puesta en el sepulcro, XIV estación," which is full of the tragic and refined macho bravura that one hears in Mexican boleros by Agustín Lara. By turns brilliant and cruel, depending on how much rum he had consumed, he fulfilled all the requirements for the cursed genius-poet-rebel, continuing the model of the nineteenth-century poets whom he most admired, Charles Baudelaire and Edgar Allan Poe. His book *Infierno de cielo y antes y después,* winner of the 1984 Rubén Darío Latin American Poetry Prize, was published posthumously in 1999.

Ernesto Cardenal is, without a doubt, Nicaragua's most internationally recognized poet. His poetry has been translated into many languages and, especially when he served as his country's minister of culture during the 1980s, he has traveled the globe, giving poetry readings to enthusiastic international audiences. Cardenal benefited greatly from the guidance he received from the *vanguardista* poets José Coronel Urtecho and Pablo Antonio Cuadra. With his mentor Coronel, Cardenal translated a major anthology of U.S. poetry (it also included Native American texts), which had a great deal of influence on successive generations of Nicaraguan poets. Cardenal also created his definition of *exteriorista* poetry in conjunction with Coronel, who, in the early 1960s, wrote a poem called "Ciudad Quesada,"which was a collage of factual data and history in prosaic free verse stripped of metaphor. *Exteriorismo,* with its emphasis on precision, objectivity, the consultation and incorporation of original sources, and moral codes is certainly a defining feature of much of Nicaraguan poetry from the 1970s through the mid-1990s. It is also mistaken, however, to think that *exteriorismo* and its opposite, *interiorismo* (exemplified by the poetry of Carlos Martínez Rivas), exist in some chemically pure form. The most successful poetry in Nicaragua always combines elements of both.

Given the relationship between the changes in Cardenal's poetry in relation to the poet's life, it is important to consider certain biographical facts. In 1954, Cardenal was peripherally involved in an attempt to overthrow the government of Anastasio Somoza García called the April rebellion. The result of this revolutionary participation was Cardenal's famous poem *Hora cero* (1960). In 1957, Cardenal decided to follow his religious vocation and entered a Trappist monastery in Gethsemani, Kentucky, where the well-known Catholic writer Thomas Merton was Cardenal's novice master. Cardenal continued his religious studies in Cuernavaca and was later ordained as a priest in Colombia. Cardenal's plan to establish a contemplative community called Solentiname on an island in Lake Nicaragua in the mid-1970s was also influenced by his ongoing correspondence with Merton. When certain young members of Solentiname expressed their opposition to the Somoza dictatorship by engaging in an armed attack of the military complex in nearby San Carlos, Cardenal was compelled to take a clearer stand in favor of the Sandinista cause. Somoza's National Guard destroyed the island community, and Cardenal went into exile in Costa Rica, where he became a spokesperson for the revolution that finally toppled the Somoza dynasty in July 1979. Because he was a priest, Cardenal's official government position as minister of culture was criticized by the Vatican during Pope John Paul's controversial trip to Nicaragua in 1983 (see Chapter 2).

Other important, influential works by Cardenal include *Epigramas* (1961), which imitate the classical style of Martial and Catullus; *Salmos* (1964), a series of poems that take as their point of departure the psalms of the Old Testament in their poetic indictment of wars, capitalism, and repressive governments; *Gethsemani Ky* (1964), imagistic poems from the Trappist monastery; *Oración por Marilyn Monroe* (1965); the long historical narrative poem *El estrecho dudoso* (1967); *Canto nacional* (1972); *Oráculo sobre Managua* (1973), published the year after the earthquake that destroyed Nicaragua's capital; and *Vuelos de victoria* (1985), a collection of poems in praise of the Sandinista Revolution. Cardenal demonstrates an ongoing interest in poetry on indigenous themes in *Homenaje a los indios americanos* (1969) and *Los ovnis de oro* (1985), which enables him to propose new models for contemporary ethical behavior based on ancient civilizations. In his more recent poetry, Cardenal has been looking into the far reaches of the universe, exploring the big bang theory and quantum physics in *Cántico cósmico* (1989) and, in a more streamlined style in keeping with his monastery poems, *Telescopio en la noche oscura* (1993). In prose, Cardenal published a religious work *Vida en el amor* (1966), an examination of the Cuban Revolution *En Cuba* (1972), and an influential book that is a practical application of the ideas of liberation theology (see Chapter 2) *El evangelio de Solentiname* (1985). During the first decade of the twenty-first century, Cardenal has been publishing his memoirs in different volumes under the general title *Vida perdida*.

GENERATION OF THE 1950S

Perhaps the most important poet of the 1950s, a generation that included Guillermo Rothschuh Tablada (b. 1926), Raúl Elvir (1927–1998), Ernesto Gutiérrez (1929–1988), Mario Cajina-Vega (1929–1995), Eduardo Zepeda-Henríquez (b. 1930), Octavio Robleto (b. 1935), and Horacio Peña (b. 1936), is Fernando Silva (b. 1927). Silva, who worked his entire life as a physician, is highly regarded as a poet and novelist with an expertise in how to incorporate Nicaraguan vernacular speech on the printed page, especially in *El comandante* (1969). His works include *Barro en la sangre* (1952), *De tierra y agua* (1965), *Agua arriba* (1968), *El vecindario* (1977), *Puertos y cuentos* (1996), *Islas de afuera* (2000), *Versos son* (2001), *Son cuentos* (2004), *La foto de Familia* (2005), and *Uno dice cosas* (2006). There is also a little-known recording of a concrete poem by Silva called *El chocorrón*, which is based on the tragic 1972 earthquake in Managua.

THE FRENTE VENTANA AND THE BETRAYED GENERATION, WRITERS FROM THE 1960S, NEW VOICES

During the 1960s, two literary groups in Nicaragua competed with very different aesthetic views. The Frente Ventana, based at the university in León and headed by Fernando Gordillo (1940–1967) and Sergio Ramírez (b. 1942), sought ways to link art with a revolutionary struggle. This generation was marked by tragic national events, such as a massacre of students in León for political reason on July 23, 1959, as well as international movements of liberation such as the Cuban Revolution. The Frente Ventana was closely linked to the idealism, commitment, and sacrifice that gave birth to the Frente Sandinista de Liberación Nacional in 1963, in conjunction with the powerful political writings of Carlos Fonseca Amador (1936–1976) that influenced the literature produced by young Nicaraguan writers at that time. The Frente Ventana published literary works and provocative manifestoes in their journal *Ventana,* which appeared from 1960–1964. One important, highly promising writer martyred in the armed political struggle to rid Nicaragua of the Somoza dictatorship was Leonel Rugama (1949–1970), whose poetry was published posthumously in the volume *La tierra es un satélite de la luna* (1983).

The other main literary group, La Generación Traicionada, was based in Managua and founded by Roberto Cuadra (b. 1940), Edwin Yllescas (b. 1941), Iván Uriarte (b. 1942), author of *Pleno día* (1999) and Beltrán Morales (1944–1986), the rebellious and fiercely critical author of *Agua regia* (1972), *Juicio final/andante* (1976), and *Sin páginas amarillas/Malas notas* (1989), who later would become more involved with the activities of the Frente Ventana. This so-called betrayed generation identified itself with the beat poets from the United States such as Allen Ginsberg, Lawrence Ferlinghetti, Jack Kerouac, and Gregory Corso and their rage against unjust wars, a lack of civil rights for many members of society in the United States, and unbridled consumerism.

Lizandro Chávez Alfaro (1929–2006) is perhaps Nicaragua's first modern novelist, although it is also true that the novel *Cosmapa* (1944) by José Román (1908–1993), set in the banana-growing region of Chinandega, can be considered the first authentically Nicaraguan work of fiction. In any case, Lizandro Chávez Alfaro is a truly remarkable writer of prose fiction, who was born in Bluefields and is unjustly overlooked outside Nicaragua. No other writer has been able to explore as effectively the psychological complexities of the inhabitants of Nicaragua's Caribbean coast. His works include *Los monos de San Telmo* (1963), a collection of short stories that won a Casa de las Américas prize, *Trágame tierra* (1969), *Balsa de serpientes* (1976), *Trece veces nunca* (1977), *Vino de carne y hierro* (1993), *Hechos y prodigios* (1998), and *Columpio al aire* (1999). This is clearly an author whose books need to be translated and circulated more widely.

The most distinguished writer associated with the generation of the 1960s is Sergio Ramírez, Nicaragua's best-known novelist. During the revolutionary struggle against the Somoza dictatorship, Ramírez was a member of the opposition Group of Twelve. After the Sandinista triumph in 1979, he was part of the new revolutionary government and later became the vice-president of his country. His award-winning books include *Tiempo de fulgor* (1970), *Charles Atlas también muere* (1976), *¿Te dio miedo la sangre?* (1977), *Castigo divino* (1988), *Margarita, está linda la mar* (1998), *Adiós muchachos* (1999), *Sombras nada más* (2002), and *El reino animal* (2006), among others.

Other noteworthy writers from the 1960s who have contributed actively to the Nicaraguan literary scene include Luis Rocha (b. 1942), currently the editor of the influential literary supplement *El Nuevo Amanecer Cultural;* the surrealist poet Francisco Valle (b. 1942), author of the important collection of prose poems *Laberinto de espadas* (1974 and 1996); Carlos Perezalonso (b. 1943); Julio Cabrales (b. 1944); and Francisco de Asís Fernández (b. 1945), co-organizer with Gloria Guabardi of the hugely successful International Poetry Festival in Granada.

Juan Carlos Vilchez (b. 1952), who published the poetry collections *Versiones del Fénix* (1998), *Zona de pertubaciones* (2002), and *En un lugar llamado dónde* (2005); Fernando Antonio Silva (b. 1957), author of *El tiempo cosechado* (1995), as well as *Tiempos de lluvia y sol, poesía reunida (1975–2001)* (2001); and Juan Centeno (b. 1957), who wrote *Amorexia* (1999) and *El otro paraíso* (2002), also have contributed as new voices in contemporary Nicaraguan literature.

WOMEN WRITERS OF THE 1970S TO THE PRESENT

Perhaps the most important phenomenon of the 1970s was the emergence of a new generation of women authors who transformed a Nicaraguan literary world that had been previously dominated by men. There were some important predecessors to these writers, such as María Teresa Sánchez

(1918–1994), Mariana Sansón Argüello (1918–2002), and, especially, the superb novelist Rosario Aguilar (b. 1938), author of *Primavera sonámbula* (1964), *Quince barrotes de izquierda a derecha* (1965), *Rosa Sarmiento* (1968), *Aquel mar sin fondo ni playa* (1970), *El guerrillero* (1976), *Siete relatos sobre el amor y la guerra* (1986), *La niña blanca y los pájaros sin pies* (1992), *Soledad: tú eres el enlace* (1995), and *La promesante* (2001). It is also important to mention the poet Claribel Alegría, who was born in Nicaragua in 1924, lived for most of her life in El Salvador and Europe, and returned to Nicaragua, where she currently resides. She has published more than 16 collections of poetry, beginning with *Anillo de silencio* in 1948. Alegría's work is well known outside Nicaragua, having been translated into English by the U.S. poet Carolyn Forché as *Flowers from the Volcano* (1982) and honored by the prestigious Neustadt Award from the University of Oklahoma in 2005. Despite these talented precursors, however, it was not until the preinsurrection period of the mid-1970s, leading to the overthrow of the Somoza dictatorship, that women writers in Nicaragua truly came into their own.

There are two writers who are especially accomplished in this new generation. One is Ana Ilce Gómez (b. 1945), author of *Las ceremonias del silencio* (1975) and, breaking a long silence, *Poemas de lo humano cotidiano* (2004). The other is Gioconda Belli (b. 1948), who began her literary career as a poet with *Sobre la grama* (1973), *Línea de fuego* (1978), winner of Cuba's Casa de las Américas prize for this book that explores themes of sexual and political liberation, *Truenos y arco iris* (1982), *Amor insurrecto* (1985), *De la costilla de Eva* (1987), *El ojo de la mujer* (1991), and *Apogeo* (1997). Her novels *La mujer habitada* (1988), *Sofía de los presagios* (1990), *Waslala* (1996), and *El pergamino de la seducción* (2005) have been bestsellers and have been translated into many languages. Her personal memoir *The Country under My Skin: A Memoir of Love and War* appeared in English in 2003.

Other notable women writers who, for the most part, began to publish in the 1970s and who remain active in Nicaragua's literary life include Vidaluz Meneses (b. 1944); Gloria Elena Espinoza (b. 1944), who published her first novel *La casa de los Mondragón* in 1998; Gloria Guabardi (b. 1945); Michéle Najlis (b. 1946); Daisy Zamora (b. 1950); Rosario Murillo (b. 1951); founder of the Grupo Gradas, director of the Sandinista Association of Cultural Workers in the 1980s, and currently Nicaragua's First Lady; and Yolando Blanco (b. 1954).

Additional recent voices on the Nicaraguan poetry scene include Isolda Hurtado (b. 1957), whose works include *Silencio de alas* (2000) and *Florece el naranjo* (2002); Karla Sánchez (b. 1958); Milagros Terán (b. 1962), author of *Plaza de los comunes* (2001) and *Sol lascivo* (2007); Blanca Castellón (b. 1968); Esthela Calderón (b. 1970), who wrote the volumes of poetry

Soledad (2002), *Amor y conciencia* (2004), and the collection of ethnobotanical poems *Soplo de corriente vital* (2008) in addition to the novel *8 caras de una moneda* (2006); Marta Leonor González (b. 1972), editor of *La Prensa Literaria,* co-founder of Nicaragua's most important new literary group 400 Elefantes, and author of *Huérfana embravecida* (1999); and feminist poet Gemma Santamaría (b. 1979).

CARIBBEAN COAST WRITERS

One especially welcome recent development, given the traditional lack of attention to Atlantic coast writers (especially if they do not write in Spanish) by the Pacific coast literary establishment, is the attention that the Nicaraguan Association of Women Writers (ANIDE) is paying to women writers from Nicaragua's Caribbean coast. A recent issue of the journal *Anide,* expertly edited by Vilma de la Rocha, highlights the work of June Beer (1935–1986), the first woman poet from the Atlantic coast, who wrote her work in both English-Creole and Spanish; Gloriantonia Henríquez, author of *Primera vigilia* (2004); Yolanda Rossman Tejada; Andira Watson (b. 1977), who published the collection of poetry *Más excelsa que Eva* (2002); Brígida Zacarías Watson, whose poetry written in the Miskitu language appears in *Miskitu tasbaia (Tierra miskita)* (1997); Erna Narcisso Walters, who writes in both English and Spanish and whose work was anthologized in *Antología poética de la Costa Caribe de Nicaragua;* Isabel Estrada Colindres, a Garífuna woman who lives in Bluefields and writes in English, Spanish, and Creole; Ana Rosa Fagot Müller, who writes in Miskitu and co-edits the journal *Tininiska;* and Deborah Robb Taylor, who publishes prose fiction and has written on the legends of the Atlantic coast.[7] Some of the work included in this selection published in *Anide* was translated into Spanish by Carlos Rigby, who was born in Laguna de Perlas in 1945, and has been a peripheral part of Nicaraguan poetry for decades. Rigby is perhaps the most well-known Caribbean coast poet, together with David MacField, who was born in Ciudad Rama in 1936 and is the author of *Dios es negro* (1967), *En la calle de enmedio* (1969), *Poemas para el año de elefante* (1970), *Poemas populares* (1972), and *Los veinticuatro: poemas y canciones* (1975). As previously mentioned in the section on writers associated with the generation of the 1960s, Lizandro Chávez Alfaro, from Bluefields, is the most appreciated writer from the Caribbean coast, although it is important to remember that he lived for many years on the Pacific side of Nicaragua, worked for the Sandinista government after the revolution, and published short stories and novels exclusively in Spanish. Given the language barriers, the extreme poverty, and the general isolation of the Atlantic coast in relation to the more densely populated western side of Nicaragua, much more needs to be done to create better understanding and cultural respect between the two, still very separate, regions.

FOUR WRITER-CRITICS

Jorge Eduardo Arellano (b. 1946) deserves special mention in this chapter on Nicaraguan literature. In addition to publishing the collection of poetry *La entrega de los dones* (1978 and 1983) and the novel *Timbucos y calandracas* (1982), Arellano has published literally hundreds of essential books and articles on every imaginable subject related to Nicaragua's sociocultural identity. His obsessive attention to bibliographic minutiae and encapsulated summaries of movements, trends, and ideas have benefited academics, researchers, and general readers for decades.

Alvaro Urtecho (b. 1951) is one of Nicaragua's most important literary critics, whose works of poetry include *Cantata estupefacta* (1986), *Esplendor de Caín* (1994), *Tumba y residencia* (2000), and *Tierra sin tiempo* (2007).

Julio Valle-Castillo (b. 1952), one of his country's premier literary researchers and art historians, is the author of *Materia jubilosa* (1986), the historical novel *Requiem en Castilla de Oro* (1996), and *Lienzo del pajaritero* (2003), a series of poems that document the myths and folk dances of Masaya.

Another writer with a strong academic background, who has taught at Tulane University and, currently, at the University of Cincinnati, is Nicasio Urbina (b. 1958), author of *El libro de las palabras enajenadas* (1991) and *El ojo del cielo perdido* (1999).

CONTINUING TRENDS

Testimonial literature remains a powerful form of literary expression in Nicaragua. Manolo Cuadra (1907–1957), who recounts his experiences as a soldier in Somoza's National Guard in the 1930s in *Contra Sandino en la montaña* (1942); Pedro Joaquín Chamorro (1924–1978), whose *Estirpe sangrienta: los Somoza* describes the repressive aftermath of the assassination of Anastasio Somoza García in 1956; Omar Cabezas (b. 1950), author of *La montaña es algo más que una inmensa estepa verde* (1982) (translated into English as *Fire from the Mountain*), an often humorous memoir of his participation in the 1970s as a guerrilla; and Juan Sobalvarro (b. 1966), who gives a brutal account of the forced military service of young Nicaraguans during the Contra war of the 1980s in *Perra vida: memorias de un recluta del servicio militar* (2005), all have written works in which personal histories resonate with the violent trajectory of Nicaraguan history and the collective memory of the people.

Statistics regarding the publication of new novels (many of which are linked to testimonial experiences in Nicaragua) are revealing. From 1990–2000, 50 novels by 30 authors appeared in print. This is a far higher rate of production than the period before the revolution of 1979. Certainly, there are historical and political factors at work here, especially given the attention that the Sandinistas gave to publishing and education during the 1980s.[8]

New literary groups continue to maintain a dialogue with Rubén Darío. Like previous literary generations in Nicaragua, the most representative current gathering of writers called 400 Elefantes understands that Darío is an inevitable point of departure in Nicaraguan letters. Founded by Marta Leonor González and Juan Sobalvarro, 400 Elefantes (the name comes from a poem by Darío) has been effective in encouraging high standards of literary excellence; creating attractive books (Sobalvarro is a talented graphic designer) by up-and-coming writers (including the excellent selection of new poets in *Novísimos: poetas nicaragüenses del tercer milenio* [2006]; as well as Henry A. Petrie [b. 1961], author of the novel *Fritongo morongo* [2007]), breaking through the barriers of Nicaragua's isolation by producing anthologies of Nicaraguan poets sharing space with poets from other Central American countries (*Poesía de fin de siglo: Nicaragua—Costa Rica* [2001] and *Cruce de poesía: Nicaragua-El Salvador* [2006]); and promoting new approaches to understanding Darío's poetry (the recently published *Nuevos asedios a Rubén Darío: 1988–2007* by Nydia Palacios Vivas).

Publishing in Nicaragua increasingly will rely on a digital rather than a printed presence. In contrast to the Sandinista years of the 1980s, when there was an effort to reprint Nicaraguan classics and new literary works as well in cheap, massive editions (10,000 copies of a book of poetry in a country of 5 million people!), the current high cost of paper, the difficulties of distribution in a country with increasingly fewer bookstores, and a general lack of readers has obliged many authors to print editions of 500 copies or less in terms of books and rely more on electronic forms of publication and publicity. Clear examples of this are the agile and informative Web site of *400 Elefantes* and the excellent electronic literary journal *Carátula,* directed by Sergio Ramírez and edited by Javier Sancho Más. Will a diminishing number of readers be willing to buy a glossy printed literary magazine filled with advertising such as *Decenio,* directed by Ariel Montoya, or even a provocative underground-type publication such as *Artefacto,* which was published during the late 1990s by Raúl Quintanilla Armijo with no advertising in its pages? The days of cultural magazines produced in massive numbers of cheap copies, such as *Nicaráuac,* from the Sandinista Ministry of Culture from 1979–1986 might well be over. It is true that a relatively low percentage of Nicaraguans own personal computers, but the democratization of the electronic culture exists in the truly astonishing proliferation of cyber cafes throughout the country.

NOTES

1. Fernando Silva. *La lengua de Nicaragua: pequeño diccionario analítico.* Managua: Ediciones de la Academia de la Lengua, 1999, pp. 5–6.

2. Rubén Darío. *Poesías completas.* Edited by Alfonso Méndez Plancarte. Madrid: Aguilar, 1961, p. 803.

3. See Rubén Darío. *Selected Writings.* Edited by Ilan Stavans. Translated by Andrew Hurley, Greg Simon and Steven F. White. New York: Penguin, 2005.

4. See Pablo Antonio Cuadra. *Seven Trees against the Dying Light.* Translated by Greg Simon and Steven F. White. Evanston, IL: Northwestern University Press, 2007.

5. See José Argüello Lacayo. *Un pobre de Jesús: El poeta de las palabras evangelizadas.* Managua: Hispamer, 2000.

6. See Alfonso Cortés. *Antología poética.* Edited by Francisco Arellano Oviedo. Managua: PAVSA, 2004.

7. See "Homenaje a la Costa Caribe de Nicaragua." *Anide* 12 (May–August 2006): pp. 5–14.

8. See Edward Waters Hood and Werner Mackenbach. "La novela y el testimonio en Nicaragua: una bibliografía tentativa, desde sus inicios hasta el año 2000," from the electronic journal *Istmo.* The article includes an extensive bibliography of testimonial works in prose fiction. http://jan.ucc.nau.edu/~ewh/WEB_PUB_LA__ NOVELA_NICA.html.

6

Media

NEWSPAPERS

THE HISTORY OF newspapers in Nicaragua is directly related to the political history of the country from the time of independence.[1] The evolution of print journalism is linked to the economic development of the country. The introduction of the printing press had obvious political implications. In Nicaragua, as is the case in the rest of Central America, newspapers originated during the colonial period. Even so, the few studies available begin in the years after independence or since the arrival of the first printing presses. The year 1844 marked the first time that a serious journalistic project began with the publication of *El Diario de Nicaragua* in Granada under the direction of Anselmo H. Rivas and Rigoberto Cabezas. After four months, owing to political differences, the two founders could not continue working together. The name of the newspaper was changed to *El Diario Nicaraguense* and was published until the 1950s. The newspaper was affiliated with the Conservative party. Supported by funds from business interests in Granada, it was a significant improvement in the presentation of the news. In 1896, a second newspaper, *El Comercio*, was founded in Granada and was published for the next 33 years with private funding and editorial autonomy.

At the beginning of the twentieth century, *La Noticia* and *El Centroamericano* were established in León, as well as *La Prensa* in Managua. *La Prensa,* established in 1926, is considered the Nicaraguan newspaper with the greatest number of years in circulation. These three newspapers, which were supported by the private sector, also represented clear political interests on the part of their owners. They appeared during the military occupation of Nicaragua by troops from the United States. The 1930s represented a new stage of evolution in print journalism, for, despite the political agitation of the time, there was a certain stability imposed by the Somoza government, which introduced innovative technologies in communication such as radio, as well as new methods of printing that included the use of photographs in magazines and newspapers. From 1930–1945, there were 15 printing operations in Nicaragua: six in León, five in Masaya, and four in Granada. The oldest extant example of Nicaraguan journalism is a copy of the *Gaceta de Nicaragua* (the official government newspaper), which began publishing in 1830 under the direction of the Agustín Viril. The newspaper lacked circulation and may have had only one edition. As the first example of Nicaraguan journalism, it is an important part of the holdings in the National Archives of Costa Rica.

León is perhaps the Nicaraguan city with the greatest number of publications in the nineteenth and the beginning of the twentieth centuries. One of these publications, *Semanario necrológico de Nicaragua* (1837), was established to inform the public about the number of deaths caused by a cholera outbreak in Sutiaba, León's indigenous community. Other publications, most of which were short-lived, include *Aurora de Nicaragua* (1837), *Nro* (1838), *Documentos sobre los negocios de la República de Nicaragua* (1838), *Boletín de Nicaragua* (1839), *El Redactor Nicaragüense* (1840), *Boletín Nicaragüense* (1842), *Eco de la Ley* (1843), and *Registro Oficial* (1845). During his stay in Nicaragua, the U.S. diplomat Ephraim G. Squier received his news from newspapers from León, especially the *Correo del Istmo* (1849), which was edited by a priest of Spanish descent and was dedicated to propaganda regarding the proposed construction of a canal in Nicaragua that would join the Atlantic and Pacific Oceans. Squier missed many things from his country, especially the newspapers. *El Correo del Istmo*, published every two weeks, was a way for him to fill that news gap. Military publications from León that began appearing in 1844 include *Aguila de Nicaragua*, *Correo del Ejército Unido,* and *Clarín del Ejército Unido.*

There were also a number of Nicaraguan newspapers published in English as a result of the presence of the United States in Nicaragua by the Accessory Transit Company, founded by Cornelius Vanderbilt in 1849 to transport people from the eastern United States to California (through the Isthmus of Nicaragua) during the Gold Rush. *Nicaragua Flag*, for example, was first published on July 26, 1851, the same year that *The American Flag*, as well as *Central American,* were established. These newspapers reflected the attempts by adventurers and mercenaries from the United States to take over the Atlantic coast of Nicaragua. The most infamous example of this in Nicaraguan history is William Walker, a nineteenth-century filibuster who declared himself president of Nicaragua and established the newspapers *El Nicaragüense*, which was published in Granada for a little more than one year, beginning in October 1855, and the *Masaya Herald*.

In the twentieth century, as previously mentioned, Nicaragua's oldest and most widely circulated newspaper is *La Prensa*, founded by Gabri Rivas and the brothers Pedro and Enrique Belli. Two years after it was established, Pedro Joaquín Chamorro-Zelaya joined the administration of the newspaper after acquiring all legal rights to its publication. In 1948, after the death of its owner, the newspaper was published by Chamorro-Zelaya's son Pedro Joaquín Chamorro Cardenal, who came to be known as the "martyr of public freedom" because of his fierce opposition to the Somoza dictatorship. Somoza was later accused of ordering Chamorro's death in January 1978 while Chamorro was driving to work. Pedro Joaquín Jr. turned *La Prensa* into the most important newspaper in the country. From the moment it was published, it called itself an independent journal, always attempting to project an image of being a moderate, balanced, and responsible newspaper. A large part of the Nicaraguan population, however, had its doubts about these characteristics, because, during the last two decades, the newspaper's editorial policies tended to favor a right-of-center ideology. After Chamorro's murder, the newspaper was published by his brother Javier, who also maintained a long-term opposition against the dictatorship. The differences among the powerful Chamorro family members began in 1980 when the right-leaning members of the family decided not to support the Sandinista government that came to power in 1979. They then carried out an ideological purge of the staff of *La Prensa* that had Sandinista affiliations or were sympathetic to the government. Consequently, the same year, a part of the Chamorro family established *El Nuevo Diario* with Javier Chamorro Cardenal as director. Jaime Chamorro Cardenal became the new director of the *La Prensa* and had the support of Pedro Joaquín Chamorro's widow, Violeta Barrios.[2]

Another influential newspaper of the twentieth century was *Novedades,* which was founded in 1937 and belonged to the Somoza family. It supported the interests of the dictator and his followers. *Novedades* ceased publishing on July 15, 1979, two days before President Anastasio Somoza Debayle fled Nicaragua in the face of the imminent Sandinista triumph.

In 1974, with the financial backing of the Suárez family, *Bolsa de Noticias* began to appear as a small informative bulletin under the slogan "We say what others don't say." It has quietly managed to increase its circulation enormously in Nicaragua.

After the triumph of the Sandinista Revolution in 1979, the newspaper *Barricada* was established, making complete use of the publishing facilities of the

Novedades. Barricada was the official publication of the Frente Sandinista de Liberación Nacional (FSLN) and used the printing equipment that belonged to the Somoza dictatorship that the Sandinistas had overthrown. The director of *Barricada* was also a member of the Chamorro family—Carlos Fernando Chamorro Barrios, who occupied this position until 1994, when he was replaced by Comandante Tomás Borge. *Barricada* circulated until January 1998. After the Sandinistas lost the elections in 1989, there was an attempt to implement an autonomy project at the newspaper from 1990–1994 in order to create more freedom between *Barricada* as an official publication of the Sandinista party and an independent publication. There was some politically sensitive investigative reporting, such as the revelation in 1993 of an arms cache in Managua maintained by guerrillas from El Salvador. Even so, the newspaper was unable to put national interests over partisan ones.[3] In 2000, a few sporadic issues of *Barricada* were published. During the height of its popularity in the 1980s, it had managed to attract readers of *La Prensa,* becoming the most widely read journal at that time. It survived into the 1990s despite the pressure of a variety of political parties that eventually forced its closure. When *Barricada* stopped publishing, the newspapers that remained were *La Prensa, La Tribuna, El Nuevo Diario,* and *El Semanario* (1990–2000). The newest journal in Nicaragua is *Hoy.* Established in 2003 by the Chamorro family, it has a tabloid format and covers entertainment, celebrities, crime, and sports.

TELEVISION

In Nicaragua, as in the rest of Latin America, privately owned television stations are the most important media forms. There are no government-owned television and radio stations. There has been, however, a tendency for private sector channels to support the policies of a particular political party in power, as for example, when Radiodifusora Nacional turned into a mouthpiece for the political party of Anastasio Somoza Debayle, the PLN. Later, during the period of the Sandinista government of the 1980s, the radio station called La Voz de Nicaragua and the Sandinista System of Television were two means of disseminating political propaganda of a specific political party (the Frente Sandinista de Liberación Nacional) instead of a more pluralistic approach that a state-run radio and television station could have had under ideal circumstances. Taxpayers in Nicaragua were not served by the three governments of Violeta Chamorro, Arnoldo Alemán, and Enrique Bolaños, who lost the opportunity to transform Channel 6 and Radio Nicaragua into media that would truly serve the public by transcending partisan interests.

There is freedom of expression in the privately owned media. Several companies meet the demand for cable television programming. National and local television and radio stations, in contrast to the newspapers that are owned by the Chamorro family, are run by different families and associations, a quality that facilitates a variety of options in terms of information and programming. In Nicaragua, as in many other countries, including the United States, the social and political beliefs of the media owners influence the ideological content of programming.

Nicaraguan television offers many options. Channel 2, with its international programming, local production, and national coverage, is the most important channel in Nicaragua. During prime time, Channel 2 broadcasts popular *telenovelas* and captures 52 percent of the Nicaraguan audience. Estesa Channel 63 is the most popular cable television channel and bases its programming on 24-hour news and news commentary. It is simultaneously broadcast on the Internet and can be viewed anywhere in the world. Telenica Channel 8 bases its programming on sensationalistic, tabloid-style journalism. Channel 4 belongs to the Frente Sandinista political party and broadcasts news, political debate, films, historical documentaries, and children's shows. Channel 10 has gained a bigger audience by incorporating programming from Univisión, which is based in the United States.

These are some of the most popular current programs and the channels on which they appear. *El Clan de la Picardía* (The Mischievous Clan) is a program that promotes different folkloric groups from all over Nicaragua. The show is hosted by well-known singer-songwriter Carlos Mejía Godoy and is aired on Sunday afternoons on Channel 2. *La Tertulia* (talk show) is hosted by the sportscaster Edgard Tiberino and Milena García, a young producer and journalist. The topics of conversation are social, political, and cultural. The program appears on Channel 2 on Sunday nights. *Esta Semana* (This Week) airs on Sunday evenings on Channel 8 under the direction of journalist Carlos Chamorro and is a program of interviews and political commentary of current interest. *El 10 en la Nación* (The Nation's Channel 10) is a daily morning show that airs on Channel 10, is hosted by the journalist Jaime Arellano, and covers politics through interviews and studio audience participation. *La cámara matizona* (similar to Candid Camera in the United States) is a popular comedy show carried out in the streets. On the program, there are video parodies of famous people in a co-production with Channel 4 and the journalist Evert Cárcamo who is also the host of the show, which airs twice a week on Channel 4.

RADIO

A wide variety of radio stations in Nicaragua serve 94 percent of the Nicaraguan population. An interesting characteristic of this audience is its age: 64 percent are less than 24 years old. The most popular station for young people is "La Tigre," which plays mostly Latino music. The national station "Mi Preferida" plays mostly reggaetón and rap music and is also a favorite among young people. The structure of the broadcasting system for Nicaraguan radio stations is divided into two main groups, taking into account differences between national and regional stations. On the one hand, there are stations that play music and have news and entertainment programming. On the other, there are religious stations, which are quite abundant in Nicaragua.

Founded on December 27, 1985, *La Primerísima* radio station belonged to the government of the Frente Sandinista for 10 years. After the electoral defeat of the Sandinistas in 1990, the station was sold to the Sandinista personnel of the station through the Nicaraguan Radio Workers group (known as APRANIC in Spanish). Its most important program with a national audience is "Somos Noticia" (We Are News), formerly "Aquí Nicaragua" (Here, Nicaragua). Its current director is William Grigsby, one of the founders of APRANIC.

Radio Pirata is an FM station that broadcasts from the center of Nicaragua at 99.9, although the difficult geography of the country inhibits perfect reception of its musical programming in certain areas.

When the AM station Radio Corporación (540 kHhz) was founded in Managua in 1965, its signal barely reached the entire capital. This changed in 1967 when the signal was boosted to cover all of Nicaragua. Its owner is Fabio Gadea Mantilla. Its programming has a pronounced conservative political content.

Estrella del Mar, founded in 1997 with the help of Cardinal Miguel Obando y Bravo, is a Catholic radio station with local programming and satellite links to PAXNET in Miami and Radio Católica Mundial in Birmingham, Alabama.

The new Radio Ya was founded in 1989 and is dedicated to general news in Nicaragua and live, on-the-scene coverage of national noteworthy items. Its programs include many social announcements and also denunciations of a variety of injustices. It belongs to the Frente Sandinista. The station sponsors many popular contests including Miss Radio Ya, the winner of which receives a grant to pursue university studies. It is perhaps the most popular radio station in Nicaragua and has programs especially for *campesinos* and workers.

Radio María is a worldwide organization devoted to the Virgin Mary and has its headquarters in Italy.

Radio Maranatha is a Protestant Evangelical station with national coverage. Its popularity reflects the rapid increase in the number of followers of these religious groups in Nicaragua.

Radio Segovia is a nonprofit station that uses the money it receives from advertising for community centers that provide free and equal access to all sectors of society with a wide range of demands and needs.

NOTES

1. Jorge Eduardo Arellano. "Inicios del periodismo en Nicaragua (1830–1884)." *La Prensa* (March 1, 2004): 10B.

2. "La Prensa: Post-mortem a un suicidio," *Revista Envío* 62 (August 1986): n.p. Available at: www.envío.org.ni/artículos/496.

3. Adam Jones. *Beyond the Barricades: Nicaragua and the Struggle for the Sandinista Press, 1979–1998.* Athens: Ohio University Press, 2002, p. xxi.

7

Cinema and Photography

COMPARED TO OTHER forms of artistic expression in Nicaragua such as poetry and visual arts, cinema has had an uneven level of quality. It developed relatively late in Nicaragua's cultural history and faces many challenges as a result of a lack of government and private sources of funding.

The period of greatest development of film in Nicaragua was the 1980s, when production was supported by Mexico and Cuba. The majority of the filmmakers at that time were trained in the government-supported Nicaraguan Institute of Film (INCINE). Most filmmakers consider this period of Nicaraguan history a true flowering of national film productions. Films made at this time reflected a period of social change, wars, and revolution. There were also films of fictional stories, which demonstrated the country's artistic range and the possibilities for future cinematographic development for creative filmmakers. During the 1980s, almost all the films competed in international film festivals and were highly praised. In national circles, films produced during this period gave the Nicaraguan people access to knowledge about what was being produced in the country. On average, at this time, INCINE produced 12 films per year in different genres and of different lengths. Notable short films during the 1980s include "El espectro de la Guerra" (The Specter of War), directed by Ramiro Argüello; "La otra cara del oro" (The Other Face of Gold), a co-production that included Rafael

Vargasruiz; "Los hijos del río" (The Children of the River), or "Wanki," by Fernando Somarriba; and "Las mujeres de la frontera" (Women of the Border), directed by Iván Argüello. Feature-length films produced in the 1980s and early 1990s include "Alsino and the Condor" (1984) directed by exiled Chilean filmmaker Miguel Littín, as well as the Cuban-Nicaraguan co-production "Sandino" (1991), also directed by Littín. Noteworthy documentary films include Ramiro Lacayo's "Bananeras" (1982), which is based on Nicaraguan poet Ernesto Cardenal's long poem *Hora 0*. María José Alvarez made a documentary film on the literacy campaign that was undertaken at the beginning of Sandinista revolution. Frank Pineda also made a film on the nationalization of Nicaraguan mines.

All film production from the 1980s is considered part of the country's national patrimony, and, for this reason, is preserved by the Nicaraguan Institute of Culture (INC) in the Palace of Culture. The INCINE disbanded in 1994, and the businesses affiliated with it were privatized, which left filmmakers disheartened and without resources, forcing them to earn a living in advertising or in the video industry. After 1994, many members of the filmmakers union attempted to reorganize as the Nicaraguan Association of Cinematography (ANCI), which achieved legal status in 1998. The film production of the 1990s was relatively scarce compared with the previous decade. There was also less interest and support by the government, which was much more conservative than the filmmakers. It was also a decade of generally harsh economic conditions in Nicaragua. Filmmaking in recent years has continued to develop primarily in two ways. First, ANCI has become a kind of trade union in which people involved with film attempt to improve the political conditions and legal framework for filmmaking in Nicaragua. Second, some members of ANCI and the defunct organization INCINE created two production companies. Frank Pineda and Florence Jaguey founded Camila Films, and María José Alvarez and Martha Clarissa Hernández established LUNA Films. Work from these groups is becoming increasingly well known internationally.

Films are also being produced independently by a group of professionals under the direction of Belkis Ramírez, who is dedicated to the production of short videos on social themes. "Victims of the Silent War," for example, is the testimony of child-victims of antipersonnel mines, a legacy of many years of civil war in Nicaragua. This documentary was produced with the support of the Horizonte 3000 organization.

Nationally produced films from the 1990s to the present are not disseminated on television, something that was not true during the previous decade when the majority of the programming was from Nicaragua.

Current Production Companies

Nicaraguan Association of Cinematography (ANCI)

ANCI is Nicaragua's only nonprofit trade union organization made up of film professionals. Created in 1988 it currently has 17 members, 7 of whom are women, a phenomenon worth noting in the male-dominated world of filmmaking, especially in Latin America. The five ANCI board members are elected every three years.

The absence of governmental politics in ANCI has led this association to initiate discussions to define a legal framework for Nicaraguan cinematography, especially with regard to Nicaragua's Law 125 concerning the Promotion of National Artistic Expression (1999), which established untenable conditions and requirements for the national production of film. As a result of this law, there is no longer any clarity in terms of the commitment that television stations have to devote an appropriate amount of airtime to promoting Nicaraguan film.

The association worked to gain access for its visual productions on television and to rotate them in national movie theaters (which was part of the policy of INCINE before it was privatized in 1990). In addition to this attempt to increase funding available for film production, ANCI also has received support from organizations such as AECI from Spain, the Danish government, and the Hubert Bals Fund (which is supported by the Dutch Ministry of Foreign Affairs, Dutch non-governmental development organizations Hivos and NCDO, the DOEN Foundation and Dutch public broadcasting network NPS). This effort toward establishing legal clarity, cultural politics, and numerous bureaucratic tasks consume most of the organization's time, which prevents it from engaging in creative work.

Of the 17 members, only 4 do film as art, producing work with their own funds and the limited support of ANCI. In the 10 years from 1994–2004, 10 film projects have been produced, mostly documentaries of different lengths, which include two documentary films in 1999 on the disasters of Hurricane Mitch. These were financed by the Direction of Forestry of the Ministry of Agricultural Forestry (MAGFOR). Another documentary called "Portraits of Women" treated the subject of domestic violence. ANCI maintains professional relations with other filmmaking groups in Latin America, the United States, and Europe.

Camila Films

Filmmakers Frank Pineda and Florence Jaguey (a husband and wife team) founded Camila Films and have produced (either separately or together) films such as "El hombre de una sola nota" (The Man of a Single Note), "Betún y sangre" (Shoe Polish and Blood), "Cinema Alcázar," and "La Isla de los niños perdidos" (The Island of the Lost Children). According to the Web site (http://www.camilafilms.com/) of the production company:

Camila Films is an independent film and video production company based in Nicaragua since 1989. Its main objectives are to reflect cultural and social aspects of life in Nicaragua and the rest of Central America. Its latest productions deal with the ways of life in the marginalized sectors of our society. Our productions have been internationally acclaimed and have won prestigious awards such as a Silver Bear at the Berlin International Film Festival in 1998 and the International Prize of the Author's Society (SCAM) in Festival Films du Réel. Paris, 2002. We have also worked in collaboration with international productions filmed in Nicaragua, such as Parallax Pictures for Ken Loach's "Carla's Song"; Universal Pictures for Alex Cox's "Walker"; and also with the BBC, Channel 4, PBS, TF1, Hallmark Channel, TVE, and others. As of 2003, Camila Films became the Camila Films Cinematographic Foundation, whose objective is to broaden its activities to include feature production and the dissemination of Nicaraguan cinematography.

Their most recent production is the film "Girls to Mothers, Chapters 1 & 2," which tells the story of Kenia, Blanca, and Viviana, Nicaraguan girls who were between 14 and 16 years old, got pregnant, and gave birth. Other documentary films treat subjects such as young people in Nicaraguan prisons, the daily life of policewomen in the Nicaraguan capital Managua, and the controversial evolution of the People's Sandinista Army.

LUNA Films

LUNA Films is a production company established by two women, who also founded INCINE and were members of ANCI from its inception. María José Alvarez, born in 1955 in Managua, is one of Nicaragua's leading filmmakers, writing screenplays and directing her own films. She is currently preparing a documentary about Nicaraguan immigrants in Costa Rica. Martha Clarissa Hernández, born in 1957, is a promising new talent in Nicaragua. Here is the synopsis of their 1994 film "Dreams Not Yet Dreamed," as described in the publicity for the 1999 International Human Rights Film Festival held in Prague (http://www.oneworld.cz):

A group of Nicaraguan girls hang out on the street around an open fire, sniffing glue and talking about their work experiences. As a result of the country's civil war, economic crisis and neo-liberal reforms of President Chamorro's government, many families in Nicaragua are forced to put even their youngest daughters to work. This documentary film tells their story in striking style, interweaving discomforting cinema verité elements with surreal video clips.

Although LUNA films is legally a private company, its creative work is more focused on films with a social impact, which tends to make it more like a foundation or nongovernmental organization (NGO) in practice. As independent filmmakers and as women, they have found it extremely difficult to raise the necessary funds to continue their work. Their 1999 award-winning film "Blanco Organdí" was miraculously produced with a total budget of $30,000, which came largely from NGOs such as The Norwegian Agency for Development Cooperation (Norad) and the Dutch organization Hivos. As one example of the challenges facing LUNA Films, it still does not have technical production equipment and is obliged to rent it. Nor does LUNA Films own a professional camera. Although there is only a small publicity team, since the 1990s, LUNA Films has made the following: "Lady Marshall" (about women from Nicaragua's Caribbean coast who earn their living fishing, a film that won first prize at the Caribbean Film Festival in Martinique); "No Todos los Sueños Han Sido Soñados" (Dreams Not Yet Dreamed); and "Lágrimas en Mis Sueños" (Tears in My Dreams), which treats the issues of teenage pregnancy and unwed mothers.

At the end of 2001, LUNA Films organized a Mobile Cine project, which allowed Alvarez and Hernández to make their documentary and fictional films more accessible in schools, universities, libraries, and cultural centers in different parts of Nicaragua.

Gota Films

Gota Films, established in 2002 by screenplay writer and film director Rossana Lacayo, is Nicaragua's most recent film production company. Lacayo, born in Managua in 1954, was a member of the Nicaraguan Institute of Film (INCINE) and distinguished herself with the documentary films "El Espectro de la Guerra" and "Sandino." She has directed more than 15 documentary films on a wide range of subjects that include Nicaragua's literacy campaign and the writers Julio Cortázar and Ernesto Cardenal. She also has worked shooting stills for full-length feature productions and is a member of the Nicaraguan Association of Cinematography. Lacayo has been interested as a director in creating films with social themes, particularly regarding women's issues. She has a degree in Economics from Duke University and has won numerous awards, including the National Prize for photography in 1982 and a prize for the best documentary film at the Granada Film Festival in 2004.

WILMOR LÓPEZ

Born in Managua in 1957, Wilmor López is Nicaragua's foremost authority on folklore, popular culture, and patron saint festivals. López studied journalism at the National Autonomous University in Managua, with an emphasis in cultural reporting. He has produced regular programming on Nicaraguan culture for national television. His work as a still photographer began in 1990, and he has exhibited his work in one-man shows in Nicaragua and abroad. López was the director of Nicaragua's National Film Archive from 1998–2000. During this period, his goals included restoring the holdings of the archive, reactivating the classic film series, and creating technical and professional training for workers at the Film Archive. A special project for López was to focus on films for children and provide a special viewing room for them. Under his leadership, many historical documentaries were produced, including "Managua in My Heart," "Old León: Patrimony of Humanity," "Rodrigo Peñalba: Teacher of the Plastic Arts in Nicaragua," and "Dances of Nicaragua." In 1999, López directed a television program for Channel 6 called "Huellas Culturales" (Cultural Trails) and produced more than 50 hour-long installments on musicians, sculptors, actors, dancers, and painters from many different parts of Nicaragua's diverse geography. López's current projects include documentaries on the folk artist Lolita Soriano and the poets Pablo Antonio Cuadra and Carlos Martínez Rivas.

NOTEWORTHY PHOTOGRAPHERS

Although Nicaragua does not have any formal academic programs for the study of photography, it has produced some excellent photographers over the last several decades. Some of these include:

- Iván García (b. 1949), a graduate of the New York Institute of Photography whose work has been exhibited in Nicaragua at the Praxis Gallery, Casa de los Tres Mundos, and the Rubén Darío National Theater;
- Oscar Cantarero (b. 1953), staff photographer for *El Nuevo Diario;*
- Claudia Gordillo (b. 1954), former war correspondent for the Sandinista newspaper *Barricada,* sole Nicaraguan recipient of a Guggenheim Foundation Fellowship, and documentary photographer of popular culture and social problems;
- Rossana Lacayo (b. 1954), also known as a documentary filmmaker and founder of Gota Films;
- Celeste González (b. 1954);
- Guillermo Flores (b. 1954);
- Margarita Montealegre (b. 1956), Nicaragua's first female photojournalist;
- Rodrigo Castillo (b. 1959), whose work includes aerial shots of remote parts of Nicaragua;
- César Correa Oquel (b. 1960);

- Mario López (b. 1961), who works with the Spanish news agency Agencia Española de Noticias (EFE);
- Alejandro Belli (b. 1961);
- Manuel Esquivel (b. 1962), who works for the Nicaraguan newspaper *La Prensa* and has been recognized by UNICEF for his photographs of child labor;
- Oswaldo Rivas (b. 1966);
- Oscar Navarrete (b. 1969), staff photographer for *Hoy;*
- Carlos Malespín (b. 1974), photography coordinator for *La Prensa*'s supplements;
- Moisés Matute (b. 1974), staff photographer at *La Prensa;*
- Ernesto Salmerón (b. 1977), winner of the V Bienal de Artes Visuales de Nicaragua in 2005;
- Pablo Aragón (b. 1977), who covers sports for *Hoy;*
- Mayerling García (b. 1980);
- and Urania Valenzuela (b. 1981), currently documenting the artisans of Estelí.

Other photographers include Guillermo Cuevas, who is best known for his remarkable photographs of the Cathedral of León, and René Rivas Barreto, Nicaragua's top photographer of models in the fashion industry and beauty pageant participants.

8

Performing Arts

THEATER

NICARAGUAN THEATER IS similar to its European counterparts in terms of its street dance-theater origins. It is the genre in Nicaragua's cultural panorama with the most precarious, relatively less developed status. The studies and archives regarding theater's first manifestations date from the Spanish colonial period. In the sixteenth through eighteenth centuries, theater was used to spread Christianity and to disseminate the Spanish language. Current examples of this include the *pastorelas,* the celebrations of the patron saints, the *judeas* produced during Holy Week, and the *posadas* produced during the Christmas season.

The monumental representative work of theater in Nicaragua (and indeed in all Latin America) is *El Güegüense,* a comedy with profound social implications that satirizes the established order during the colonial period. In 2005, this work was declared a Masterpiece of the Oral and Intangible Heritage of Humanity by UNESCO. "The Ballet of the Güegüense or the Macho Ratón" is performed annually January 17–27 in the city of Diriamba. *El Güegüense,* whose author is unknown, is a collection of 314 stories, or monologues (*parlamentos*), the earliest of which date from the beginning of the eighteenth century, and are written in a mixture of three languages: Spanish, Basque, and Nahuatl, an indigenous language spoken throughout Mesoamerica. The Nahuatl word *güegüe* means an elder who commands respect.

The unique quality of this literary work is that it moves readily between two primary languages, Nahuatl (the indigenous language widely spoken during the colonial period by the descendants of the Aztecs) and Spanish (the language imposed on the indigenous people throughout the Americas by the conquistadors, who followed Columbus, beginning in the sixteenth century). The racial mixing of Spaniards and Indians is also reflected as linguistic mixtures in a mutual, ongoing process of evolution and displacement. There was, of course, a wide variety of indigenous languages spoken throughout Central America. Some linguists believe that there may have been 450 languages and more than 2,000 dialects spoken by the aboriginal inhabitants of the region.[1] The conquistadors, in fact, admired the ability of the indigenous groups to learn and create new languages.

Three figures from *El Güegüense,* a work that UNESCO has declared a Masterpiece of the Oral and Intangible Heritage of Humanity. © Wilmor López. Used by permission.

The Macho Ratón figure from the colonial-era play called *El Güegüense* that is performed every year in the city of Diriamba. © Wilmor López. Used by permission.

The Güegüense is the protagonist of the play who uses his wit and verbal skill to get himself out of trouble when he is charged by the local colonial authorities of entering their territory without a proper permit. The Güegüense might appear to be cooperating with his accusers, but he is really outsmarting them, mocking them with words that have double meanings in two languages and subverting their power with obscene gestures. Performances of *El Güegüense* are generally on the street, with eight characters presenting the stories. Although it is a satirical drama, it combines theater with music and dance. It incorporates 14 musical pieces known as *sones;* four more mentioned in the text may have been lost. Each *son* is accompanied by a dance. The characters, in colorful costumes, are distinguished by different symbols such as the Güegüense's whip and the Macho Ratón, who wears a mask shaped like a horse's head. Numerous folkloric groups have staged the sections of dance from this play throughout the world.

The 13 characters in the play include Alguacil Mayor (Bailiff), Gobernador, Güegüense, Don Ambrosio, Don Forsico, Escribano (Court Clerk), Suche Malinche, two women, macho viejo, macho quajiqueño, macho mohino, arriero (muleteer), and regidor (Alderman). Only men have spoken parts in the play. Animals, especially the machos, or horselike bulls, are personified. All the characters wear masks and the play has a festive ending.[2]

As the trauma of the conquest gradually passed, *El Güegüense,* as a work of street theater, became a primary oral work with two objectives: to entertain the Indians and to teach the Indians how to read. It is fascinating, however, to examine the three known manuscripts of *El Güegüense* to understand the evolution of Nicaraguan speech in relation to the dynamics of colonial rule. The manuscript is a hybrid of primarily two languages, which might be called Españáhuat, a mixture of Spanish and Náhuatl. *El Güegüense* represents a moment when the Spanish language was perforated by the linguistic force of the native language without ever losing its lexical, syntactical, and morphological dominance over the Náhuatl language of the region. In many ways, this linguistic combination reflects the reality of *mestizaje,* the new *mestizo,* or mixed race culture, of the colonial period.

It is worth exploring this idea further, for it illuminates many fundamental qualities of Nicaraguan culture and customs. The *mestizo* represents a third individual, who, as a product of the conquest, emerged in society as an object of scorn and ridicule. The mestizo was the living proof of the conquistadors' virile and arrogant weakness as men who were armored and supposedly divine. As neither Indian nor Spaniard, the mestizo was excluded from both groups, the mixture of a double shame.

It is precisely in this world that the protagonist of *El Güegüense* makes his way, carrying his own mixed race heritage, creating a space for himself and his racial identity. The Güegüense, in speaking, affirms that this new race is constituted by hardworking, astute people who have a biting sense of humor. The monologues of the play do not exist simply to tell some story, but rather to describe the larger sense of Nicaraguan culture and customs. The Güegüense, as a character moving between many different places as he bought and sold goods, saw his own language and ways of interacting with people change. Nevertheless, he was capable of adapting and incorporating these transformations into a new idiosyncratic way of life. Reading between the lines of what he says, there is always the protest, an opposition to the way he has to use his merchandise to support the public representatives of a king, who under no circumstances represents him and people of his mixed ethnic background.

The Güegüense is a traveler looking for a way to survive in a world divided into Spaniards from Spain, Spaniards who were born in the New World (*criollos*), Indians, and mestizos. The *criollos* view the Güegüense as a source of money to replenish their own dwindling funds as a result of an excessive, decadent lifestyle. They want to force the Güegüense to pay taxes on his business. This payment of taxes forms part of an invisible language in the play. The Güegüense describes the corruption and predatory nature of the government officials and how they want to confiscate the earnings of an ethnic group that they themselves have scorned, although the mestizos are indispensable and vital to the economic well-being of colonial rule. The words of the Güegüense also reflect how the mestizos learned to develop a new kind of work based on clandestine commerce. In linguistic terms, Castilian Spanish meant the displacement of many indigenous languages, but it also signified the birth of a new form of Spanish enriched by the native vocabulary and a firm but sweet accent derived from the languages and their dialects of Indian ancestors.

And perhaps things have not changed all that much if one considers the many current comings and goings of Latino-mestizos, who continue to create their own linguistic spaces and new forms of oral communication. The hybrid language "Españáhuatl" from the time of *El Güegüense,* has more than a little in common with Spanglish, a new language evolving in the United States that is also scorned and criticized.

In Nicaragua, *El Güegüense* exists, but is always in need of cultural reaffirmation. The city of Diriamba, the so-called cradle of the Güegüense, with its annual performances of the play using the original *parlamentos,* is an important way of keeping this theatrical tradition alive in the contemporary world. Dr. Jorge Eduardo Arellano is also to be commended for his work in organizing the production of this play in December 1999 at the Rubén Darío National Theater under the direction of César Paz, with live music by the Nicaragua's National Orchestra conducted by Pablo Buitrago and dancers from the Ballet Folclórico Nicaragüense. After the UNESCO declaration in 2005 that recognized the importance of *El Güegüense,* there have been efforts to teach it to younger generations in Nicaragua. Especially noteworthy in this regard were the classes given by Arellano and others in the Universidad Americana (UAM) in July and August 2006. The seminar was called "Let's Get to Know Our Güegüense" and successfully highlighted the play's music, beautiful dances, and costumes, as well as its incomparable masks filled with the magic representing the unpredictable, mocking, and joyful Nicaraguan spirit.

Postindependence Theater in Nicaragua

After Nicaragua achieved its independence from Spain, specifically during the so-called thirty years of Conservative government that began in 1857, the Rubén Darío Municipal Theater was built in 1885. This structure was destroyed by a fire in 1956, and its ruins were used as a military barracks, boxing ring, and warehouse. When, on August 6, 1983, the building was declared a site of National Historic and Architectural Heritage, the mayors and citizens of León began a fundraising campaign to rebuild it. Under the leadership of Mayor Rigoberto Sampson, the theater was finally completed and inaugurated in 1997 as the José de la Cruz Mena Municipal Theater, in honor of the composer of Nicaragua's *pentagrama nacional* (national anthem), who lived from 1874–1907. The administration of the building was taken over by

Friends of the Theater Association that functions under the leadership of a board of directors and an executive director (currently María Manuela Sacasa de Prego). Granada's theater was built in 1889 and was damaged in 1894 by an explosion at a nearby military barracks. In both León and Granada, stages were improvised in the mansions in which the theaters were located for music recitals, productions of Spanish Romantic plays, and theater companies generally from Spain.[3]

Managua was named the capital of Nicaragua in 1852. In 1898, "El Castaño" ("The Chestnut Tree") was the city's first theater and was built with private funds. Later, in 1905, the Variedades Theater was built for the projection of silent films. Two other minor theaters were built in 1911. On March 31, 1931, an earthquake destroyed much of Managua's infrastructure, including its theaters, and left the capital without theatrical performances for 30 years.

Playwriting in Nicaragua developed during the period of the country's *vanguardista* literary movement during the 1930s (and continuing into the 1940s) with four main works that incorporate both traditional and modern characteristics: *La chinfonía burguesa* (The Bourgeois Chymphony) (1936) by José Coronal Urtecho and Joaquín Pasos, which is filled with social satire and exaggerated verbal fireworks; *Por los caminos van los campesinos* (*The Peasants Go Down the Roads*) (1937) by Pablo Antonio Cuadra, a tragic play about life in Nicaragua's rural areas; *La novia de Tola* (*Tola's Fiancee*) (1939) by Alberto Ordoñez Argüello; and *La Cruz de Ceniza* (*The Cross of Ash*) (1946) by Hernán Robleto.

Years later, three historical theatrical works by Enrique Fernández Morales (1918–1982) were produced: *La niña del río* (*The Girl from the River*) (1943), about the Nicaraguan national heroine Rafaela Herrera, who defended El Castillo de la Concepción on the San Juan River from an attack by the English in 1769; *El milagro de Granada* (*The Miracle of Granada*) (1954), about the apparition of the Virgin of the Conception on the waters of Lake Nicaragua; and *El vengador de la concha* (*The Avenger of the Shell*) (1962), which is based on the war against William Walker and the filibusters from the United States in the 1850s. He is also the author of the dramatic monologue *Judas* (1970).[4]

What followed were some isolated cases of genuine quality that include playwright Rolando Steiner (1936–1987) from Managua, who wrote *Antígona en el infierno* (*Antigone in Hell*) (1958) and *Pasión de Helena* (*Passion of Helen*) (1963), both of which demonstrate the strong influence of classical Greek theater. Steiner is also the author of *La agonía del poeta* (*The Agony of the Poet*) (1977), about the final days of Rubén Darío, and *La noche de Wiwilí* (*The Night of Wiwilí*) (1982) that treats the peasant massacre that occurred after Augusto C. Sandino was murdered in 1934. Other playwrights include Alberto Icaza born in León in 1943, who wrote *Asesinato frustrado* (Thwarted Murder) (1970), and Miguel de Jesús Blandón, author of a satirical work entitled *El nacatamal de oro* (The Golden Nacatamal) (1982).[5]

Given societal needs at the end of the 1960s, construction began on a building that would be called the Ruben Darío National Theater when it was inaugurated on December 6, 1969. Since that time, it is a space that has maintained high artistic standards. The so-called Golden Age of theater in Nicaragua was from 1962–1978, when the greatest number of shows were produced.

During the decade of the Sandinista revolution (1979–1990), because cultural activities were subsidized by the government, theater had its most important moment in Nicaragua's history. There were many different kinds of artistic representations at the highest level including the singers Mercedes Sosa, Amparo Ochoa, Isabel Parra, Joan Baez, Silvio Rodríguez, Pablo Milanés, Ali Primera, Joan Manuel Serrat, Chayanne, and many others. There were readings in the theaters by internationally renowned writers such as Julio Cortázar, all of which became an everyday part of the cultural life at that time. Dance companies such as the Bolshoi from Russia and the National Ballet of Cuba with Alicia Alonso as the prima ballerina were shows open to all those who loved the fine arts.

Playwrights during the decade of the Sandinistas included Alan Bolt, among others. During this time, the Popular Theater was born, which was a movement composed primarily of actors and actresses with skills for working in urban as well as rural areas, and were mostly young people. Along with the Popular Theater group, there was a large increase in theater groups that focused more on projecting politicized art than a deeper aesthetic experience.

One strong, professional group that was established at this time was Justo Rufino Garay Theater Group and the Guachipilín Puppets Collective, whose work was most appreciated by young audiences. Many skilled actors such as Eveling Martínez and Salvador Espinoza performed at this time, as well as the majority of the people who constitute the members of groups that currently exist.

CONTEMPORARY THEATER

The First Festival of Nicaraguan Theater was held in 1991 and was a noteworthy event in Nicaragua's history of theater New works by Nicaraguan playwrights demonstrated that there was a continuation of hard work that is limited only by a lack of funding. Sixteen plays were staged in the festival, six of which were new. Plays by Blanca Rojas, Carlos Maturana, Isidro Rodríguez Silva, and Francisco Silva were especially noteworthy.[6]

During the last decade, there have been sporadic incursions of groups creating their own works. What predominates is the so-called *teatro de autor,* author's theater, which simply means the interpretation of the great works of universal theater, but with the added sense of adapting original creations by introducing similarities to Nicaraguan reality. An example of this was Shakespeare's *Macbeth* by the EKO Group and Oscar Wilde's *The Importance of Being Earnest* presented by the Teatro Experimental Managua (TEM). The theater-puppet group Títeres Guachipilín has been active since its creation in the 1980s and has increased its repertoire of characters with the staging of its own works, adapting the less-challenging pieces for children. Among their characters are those representing the inhabitants of the Caribbean coast with their dances, costumes, music, and customs.

Justo Rufino Garay was established in November 1979, under the auspices of the Sandinista government television station. Its director and founding member is Lucero Milán (in collaboration with Enrique Polo). It is the only group with its own space (which has a capacity for 150 people) for staging productions of their own work and also that of other groups. In addition to the stage, the group also has an acting school and a small art gallery. The company has staged 40 plays and has presented its work in more than 25 different countries in Europe and Latin America. The recent piece, *La casa de Rigoberta mira al sur* (*Rigoberta's House Faces South*), has been presented in Brazil, Colombia, El Salvador, and Ecuador.[7] Each year, the group hosts a festival of dramatic monologues with Nicaraguan participants and invited international guests.

The EKO Group's director is Salvador Espinoza, who is also the principal actor of the troupe, whose most well-known performance is the monologue "Case 315." The group has recently staged multidisciplinary work that combines theater, dance, and music under the guest director Enrique Polo. It also has performed a theatrical adaptation of the 1917 short story, "A Report to an Academy" by Franz Kafka.

The Teatro Experimental Managua (TEM) was founded in 1961 by Gladys Ramirez de Espinoza in conjunction with Gloria Pereira de Belli, Mimi Hammer, Adelita Pellas de Solórzano, and Tina Chamorro Benard. After decades of producing many plays, the group is currently in the process of reorganization.

The Títeres Guachipilín Group has been in existence for more than 25 years. It is the only group of its kind, working with puppets and specializing in theater for children in Nicaragua. It is directed by Gonzalo Cuéllar. The actress Zoa Meza has adapted the scripts since the group's beginnings in the 1980s. Recent work includes the staging of the children's play *El perro que no sabía ladrar* (*The Dog Who Didn't Know How to Bark*) by the Italian writer and teacher Gianni Rodari. The technique used by this group is related to the puppetry of ancient Japanese theatrical traditions. For example, the musicians appear next to the puppeteers, dressed entirely in black hoods and visible to the audience. The puppets perform on tables or platforms.[8]

The Grupo Nixtayolero began its work in the 1980s under the direction of Valentín Castillo. Their artistic work has three main tenets: using Nicaraguan traditions and cultural expressions, engaging in issues of contemporary social life, and developing artistic quality. Their plays reflect Nicaragua's cultural richness in that they are nourished by the traditions, symbols, and magical realism that form the basis of a Nicaraguan national identity. Recently, the group has participated in international festivals in Mexico and Scotland, where they have been applauded for staging plays about the frustrating process of development in Third World countries.[9]

The Ceiba Group was established at the end of the 1990s by José Wheelock, who has directed and staged several well-received works including *La canción del espacio* (*The Song of Space*), *El Güegüense*, and *La soldadera y sus muertos*. One of its main goals is to create a compelling mix of theater and dance. The director enjoys staging his works in open spaces.

The Espiga Nueva Theatre Group was founded in the city of León in the 1980s by director Filiberto Rodríguez. It consists of musicians, dancers, and actors who have their own space for performances, as well as an acting school. They have also presented their work in Holland, Spain, Sweden, and El Salvador. Recent productions include *El Naufragio* (*The Shipwreck*) with a theatrical run of five packed performances for students in secondary school in León's José de la Cruz Mena Municipal Theater, which can accommodate 500 people. Their work mixes humor with everyday events and themes of social importance. They are currently the main theater group for León's Municipal Theater, and gave a very successful performance of the Nicaraguan legend of the golden crab for a student audience in 2007.

The Ronda de Barro Group began functioning in León in the 1990s, consisting primarily of members of the Sarria family who received their acting experience in the street theater groups of the 1980s. In their house, there is a small stage where they rehearse and stage new works. They also give classes in dance and theater. Gioconda Belli's play *El taller de los insectos* (*The Insects' Workshop*) is the most important work on a national and international level that this group has produced.

DANCE

Dance in Nicaragua is perhaps understood most fully when it is examined from its beginnings in relation to indigenous dances used to invoke the gods.

Young people wearing indigenous costumes and performing a traditional dance in Masaya, with the church of San Jerónimo in the background and surrounded by numerous spectators who gather to watch this important cultural event each November. © Wilmor López. Used by permission.

Although there are studies that have made it possible to begin to re-create these ancient rituals, this section of the chapter focuses on folkloric dance from the colonial and contemporary periods.

Monimbó, in the department of Masaya, is widely considered to be the cradle of Nicaraguan folklore. The *fiestas patieras* (small festivals in the patios of private houses) of the *inditas* (little Indians) that are held here are perhaps the current dance representation that is most closely linked to the indigenous celebrations before the arrival of the Spaniards. In the patios of the houses, the people gather in their best costumes and dance in couples to marimba music. Another noteworthy tradition from this area is the dance of the *negras* (black women), which is performed by male couples, although one of the men is disguised as a woman. It is said that this custom has its origin in the belief that on one occasion the men in a *fiesta patiera* asked the women to dance, but the women were offended and rejected their invitation. The men, bothered by this rejection, developed the dance to show the women that they were not necessary for dancing. Two men form a couple dressed in luxurious costumes, with both men wearing masks and carrying beautiful fans. In the northern part of Nicaragua, people dance mazurkas (*mazurquitas norteñas*) and polkas, which reflect the influence of European culture in Nicaragua. On the Caribbean coast, festivals such as the Palo de Mayo are characterized by swaying erotic movements.

Dance combined with music produces a kind of endless honeymoon for its participants with an almost infinite variety of forms. Many dances in Nicaragua were part of street theater, which is certainly true of *El Güegüense*, dating from the colonial period. At the end of the nineteenth century and the beginning of the twentieth century, waltzes in Nicaragua filled the salons with delicate swirls and overflowing dresses of European influence for many years. From the 1940s through the 1970s, classical ballet was fashionable. Many schools in Nicaragua suddenly began to teach classes on this delicate and academic form of dance. Dance in Nicaragua as a staged art began in the 1960s with the opening of the School of Fine Arts and the inauguration of diverse nightclubs in the vital downtown area of old Managua (before the massive destruction of the 1972 earthquake) and in the country's major cities such as Granada and León. As the School of Fine Arts gained prestige and influence, the nightclubs allowed the spaces to be used for shows produced in Nicaragua.[10] During this period, Alcira Alonso was a prominent choreographer who collaborated in conjunction with the dancer Heriberto Mercado.

The first folkloric dance groups of high artistic merit emerged in the late 1960s as a result of the perseverance of Chonita Gutiérrez and Camilo Zapata. Under their influence, folklore transformed into dance achieved the recognition it deserved. Irene López, Bayardo Ortiz, and Antonio Dávila created national interest to form groups that staged the beautiful choreographies of national identity that folkloric dance represents. In León, the persistent work of Prof. Rosalpina Vázquez facilitated the presentation of traditional dances from the indigenous community of Sutiaba in León. Both Irene López and Rosalpina Vázquez were cited by UNESCO in 2005 as two people who have conducted important research that has helped save Nicaraguan folklore from extinction.

In the 1970s, folkloric dance appeared with a greater level of organization in more professional groups. The folkloric ballet group called Macehuatl directed by Ronald Abud (from Jinotepe) and Alejandro Cuadra made up the first folkloric group composed of university students in Managua. In Masaya, Haydee Palacios's role in taking folkloric dance to the National School of Commerce and different secondary schools, such as Ramírez Goyena and Primero de Febrero, helped to legitimize this kind of dance as an art form.

In the 1980s, given the Nicaraguan government's interest in funding a diverse range of cultural activities, there were many dance groups, not only in folklore, but also for free dance, salsa, mambo, rumba, tango, merengue, disco, and others. Dancers organized themselves, creating the Association of Dance Artists. During this period, the National School of Dance was established, creating the opportunity (for the first time in Nicaragua) to practice modern and contemporary dance with professional teachers, many of whom enjoyed international prestige, such as Patricia López, Evangelina Villalón (from Mexico), Elena Gutiérrez (from Chile), and Gerardo Lastra (from Cuba). Also, under the direction of Gloria Bacon, a graduate of the National School of Dance, Nicaragua's first School of Contemporary Dance was established. The diverse range of dance genres began with Variedades, created by Iván Luis Palomo and Miguel Angel Tercero. In addition, ballet occupied such an important place in Nicaraguan culture during the 1980s that the dancer Ana Amalia Sierra was able to create the National School of Ballet, which was closed by the government of Nicaraguan President Arnoldo Alemán.

Among the prominent folkloric dance groups of the 1980s, Macehuatl, under the direction of Alejandro Cuadra, was the first group to create a fusion between classical and modern dance techniques with innovative choreographies that re-created the different regional traditional dances in Nicaragua. Examples include their performances of *El Güegüense, El baile encintado* from the Caribbean coast, *Las inditas* from Diriamba, *El viejo y la vieja* from Masaya, *La sirena Miskita* from the Autonomous Region of the North Atlantic, and *La danza de los pescadores* from Managua. The Macehuatl group gave all these folkloric pieces their own personality as major works of art, primarily as a result of their great aesthetic content. In their choreographies, one can enjoy the contrasts of tradition and mischief. Internationally, even after the death of the director, the group has been a cultural ambassador of Nicaragua, precisely because of the professional legacy that Alejandro Cuadra gave to the members of the group. The current director of Macehuatl is René Jaime.

Other noteworthy groups from the 1980s include the Gaspar García Laviana group led by Aldanaro Jarquín, Flor de Sacuanjoche under the supervision of Nina Moreno, El Güegüense directed by Javier Duriez, the Nahuatl group headed by Xiomara Gutiérrez, the Anáhuac company under the leadership of Guillermo Urbina, and Blanca Guardado's Ballet Folclórico Tepenáhuatl.[11]

In the different festivals of the patron saints, the people commonly express themselves through dance. The popular festival in which dance is the main ingredient in the municipality of Bluefields, in the Autonomous Region of the South Atlantic, is called the Palo de Mayo, which is celebrated at the end of April and the beginning of May. It is also known as the fertility dance. In Nicaragua, at this time of year, the fields are filled with flowers. The arrival of the first rains creates this magic of diverse fertility everywhere and forms a part of the cult of tree worship. It is presumed that the roots of this festival are English, as this part of Nicaragua was conquered by England. The celebration does, in fact, include a program similar to the English May Day in two parts—one for children and the other for adults. But it is important to point out that even though its roots might be English, the blacks of African descent, the Miskito Indians, and the mulattoes gave their own touches to the dance, music, and song lyrics that are markedly different from anything of English origin. The dance is done around a tall tree trunk or *palo,* as it is commonly called. This pole is adorned with flowers, fruit, and ribbons of brilliant colors. The pole is sunk into the ground where the festival will be held. Nowadays, this happens on weeknights and the dancers move around the pole, weaving the ribbons together that each dancer carries in his or her hands after 8:00 P.M. When all the ribbons have been woven together, the dance is done in reverse to undo the weaving.

In this strange and beautiful dance, one can find the signs of spirit-worship, for the pole, as well as the flowers and fruit, are said to possess sensitive spirits born from Mother Nature. It is the dance of the spirits that inhabit the trees that are the givers of life itself, for offering their fruit as food and their bodies as dwellings helps humanity maintain a perennial relationship with them. Dancing creates unbreakable links that last until the next

A group of men and women street dancers from the Caribbean city of Bluefields. © Wilmor López. Used by permission.

Queen of the May festival on Nicaragua's Atlantic coast. The festival lasts the entire month with
dancing, food, music, and a carnival-like atmosphere. © Wilmor López. Used by permission.

end of April or beginning of May when the cycle again offers flowers, trees,
and fruit.

In the 1990s, the Casas de Cultura (cultural spaces in cities and towns for
public use, created largely in the 1980s) continued to provide space to dance,
theater, and music groups for both rehearsals and performances. But it was
never easy. Many dancers and their groups had to persevere in their search to
survive and create quality work. Examples of the Nicaraguan dance groups
that continue to thrive include the Ballet Nueva Compañía directed by Prof.
Ernesto Lanzas in León, which specializes in a variety of free dance; the Ballet
América in Managua, which works primarily with folkloric dances incorporating abundant traditional costumes transformed into beautiful *trajes de
fantasía;* and the Danza Arabesco group in Matagalpa, which stages rumbas,
flamencas, and classical ballet.

Currently, dance as teaching also survives in the Adán Castillo National
School of Dance that belongs to the Nicaraguan Institute of Culture. There
are also the Nicaraguan Academy of Dance, which is part of the Association

Float from the Bluefields carnival, whose theme is related to the region's products such as coconuts. There is also a cayuco that is used for fishing. © Wilmor López. Used by permission.

of Dance Artists, and the Open Space School of Contemporary Dance. The majority of the groups, whether they work in contemporary dance, folkloric dance, or classical ballet, and whether or not they are professionals, are affiliated with the Association of Dance Artists. Many groups in other departments of Nicaragua are well maintained through the personal efforts of people such as Lelia González, Diamante Marenco, Auxiliadora Valle, Felipita Cermeño, Rosalpina Vázquez, and Ronald Abud, among others.

There is also the Danza Contemporánea de Cámara, which was founded in 1980. Beginning in 1991, the government of Violeta Chamorro cut its budget. Faced with the closing of the National School of Dance, the group created the Open Space School. They continued working independently, surviving on the small amount of income from classes and from the generous cooperation of Hivos in Holland. They entered the twenty-first century as a group with the strength and wisdom to face future challenges. The group, under the direction of Gloria Bacon, is composed of eight dancers and one technician. Five of the dancers are women. They perform not only on stages in theaters, but also in parks, plazas, church atriums, and markets. Because they have an original way of doing dance that can be appreciated by everyday people from all walks of life, they are now popular and well respected. In 2001, this group organized Nicaragua's VII International Festival of Dance. They presented their choreographed piece "Tierra, pasión y vida" (Land, passion, and life) in which they combined body movements with a video background, showing different anguishing and desolate Nicaraguan landscapes, thereby providing a warning concerning the ecological destruction of the planet. They have participated in international competitions in Venezuela, Cuba, Mexico, Holland, Spain, and elsewhere.[12]

The most well-known Nicaraguan groups that perform contemporary dance include Danza Contemporánea de Cámara de Nicaragua, Teatro Danza Desequilibrio, Danza Contemporánea from the Universidad Nacional Autónoma de Nicaragua in Managua, Yaxall from the Universidad Nacional Autónoma de Nicaragua in León, Danza Contemporánea Experimental from the Universidad Agraria Nicaragüense in Managua, and Danza Contemporánea from the Universidad Americana in Managua.

There are also many male and female dancers who are doing outstanding work in this field, including Francisco González, Sterling Vázquez, Isidro Vargas, Oyanka Cabezas, and Nadia Flores.

Other Dances Associated with Specific Parts of Nicaragua
Northern Region (Jinotega, Nueva Segovia, Madriz, Ocotal)

The traditional regional costume that identifies this area are the white dresses worn by the women and the white *cotona* shirts and white pants worn by the men. For footwear, the men use *caites* made of leather. They dance mazurkas that are played on violins and guitars. The polkas and rancheras are two other types of music associated with the northern region. The *Danza de las Húngaras* (Dance of the Hungarian Women), performed in the central part of this zone, close to Matagalpa, is a remnant of the presence of the gypsies in this area during colonial times. The costume for this dance is luxurious, with handkerchiefs tied around the head and dangling gold coins. The women wear large dresses with big folds of satin material with a flower print. The blouses have *vuelos* in the bust and bunched and gathered sleeves. They wear closed shoes of black leather with medium square heels. Men are dressed in black pants and a long-sleeved shirt of a single color and, over it, a flowery vest made from the same fabric as the women's dresses. They wear black boots and, on their heads, handkerchiefs with coins.

Central Nicaragua

This area includes the departments of Chontales and Boaco, a zone known for its cattle and horses. It is a normal part of everyday life here to see the

Two riders passing the Dolores church. It is common to see people on horseback during the festivals commemorating a town's patron saint. © Wilmor López. Used by permission.

men with their sombreros and leather boots riding on horseback. The traditional dance costume consists of the following for women: a long bell-shaped checkered dress, which can also be a skirt and a blouse; a shawl; and red flowers in hair that is tied in a bun. The men wear long-sleeved shirts that are checked or of a single color, blue jeans, leather boots, wide leather belts with silver or gold buckles, and a sombrero. The dances show the influence of Mexican folklore, as the music is the kind played by mariachis and philharmonic bands. For this reason, the dances are in the style of *corridos* and *sones de toros.* The dances reflect the festive atmosphere of parades of horses, cockfights, and closed-off streets for bullfights and rodeos.

The Island of Ometepe

A large island consisting of two large volcanoes jutting from Lake Nicaragua, Ometepe is the place where the Dance of the Zompopos (Dance of the Leaf-cutting Ants) is performed. It is possible to consider this dance in ecological terms, which is reflected by the dancers' costumes. The men are dressed in loincloths and are barefoot. The women also wear these loin cloths with a top to cover their chests; they also dance barefoot. They carry leafy mango branches in their hands, which move to the ancestral rhythms of drums. They imitate a group of these ants in their dance, as they go looking for food in preparation for the rainy season when they have to remain in their underground lairs. Among the members of the group are soldiers who carry a piece of wood in their hands instead of a branch with which it can wage war if the group meets another group of *zompopos* that is also in search of food. The hips of the dancers move rhythmically to the sound made by the drums that gradually increases in intensity.

The Pacific Side of Nicaragua

Here dances are done in couples. The traditional costume for women consists of the *huipil,* which is a blouse open to expose the shoulders, surrounded by *vuelos* that are adorned with braided, colored ribbons. The skirt is long and gathered at the waist, with *vuelos* in the lower part that is adorned like the blouse. The women wear their hair in two braids adorned with ribbons and flowers. The men wear *cotona* shirts and pants. The clothing is made of white manta and can be of any color. Only in the national costume is the material of white *manta* and *trencilla* of blue ribbons, though in the same style as the traditional costumes of the Pacific. Both men and women wear leather *caites.* The men wear a hat and carry a machete. The couples dance to the sound of marimbas and guitars playing songs such as "Aquella indita" and "Solar de Monimbó."

Another typical dance of the Pacific zone is the Dance of the Mestizaje. As the name suggests, it is the dance that shows (including in its costumes) the mix of the two cultures, Spanish and Indian, which gives rise to a new culture. The indigenous presence in the dance consists of dancing barefoot, with the female dancer holding a ceramic vase in her left hand. The blouse is decorated with sequins, lace, and brilliant material. The skirt is wrapped tight against the body to the knee with a shawl that allows the edge of the lace around the *fustán* to be seen. There are three elements representing Spanish culture: on her head, the woman wears a mantilla and a *peineta;* in her right hand, she carries a fan. In general, only women dance, although there are versions for couples. The most commonly played music (on marimba and guitar) for this dance is "La danza negra" and "El mate amargo."

The development of dance as an area of Nicaraguan fine arts is the result of the iron discipline of the great number of young men and women dancers who, receiving little payment for their professional effort, keep tradition alive with the movement and rhythms that continue filling the empty space onstage.

MUSIC

In the history of world music, Nicaragua occupies a prestigious place. It has produced many distinguished musicians who have spread their music throughout the world. Their ingenious sounds are accompanied by the voices of men and women who are often of humble origins. Nicaraguans are nationalistic, sometimes sarcastic and roguish, as well as romantic by nature. The songs they produce confirm this worldview.

The first musical document in Nicaragua dates from the end of the seventeenth century and corresponds to the melodic lines of the theatrical work *El Güegüense.* The musical instrument native to Nicaragua is the ocarina, a ceramic flute that comes in different shapes and sizes. It has five holes that produce its music. The marimba is an instrument originally from Africa, but in Nicaragua it was developed and adapted to become the instrument called the *marimba de arco.* This instrument is used in almost all Nicaraguan folkloric dance pieces. Other important instruments in the musical history of Nicaragua include the guitar, the *atabal,* and the violin, which are all part of a European tradition.

In the first half of the nineteenth century, the true development of Nicaraguan music occurred. It was at this time that certain musical families such as Vega-Matus from Masaya really stood out in terms of their members who were violinists, singers, guitarists, and composers who wrote the first national anthem in 1876. They were also teachers and the founders of León's first school of music methodology. From this family, Alejandro Vega Matus was an important composer of waltzes. The Zúñiga family, which had flautists and composers of nocturnes and concerts, academic music, and popular dance music was also important. Another essential contributor to Nicaraguan music was the Ruiz family from Masatepe and Masaya who founded their own orchestra and created sacred and secular music. Carlos Alberto Ramírez Velásquez, a composer of waltzes and religious music, was also a member of this orchestra.[13]

José de la Cruz Mena (1874–1907) was born in a musical family in León and is known in Nicaragua as the composer of the immortal waltzes "Ruinas," "Rosalía," "Bella Margarita," "Tus ojos," and "Amores de Abraham." At age 21, he contracted leprosy, but this did not stop him from continuing to compose his jewel-like songs in different rhythms such as waltzes, *paso dobles,* marches, requiems, and *sones de pascuas* and religious music approved by the Vatican. He died at the age of 33 on the banks of the Chiquito River in the city of León, completely blind and with his hands destroyed by the illness that killed him. He is called "The Divine Leper," and the Municipal Theater of León is named after him.

Managua musician Luis Abraham Delgadillo (1887–1961), author of numerous symphonies, operas, ballets, and concertos, founded the National School of Music and a symphony orchestra. Alejandro Vega Matus and Carlos Alberto Ramírez, together with José de la Cruz Mena and Luis Abraham

Delgadillo, make up the four most important academic composers in the history of music in Nicaragua.

With Camilo Zapata, born in Managua in 1917, there was further development in popular Nicaraguan music the middle of the twentieth century. He created the Nicaraguan *son,* composing at the age of 14 his first song called "Caballito Chontaleño." With this innovative popular current as a kind of "birth certificate" of a cultural identity that is truly Nicaraguan, he created important songs such as "Minga Rosa Pineda," "Flor de mi colina," and "El Nandaimeño." In the twentieth century, there are trios, singer-songwriters, groups, and rescuers of music native to Nicaragua. Important figures include Tino López Guerra from the city of Chinandega, author of *corridos* that pay homage to important cities in Nicaragua such as Managua, Matagalpa, Chinandega, León, and Masaya. Erwin Krüger is called the musical watercolorist because of all the richly painted landscapes in his songs. Justo Santos, an excellent guitarist, was the creator of "Mora Limpia," which became a musical work of art that is unsurpassed. Victor Manuel Leiva and Otto de la Rocha are singers of the daily spice of life that Nicaraguans learn to incorporate in their everyday activities. José Gastón Pérez left contributions in the tradition of the Latin American *bolero.* To this list of names, one must add Jorge Isaac Carballo, Jorge Paladino, Sergio Tapia, Tránsito Gutiérrez, and a group of singing doctors called the Bisturies Armónicos (The Singing Scalpels).[14]

During the years of the dictatorship in the 1960s and 1970s, characterized by a fierce repression of the people, there was a countervailing force of Nicaraguan protest music that mirrored what was happening in similar political contexts in other Latin American countries. The brothers Carlos and Luis Enrique Mejía Godoy, originally from the municipality of Somoto, burst onto the music scene with their politicized songs of denunciation. They incorporated the richness of regional songs, the political *corridos* about Sandino's struggle, folk songs, and *copleras,* setting poetry to music. Their original songs of protest and bearing witness, such as "El Cristo de Palacagüina," "Navidad en Libertad," and "Madre Nicaragüense," among many others are a great gift to the Nicaraguan people. With that music, they traveled the world, offering concerts and doing fundraising that benefited the Frente Sandinista at a time when they were fighting to overthrow the Somoza dictatorship. The Mejía Godoy brothers became the inheritors and best representatives of this kind of music. Carlos Mejía formed the group called "Los de Palacagüina." Together with the composer from León, Pablo Martínez Téllez, they wrote and performed the most internationally well-known piece of music entitled "Misa Campesina," a work that was censored by the dictatorship and the Catholic Church because of its progressive political content. The recording "Hilachas de sol" by Luis Enrique Mejía was also censored.

These works circulated widely underground. The songs from Carlos Mejía's album, "Guitarra Armada" (1979), gave listeners hope and inspiration and even taught them how to strip down and reassemble rifles such as the M-1, as well as how to make homemade bombs that could be used in the struggle against the dictator. These catchy tunes with easy-to-remember lyrics were broadcast from mobile transmitters of the clandestine radio station Radio Sandino during the crucial final months of the insurrection.[15] In 1978, Carlos Mejía's song "Quincho Barrilete," performed by Guayo González, put Nicaragua on the cutting edge of new music when it won the first prize in the OTI (Organization of Latin-American Television, in Spanish) International Festival of the Song, which was held in Spain that year. The song tells the story of a child laborer who earns a living making kites from paper. One day he decides to join the revolutionary struggle just like the majority of the Nicaraguan people who dream of achieving freedom.

During this decade of political unrest, there were also alternative rock bands such as Los Rockets, Los Hellions, Bad Boys, Los Fermons, Los Hermanos Cortés, Llama Viva, and Los Music Masters. There were also excellent independent musicians such as the guitarist Wilfredo Galo, the keyboardist Higinio Flores, the singer Mario Roa, and the arranger Ricardo Palma.

During the cultural boom of the 1980s associated with the Sandinista government in Nicaragua, there were many singer-songwriters of unquestionable value who introduced a strong poetic and lyrical content in their musical arrangements. For example, the brother and sister Katia and Salvador Cardenal formed the duo called Guardabarranco (named after Nicaragua's national bird). This group truly captured the public's imagination with the magic of a new kind of protest song that was linked to the new song movement and the Latin American Trova. Guardabarranco traveled to more than 15 countries over 10 years, representing Nicaragua in international festivals. Their song "Autor anónimo," dedicated to the young men who were doing their obligatory military service during the Contra War, become an anthem among these young people. On two occasions, 1986 and 1990, Guardabarranco won the OTI festival in Nicaragua. In the 1990 OTI festival in Mexico, they won second prize for the song "Dame tu corazón."

This same generation includes performers such as Engels Ortega, Salvador Bustos, and Mario Montenegro, who has dedicated his heart and soul to composing music for children. Nicaraguan participants such as Pancasán, Volcanto, Libertad, and Grupo Zinica often did well in international music festival competition. Popular musical groups such as the Urrutias from the mountains of Estelí, Los Alegres Saraguasca from the rugged mountains of Jinotega, and Los Alegres de Ticuantepe filled stages and public plazas with enthusiastic crowds.

A group of musicians called Don Felipe Urrutia and his Cubs, practicing their songs in a home located in the town of El Limón. © Wilmor López. Used by permission.

Norma Helena Gadea, one of the greatest women singers during this period, also achieved well-deserved fame. She continues to travel the world, interpreting primarily songs by Latin American composers associated with the Nueva Trova, such as the Cubans Silvio Rodríguez and Pablo Milanés.

El Indio Pan de Rosa, a poor farm worker and roving singer, composed songs for the National Literacy Campaign in the period immediately after the revolutionary triumph in 1979. At this time, all the singer-songwriters were composing under the influence of the euphoric mood of the revolution. Everyone wanted to sing about this triumph of the people over an oppressive government. Poets, too, composed verse to the revolution. The contests for music that celebrated the countryside and farm workers were held in support of the revolution. At first, this was a positive force for the artists. These singer-songwriters and poets, however, soon began to find themselves in creative circles that were too limited. Only those musicians who managed to break free from those constraints continued to compose with quality and freedom. The rest remained behind, singing and repeating their songs of that time, praising a revolution that no longer existed.

After the defeat of the Sandinistas in the elections, new groups appeared on the Nicaraguan music scene.

Staccato was founded in 1992 by Eduardo Araica and Milton Guillén. Other members of the group included Luis Emilio Martínez, Gabriel Fonseca, Hugo Castilla, Freddy Martínez, and Fernando Escorcia. From their beginnings, the group proposed its own style based on flamenco rhythms and classical guitar, of which Eduardo Araica was a virtuoso. They have many enthusiastic fans as a result of the high quality of the music they offer.[16]

The rock group C.P.U. (the acronym in Spanish, Contra Políticos Ultrajantes, means Against Offensive Politicians) was founded in the mid-1990s and is composed of five members whose audacious songs touch on social issues such as corrupt politicians and the lack of opportunities for young people. Their concerts provoke a kind of frenzied acceptance among their young audiences. The lead singer is Alejandro Mejía (son of Luis Enrique Mejía Godoy) who has a disturbing, delirious style of Latin rock. The titles of some of their songs that are heard on the radio and sung by thousands of young people include "Nica en Costa Rica," "El Racista," "Cristo Viene," and "Obras no palabras." The songs deal with the discrimination and racism suffered by Nicaraguans who immigrate to the neighboring country of Costa Rica in search of work that Costa Ricans do not want to do themselves. Others are biting commentaries on the Evangelical Christians that have an ever-larger presence in Nicaragua and other Central American countries. The song "Obras no palabras" (Actions not Words) subverts the slogan that Nicaraguan ex-President Arnoldo Alemán used during his government (1997–2002) characterized by multiple, massive acts of corruption.

América Vive is a group that has taken up the flag of the testimonial song. Their members are primarily students and former students of the National Autonomous University of Nicaragua (UNAN). Their songs are by the Cuban Nueva Trova, Chilean Víctor Jara, the Venezuelan group Los Guaraguao, and Ali Primera. The influence of Andean music is also characteristic of their work, which is performed professionally with the magic of instruments such as the *zompoña, charango,* guitar, flute, *atabal,* and numerous other wind instruments. These, together with the voices of the singers, create an ambience that is both very Latin American and Nicaraguan.

The newest additions to the music scene include these groups.[17] Sol Azul was established in July 2000. Its members—Clara Grün, Sergei Cáceres, Silvio Pereira, Alvaro Gutiérrez, and Tránsito Gutiérrez—are between the ages of 19 and 25. In 2001, they participated in a music festival in Panama.

Amalgama has five members, each of whom is a talented singer-songwriter in his own right: Luis Pastor González, Carlos Luis Mejía (son of Carlos

Mejía Godoy), Napoleón Escorcia, Rigo Osorio, and Luis Manuel Guad-
amuz. Their primary motivation is to share their art as a serious discipline.
Luis Pastor has been known as a soloist since 1996. His music is oriented to
the Latin American Nueva Canción.

El Grupo Armado is the new name of the group formerly known as C.P.U.
It has new members but the same lead singer (Alejandro Mejía) and a similar
biting, satiric approach to their songs.

Zona 21 is a group of excellent young musicians from León that has a wide
audience of all ages. Their repertoire includes songs that are part of the heritage of Nicaraguan folklore with a touch of Latin American and Nicaraguan
pop music. Their song "Cantinero" made them well known throughout the
country.

División Urbana is a group recognized for its modern arrangements of
traditional songs of Nicaraguan identity, for example, "Nicaragua Mía." This
group, together with Perrozompopo and Zona 21, toured in concert as a kind
of civic act during the presidential election of 2006 in different departments
of Nicaragua. The concerts were free and directed toward young people, call-
ing on them to exercise their right to vote. The slogan of their concerts was
"Vote! Break the Silence!"

The most important musical groups in Nicaragua contracted to play at
a wide range of parties for weddings, birthdays, and other occasions are
Los Mokuanes, Macolla, La Nueva Compañía, Las Nenas, and Dimensión
Caribeña.

Some of the most distinguished soloists in Nicaragua include these performers. Ofilio Picón is a singer-songwriter and founding member of the
group "Los de Palacagüina." Known for his masterful guitar playing and
rich baritone voice, Picón has set to music the poetry of some of Nicaragua's greatest writers such as Rubén Darío, Salomón de la Selva, Alfonso
Cortés, José Coronel Urtecho, Pablo Antonio Cuadra, Ernesto Cardenal,
and Carlos Martínez Rivas. He plays in a group established in 2001 called
"Ventana."

Ramón Mejía, also known by his nickname Perrozompopo, belongs to the
musical family Mejía Godoy. His music reflects influences from the Caribbean, Brazil, and soft rock and has captured the attention of national and
international audiences. His song "Cuando tardas y demoras" was extremely
popular on the radio.

Abraham Castellón is a singer-songwriter who won the 2005 National Festival of Testimonial Music. He has toured in Spain, El Salvador, and Holland. Other singer-songwriters worthy of mention are Danilo Norori, Juan
Centeno, Frank Torres, Moisés Gadea, Jairo González, Elsa Basil, Osiris

Rodríguez, Lenín Triana, Richard Loza, Philip Montalbán, Evenor Lorío, Marlon Sosa, Gabriela Baca, Carola Delgado, Alfonsina Cardenal, Mario Sacasa, and Cristyana Somarriba.

The most prominent women singers in Nicaragua are Norma Elena Gadea, Katia Cardenal, Lya Barrios, Flor Urbina, Martha Vaughan, Deyanira Toruño, Eveling Martínez, Keyla Rodríguez, María Eugenia Urroz, Julieta Jirón, Martha Baltodano and Marina Cárdenas.

Music on Nicaragua's Caribbean Coast

In this region of Nicaragua, the music that predominates is characterized by Afro-Caribbean rhythms, calypso, and reggae. These three musical currents converge to create the melodies used in the Palo de Mayo festivals. These musical varieties are also used for compositions not associated with the May celebrations.[18]

The Wallagallo is a healing ceremony performed in this region, incorporating musical elements that are from the Black Caribs, and is unique to the Nicaraguan Caribbean.

Chamber Music in Nicaragua

The development of chamber music began in the 1980s and increased in prominence in the 1990s. It currently enjoys greater popularity than ever before. These musicians have adopted a clear strategy for giving concerts throughout the country to stimulate as much interest as possible in this kind of music.

The groups listed here are the most prominent groups of chamber music with national and international reputations. Camarata Bach was founded by the well-known flautist Raúl Martínez, together with Ramón Rodríguez, who is currently the group's director. Between 2001 and 2002, they performed a series of didactic community-oriented concerts sponsored by the embassy of Finland. The project made their program of international, Latin American, and Nicaraguan classical music available to nearly 10,000 people with limited resources who otherwise would not have been able to attend the performances.[19]

Grupo de Cámara Kinteto began in 1994 under the name "Grupo de Cámara César Jerez," which was associated at the time with the Universidad Centroamericana (UCA). In the process of improving as a group, they were sponsored by the Norwegian Authority for Development. Their repertoire includes national and universal classical composers, as well as composers of vernacular and popular music.[20] Other chamber groups of distinction include the National Orchestra, the Coro de Cámara, the Coro Lírico, Quinteto de Bronce, Grupo Solfa, and the Quinteto Nica Brass.

Support for Music in Nicaragua

In 1991, the Association of Nicaraguan Singer-Songwriters (ASCAN by its Spanish acronym) was founded. Immediately afterward, it received funding from the Swedish Authority for International Development. With this support, it was possible for the Nicaraguan organization to sponsor a series of concerts in 1991–1992 in the poorer barrios of Managua and departments from the country's interior such as Jinotepe, Estelí, and Masaya. They also offered a large concert in the Rubén Darío National Theater with the participation of all its singer-songwriter members. Later, companies from the private sector supported concerts in León and Granada, cultural centers, and universities in Managua. ASCAN is comprised of the majority of the country's musical artists. It is the product of the initiative of several musicians and singer-songwriters determined to continue with their individual projects but convinced that together as an organized nonprofit group they can accomplish more. The primary objective is the development of activities to promote and disseminate Nicaraguan music by means of concerts, national and international tours, and the recording of compact discs and DVDs. One of the goals is to allow its members to participate in social causes. In this way as an organization, ASCAN achieved a major accomplishment, which was to have the National Assembly of Nicaragua approve a law that protects artistic copyrights.

There are a number of other organizations that support musical activities in Nicaragua.[21] The Mejía Godoy Foundation was founded in 1997 by the Mejía Godoy brothers with the purpose of gathering their musical family "under the same roof." They are based in the "Casa de los Mejía Godoy," which is a cultural café for concerts that offers the singer-songwriters a space for their artistic expression. It facilitates the gathering of a great Nicaraguan family that has been divided many times by politics. The foundation also extends its role toward social projects that relate to education, reproductive health, and domestic violence in places in the capital where people are especially vulnerable to these issues.

Every August since 1999, the Achuapa International Music and Solidarity Festival has been an annual event in this rural town of 3,500 residents in the Department of León, where horses outnumber cars 100 to 1. An amazing variety of internationally renowned performers from the Basque country, Brazil, Chile, Cuba, Denmark, England, Scotland, Spain, and the United States share the stage with talented local musicians such as José Adán Hernández Rocha, Don Felipe Urrutia y Sus Cachorros, Amancio Pérez, Los Alegres de

Santa Rosa, and Los Rústicos. Co-founded by Arizona resident Lillian Hall and Achuapa's most well-known troubadour Brigido Soza with help from international groups such as ProNica, Inc., Canadian Friends Service Committee, and Canadian International Development Agency, among others, the festival is a shining example of grassroots organizing, fun and music for social change.

Since 2001, the Nicaraguan Institute of Development (INDE) has sponsored different activities that strengthen cultural and social development among young people, coordinating these events through the offices of local mayors.

The Alianza Francesa organizes an annual music festival in June with the participation of amateur and professional musicians in concerts held in streets, plazas, bars, and cultural centers, with the goal of promoting different groups and soloists and getting music out to the people.

FLADEN-Nicaragua (an acronym in Spanish that means Latin American Forum for Music Education) is a nonprofit organization that works to develop music education in Nicaragua, a country where, owing to a lack of institutionalized support for this activity, there is a great deal of music illiteracy. It is an independent organization that is not linked to any particular political party and is not supported by the government. It is financed by its members and by the generosity of different sponsors. The Friends of the José de la Cruz Mena Theater Association in León was founded in 2000 with the purpose of promoting artists from León and the rest of Nicaragua on the theater's impressive stage. The "Rondas Culturales" program that the association has developed over the last six years is directed primarily toward children, adolescents, and young people from the Pacific side of Nicaragua. It helps recognize new talent in a wide range of educational centers at the preschool, primary, and secondary levels. Every 15 days, four different schools come to the theater to compete in contests in the fields of music, variety dance, declamation, and folkloric dance. The participants are evaluated by a jury that selects one winner per category, who in turn compete as semifinalists and then as finalists as the contests reach their conclusion. Winners are given a trophy, a diploma, books for their school libraries, and small grants. If the winner is in the category for singing, the prize includes the right to record a master CD using the theater's equipment. In this way, the young singer can obtain a demo to present to radio stations.

The Centro Cultural Ruta Maya is a Managua coffeehouse that serves as a gathering place for the most current music in Nicaragua. It also promotes established talents, as well as new singer-songwriters, actors, comedians, and poets.

Radio Güegüense is a station that, for more than 40 years, has disseminated world classical music in addition to the music of Nicaraguan composers of classical and contemporary music. The radio station is renowned for the work of its founder Salvador Cardenal (grandfather of the two members of the Guardabarranco group) and his program "Music Lessons from One Amateur to Another," even though it is obvious that he is an expert in his field. Currently, the station is directed by his granddaughter María Belén Cardenal.

For a certain period of time, the station received some government funding and later some support from the private sector. Later, however, the lack of economic support for a cultural institution in the important world of Nicaraguan radio left the station in a critical situation, the worst in its many years of existence. The artists responded by joining forces, doing concerts, auctions, and talkathon fundraisers to cover the station's deficit and keep it on the air. The goal was met and music and art lovers will be able to enjoy Radio Güegüense for many more years.

It is clear that the Nicaraguan government has not given music or the other arts in Nicaragua the support they deserve. For the most part, the survival of the traditions that sustain the cultural identity of the country depends on the artists and simple people with few resources. They seem to be the ones in charge of finding the means necessary to achieve that overarching, essential goal.

NOTES

1. Jorge Eduardo Arellano, lecture, Biblioteca Pablo Antonio Cuadra, Universidad Americana, July 29, 2006.

2. See Pablo Antonio Cuadra, ed. *El Güegüense*. Managua: Cuadernos del Taller San Lucas, 1942; Jorge Eduardo Arellano, "El Güegüense, patrimonio de la humanidad," *Boletín Nicaragüense de Bibliografía y Documentación* 129 (October–December 2005); Adelaida Rivas Sotelo, "*El Güegüense:* hito de la tradición dramática del mestizaje, sones y corridos," *La Prensa* (special supplement) (November 29, 2006).

3. Isolda Hurtado. *Diagnóstico del arte contemporáneo en Nicaragua*. Managua: Gráfica Editores, 2002, p. 51.

4. See Sergio Ramírez, *Enciclopedia de Nicaragua*. Barcelona: Océano, 2002, and also Julio Valle Castillo, "Las lecciones de Enrique Fernández Morales," *El Nuevo Diario,* December 2002.

5. Ibid.

6. See Jorge Eduardo Arellano. *Literatura nicaragüense*. Managua: Distribuidora Cultural, 1997.

7. Hurtado, 54.

8. Auxiliadora Rosales, "Picardía titiresca," *La Prensa* (Revista) (June 14, 2001): 3C.

9. Isidro Rodríguez Silva. "El trabajo teatral de Nixtayolero (entrevista al director Valentín Castillo)," *Nuevo Amanecer Cultural* 1007 (June 23, 2001).

10. No author. "Un poco de historia de la danza en Nicaragua," *Nuevo Amanecer Cultural* (April 29, 2000).

11. Ibid.

12. Hurtado, 61.

13. Hurtado, 41.

14. Alfredo Barrera. "La música, arte armonioso," *La Prensa Literaria* (Managua) (June 23, 2001).

15. See Robert Pring-Mill. "The Roles of Revolutionary Song—A Nicaraguan Assessment," http://www.jstor.org/view/02611430/ap030007/03a00060/0.

16. Carlos Martínez and Oscar Cantarero. "Staccato celebra 9 años," *El Nuevo Diario* (Variedades) (Managua) (October 2001).

17. Hurtado, 44.

18. Barrera, ibid.

19. Hilda Rosa Madariaga. "Más de 600 estudiantes en concierto didáctico," *La Prensa* (Managua) (June 2001): 2C.

20. Isidro Rodríguez Silva. "Grupo de Cámara Kinteto: en la formación de instructors nacionales de la APC," *Nuevo Amanecer Cultural* (Managua) (January 2001): 5.

21. Hurtado, 47–49.

9

Visual Arts

LIKE THE OTHER cultural areas presented in this study, contemporary visual artists in Nicaragua also have indigenous precursors. In Nicaragua, the past is a kind of fertile, moist soil that nourishes the present. The connection between Nicaraguan artists such as Armando Morales, born in Granada in 1927, and Leoncio Sáenz, born in Palsila, Matagalpa in 1935, and ancient aboriginal cultures may be obvious (as in the case of Sáenz) or much less so (which might be said of Morales). Sometimes the link may reside less in formal, structural, or thematic qualities than in an ability to assimilate diverse cultural influences and act as a collecting site for the emigrating symbols that move with their human carriers across temporal and spatial borders.

In terms of indigenous antecedents, the island of Ometepe in Lake Nicaragua is full of indigenous art in the form of petroglyphs, many with the circles, spirals, and abstract geometric and zoomorphic forms that are a recurring motif in contemporary Nicaraguan art. It is as if the island, independent and isolated, were a huge gallery on display to the elements, a vast stone poem. Many Nicaraguans consider the island the indigenous and geographic heart of the country. In ancient times, the Chorotegas and Nahuas, subjugated by the Olmecs in Socunusco, Mexico, decided to seek their freedom in a massive southern migration that led them to a prophesied freshwater "sea" and an island composed of two volcanoes. Centuries later, the same site was the background for the meeting and dialogue between two distinct ethnic groups: the Spanish conquistador Gil González Dávila and the indigenous cacique Nicarao. This is the interracial base, the ethnic mixture, or *mestizaje,* that continues to define Nicaragua's cultural identity, often in violent, traumatic ways.[1]

Although Roberto de la Selva (1895–1957), brother of renowned poet Salomón de la Selva, is considered the first modern Nicaraguan artist, someone who learned his painting and carving techniques from indigenous artists in Mexico and Guatemala before he moved to New York in 1926, it can also be said that the real founder of the modern visual arts movement in Nicaragua was Rodrigo Peñalba (1908–1979). Peñalba returned to Nicaragua after studying in Mexico, Spain, Italy, and the United States to found Nicaragua's National School of Fine Arts, which he directed from 1948–1973. He taught three successive generations of students, some of whom, like Armando Morales, went on to become internationally recognized artists, moving beyond the borders of Nicaragua in terms of cultural references while, at the same time, creating from the core of their own diverse ethnic and historical national backgrounds.[2] In terms of the difficult process of educating artists in a country with such limited resources, it is also important to highlight the presence of Enrique Fernández Morales (1918–1982), who traveled extensively abroad and returned to Nicaragua with books, articles, and catalogs of modern art and distributed them among artists and intellectuals. As a collector, he was instrumental in reevaluating national artistic traditions, especially those that, in his opinion, had been unjustly ignored. He was instrumental in encouraging artistic creation by personally promoting a number of painters.[3]

The second generation of artists to work with Peñalba formed the innovative Praxis group in Managua in the early 1960s, which included, among others, Alejandro Aróstegui (b. 1935), César Caracas (b. 1935), Omar D´León (b. 1929), Arnoldo Guillén (b. 1941), César Izquierdo (b. 1937), Genaro Lugo (b. 1935), Leoncio Sáenz (b. 1935), Fernando Saravia (b. 1922), Orlando Sobalvarro (b. 1943), Luis Urbina (b. 1937), and Leonel Vanegas (b. 1942). By this time, Armando Morales (b. 1927) had left Nicaragua with a Guggenheim Fellowship to take up residence in New York City and rarely returned to his native country. Over the next 15 years, Praxis would pass through at least four distinct stages of development. From 1963–1966, the leading figure of the group was Alejandro Aróstegui, born in Bluefields in 1935, who helped write manifestos in conjunction with art critic Amaru Barahona in which abstract art was coupled with sociohistorical concerns. From 1966–1969, while Aróstegui was in the United States, César Izquierdo, born in Guatemala in 1937, and Arnoldo Guillén, born on Ometepe in 1941, guided Praxis more as a gallery than as an artistic movement. When Aróstegui returned to Nicaragua, he revitalized Praxis from 1970–1972 in a process that lasted until the massive 1972 earthquake that destroyed Nicaragua's capital Managua. After this national tragedy, the Praxis group engaged in a new search for a collective national identity and explored new artistic techniques.[4]

The 1970s also was the decade that, for the first time in Nicaragua, a generation of women painters emerged including Violeta Báez, Liliana Neret, Rosario Chamorro, Claudia Lacayo, and perhaps most important, Ilse Ortiz de Manzanares, the first woman to receive Nicaragua's National Prize for Painting from the Institute of Hispanic Culture in 1975.[5]

Another tendency of this era was the prominence of primitive or naïf art in Nicaragua. The true founder and precursor of this simple art that incorporated landscapes and historical scenes was Asila Guillén (1887–1964), who began painting what she had been doing in embroidery at the age of 73. Her works include "Northern Region of Nicaragua" (1962) and "Columbus Arrives at Cabo Gracias a Dios" (1963). Two other women, Salvadora Henríquez de Noguera and Adela Vargas, are also important early naïf artists, followed by Manuel García, a painter known for a sense of balance and harmony in his depiction of intensely colored, everyday Nicaraguan scenes that demonstrate a close attention to detail in carefully rendered mountains, houses, people, animals, and botanically accurate trees. The most important gathering of these artists, who were directed by painter Róger Pérez de la Rocha (b. 1949), was in the 1970s at Ernesto Cardenal's archipelago community at Solentiname on Lake Nicaragua. Especially noteworthy among the Solentiname naïf artists are Tomás Peña, Alejandro Guevara, and José Arana. Much of the other primitive artwork, however, was mass produced and priced to sell quickly.[6]

Post-earthquake paintings from the 1970s in Nicaragua reflected a return to pre-Columbian sources. Many artists seemed to be seeking consolation for the future in the past. This is especially true of work by Aróstegui with his "Petroglyphs" (1974) and "Nicaraguan Ceramics" (1975), Orlando Sobalvarro (b. 1943), and Pérez de la Rocha, who painted murals with indigenous themes in public places, as well as the 1975 stylized forms in ochre colors in "Ometepe Petroglyph." Leoncio Sáenz also did a series of influential works based on designs from aboriginal ceramics for a supermarket at the Plaza España in Managua.

Two of the most important exhibits of Nicaraguan contemporary visual arts occurred in 1976 at the Galería Tagüe in Managua and in 1995 at the Duke University Museum of Art. The 1976 exhibit was organized on the theme of *El Güegüense,* the most important work of theater from the colonial period. Some of Nicaragua's best painters, including Sáenz, Aróstegui, Carlos Montenegro (b. 1942), Sobalvarro, D'León, and especially César Caracas (for whom *El Güegüense* became a consistently recurring theme) succeeded in moving Nicaraguan painting into a new world of vibrant colors away from the austerity of the 1960s and also affirming a rebellious national identity.

On the one hand, Nicaragua's twentieth-century visual artists (with their paintings of abstract landscapes, still lifes and historical figures) represented a definitive rupture with the obligatory conception from the colonial period that art was meant to be at the service of the dominant structure and its ideology: colonial painting was reserved for the depiction of saints, virgins, the sacred family, and the Holy Trinity. On the other hand, many contemporary Nicaraguan painters continued to express their spiritual values and deep religiosity through their painting. Every year, for example, there is a major exhibit of paintings depicting La Purísima, which coincides with this important religious holiday in Nicaragua.

The major overview of Nicaraguan visual art in 1995 at Duke included works by Aróstegui, D'León, Ricardo González (b. 1952), Reinaldo Fernández (b. 1969), Claudia Lacayo (b. 1935), Armando Morales, Federico Nordalm (b. 1949), and Rosario Ortiz de Chamorro (b. 1949). Here, the curator in her selection of artists seemed intent on defying stereotypical subjects of Latin American art (the Catholic Church, pre-Columbian and colonial pasts, African influences, and political oppression) in favor of artists whose work deflects attention from the reality of the present to create a personal, more private, and sometimes magical world.[7]

For some, including the curator of the Duke University exhibit, art produced during the time of the Sandinista government from 1979–1990 was mediocre and limited to orthodox interpretations of the revolution's leftist ideology.[8] For others, it was a period of a vibrant creative spirit that included greater access for Nicaragua's general population to produce art, as well as to appreciate different kinds of art, such as murals with a strong historical content in public places. In Sandinista Nicaragua, more than 300 murals were created as visual manifestations of the revolution and the promise of a better future for an impoverished nation. It was during this decade, too, that elitist aesthetics were challenged by the creation of Centers for Popular Culture throughout the country in big cities and small towns alike in addition to the Ministry of Culture directed by Ernesto Cardenal and the Sandinista Association of Cultural Workers (ASTC) headed by Rosario Murillo.[9] When the Sandinistas lost the elections in 1990 to the UNO government headed by Violeta Chamorro, most of these public murals by artists such as César Caracas, Alejandro Canales, Leonel Cerrato, and Manuel García, as well as internationalist brigades from Panama, Chile, and Denmark, were obliterated by anti-Sandinista vandals.

ARMANDO MORALES

Armando Morales is, without a doubt, Nicaragua's most highly regarded and internationally renowned artist, whose work is part of major collections in the United States and Europe. Morales, born in Granada, Nicaragua, in 1927, was trained by Rodrigo Peñalba in Nicaragua's National School of Fine Arts from 1948–1953. By 1960, he moved to New York City, where he was influenced by the abstract aesthetics that predominated there at that time, especially in the work of Mark Rothko. Although he did not return to Nicaragua on a regular basis or for any extended period, Morales insists that he draws heavily on memories and scenes of life from his native country in his painting.[10] In the early abstract work "Landscape" (1964), for example, it is possible to imagine a Nicaraguan scene of village walls and dense vegetation in the interconnecting white and green planes.[11] Something similar would also be true in a more readily discernible way in "Selva Tropical 1" (1987). For Morales, these newer paintings have an ecological importance as well.

Morales's evolution as a painter passed through a series of stages, including the figurative, the semi-abstract, pure abstraction, a new figurativism, and a richly colored lyrical realism.[12] Two major motifs in his paintings include female nudes (which are often dismembered, mutilated, and manikin-like) and zoomorphic forms. Both of these motifs are apparent in "Three Nudes and Three Dogs" (1993).[13] Newer work by Morales rejects some of the painter's atemporal qualities to incorporate historical themes that define Nicaraguan identity. For example, from July to October 1993, while Morales was living in Mexico, the artist produced a powerful series of seven lithographs, depicting key moments in the dramatic life and premature martyrdom of Augusto César Sandino (1895–1934), the Nicaraguan hero who, with a small group of dedicated soldiers and by using guerilla tactics, resisted and defeated the U.S. Marines who were occupying Nicaragua in the late 1920s and early 1930s. These lithographs, with their depiction of Sandino's Homeric, epic struggle, composed with admiration and fear in addition to a fierce tenderness and a sense of nationalistic pride may be the most accomplished work ever produced by a Nicaraguan artist.[14]

ALEJANDRO ARÓSTEGUI

Alejandro Aróstegui was born in Bluefields on Nicaragua's Atlantic coast in 1935. Beginning at the age of 19, he spent almost 20 years studying architecture and art at Tulane University; the Ringling College of Art and Design in Sarasota, Florida; the Academia de San Marcos in Florence; and the École des Beaux Arts in Paris.[15] He returned to Nicaragua in 1963 to study in the National School of Fine Arts directed by Rodrigo Peñalba. At this time he also helped establish Nicaragua's most important artistic movement in the visual arts, the Praxis Group. From his beginnings as an artist, Aróstegui's work has manifested a social awareness. Early works such as "Laguna" and "Personas lacustres," both from 1964, reflect a concern for those who live in misery along Lake Managua's polluted waters and garbage-strewn shore.[16] These paintings, in their steely, thickly textured, almost monochromatic use of paint, also reflect the coloring of the lake's waters. In the 1970s, in addition to exploring pre-Hispanic themes in his painting, Aróstegui began to create his signature pieces that include smashed cans as icons, perhaps, of a materialistic, consumer-oriented, and ecologically irresponsible society.[17] Ultimately, however, the cans that Aróstegui incorporates in his textured surfaces (as he does in the still lifes "Three Objects on a Table" and "Table with Four Objects," both from 1986) become precious objects, sacred in their very ordinariness, an emblem, a reminder of the precarious, alienating nature of the deteriorating world we inhabit and destroy with our contemporary culture and customs.[18]

Other prominent Nicaraguan painters who began to achieve prominence in the 1960s with the Praxis Group include César Caracas, best known for his work that is derivative of the Mexican muralist José Clemente Orozco and his interpretations of the mischievous mestizo literary figure from the colonial period El Güegüense; Omar D'León, appreciated for his sensually charged still lifes of Nicaraguan fruit; and Leoncio Sáenz with his magical, mythical treatment of neo-indigenous themes.

Noteworthy independent and post-Praxis artists include Bernard Dreyfus (b. 1937); Rolando Castellón (b. 1937); Carlos Montenegro (b. 1942); Alberto Ycaza (b. 1945); Alfonso Ximénez (b. 1948), whose paintings are a poetic treatment of mestizo houses; Róger Pérez de la Rocha (b. 1949), whose dark and somber portraits of Sandino appeared in a kind of semi-official capacity in many public places during the Sandinista government period in the 1980s; Silvio Bonilla (b. 1950); Bayardo Gámez (b. 1951); and Otto Aguilar (b. 1958), who resides in Berkeley, California. Luis Morales Alonso (b. 1960), currently the director of the Nicaraguan Institute of Culture, won first prize in the III Bienal de Artes Visuales in 2001 with his work "Colección de CDs contra la amnesia" (Collection of CDs to Counter Amnesia). It is an installation of modules with metal discs covered with wax enclosed in two pieces of glass and mounted on six pedestals. Each CD uses different images to narrate a series of episodes of Nicaraguan history on the front and back of the discs. The astonishing Ortiz-Gurdián Collection in León also includes two striking paintings by Javier Valle Pérez (b. 1973), "La Tríada" (2001) and "Trópico del Inconsciente Despierto" (1999).

Up and coming painters on the Nicaraguan visual arts scene include María del Pilar Fonseca Alcalá (b. 1970), Mario Cruz Sánchez (b. 1972), and muralist and portrait artist Vladimir Hernández (b. 1975).

NOTES

1. Pablo Antonio Cuadra. "Prólogo," in Joaquín Matilló Vila. *Ometepe: isla de círculos y espirales*. Managua: Centro de Investigaciones Rupestres, 1973, pp. 1–2.

2. Sofía Lacayo. *Patria: Contemporary Nicaraguan Painting*. Durham, NC: Duke University Press, 1995, p. 6.

3. Jorge Eduardo Arellano. *Historia de la pintura nicaragüense*. Managua: CIRA, 1990, p. 11.

4. Arellano, 70.

5. Arellano, 70.

6. Arellano, 72–76.

7. Lacayo, 3.

8. Lacayo, 8.

9. David Kunzle. *The Murals of Revolutionary Nicaragua, 1979–1992*. Berkeley: University of California Press, 1995, pp. 12–13.

10. Lacayo, 21.

11. Ricardo Pau-Llosa. "Landscape and Temporality in Central American and Caribbean Painting." Available at: http://pau-llosa.com/Gallery/1984Landscapes6. html.

12. Arellano, 95.

13. Lacayo, 22–24.

14. Pablo Antonio Cuadra. *Crítica de arte*. Managua: Fundación Uno, 2005, p. 169.

15. Raquel Tibol. "El rigoroso proyecto estético de Alejandro Aróstegui," *La Prensa Literaria* (July 12, 2003): p. 1.

16. Arellano, 100.

17. Lacayo, 29.

18. Tibol, 4.

10

Architecture and Housing

ARCHITECTURE

NICARAGUAN ARCHITECTURE IS far different from the famous skyscrapers of modern cities in the developed world. In Nicaragua, the architecture is simple. In the majority of Nicaraguan cities, one-story buildings predominate, primarily because of all the fault lines throughout a country located amidst ranges of mountains that have active volcanoes. Each part of the country has different architectural qualities that characterize it. The existence of the colonial house is visual testimony to the Spanish presence. This chapter covers the architecture that exists throughout Nicaragua, examining a variety of specific and general structures.

Currently, the architecture that can be observed in Nicaragua can be divided into four main groups. First, the historicist category corresponds to religious architecture, in particular to the kind with baroque, neobaroque and neoclassical characteristics, which were developed in the nineteenth and early twentieth centuries. Next the neocolonial style describes many large Nicaraguan houses that have a corridor surrounding an internal patio or courtyard. This delineated space is, in turn, divided into rooms, similar to the construction of nineteenth-century churches. The third group, the art deco style, developed at the beginning of the twentieth century. Finally, the prefabricated style met the needs of many Nicaraguans after the 1972 earthquake destroyed the capital Managua.[1]

An adobe house with a corridor construction built at the beginning of the twentieth century. © Wilmor López. Used by permission.

A case can also be made for a fifth kind of architecture that corresponds to the postwar period after 1990. It is most prevalent in Managua, especially in the projects that resulted in the construction of modern buildings such as the Metropolitan Cathedral, and is characterized by decorative elements, with a greater emphasis on color. This is also true of some hotels, state buildings (such as the Chancellery and the Presidential House), shopping malls, and office buildings.

Without a doubt, the two buildings that best represent the country's architecture, as well as the pride of its citizens (in addition to the Cathedral of León), is Managua's Palacio de la Cultura, built originally in 1871 as the Palacio de Gobierno. At that time, it was a square, low, unremarkable building with Spanish-style balconies but no outside ornamentation and generally lacking in architectural style. This building was destroyed by the 1931 earthquake. That same year, an 11-year construction project began on the current building. This structure represented a qualitative leap in terms of its aesthetic form and architectural design, which is based on a correlation to geometry with a neoclassical influence. It has a trapezoidal form with four stories and

The National Palace of Nicaragua, where many important cultural events (especially dance presentations, music concerts, and painting exhibits) take place. © Wilmor López. Used by permission.

four tower-like structures on the four corners. It is located in the northern part of Managua and flanked by the ruins of the Apostle Santiago Cathedral, the Gran Hotel Cultural Center, and the Rubén Darío National Theater, in addition to the Central Park and the President's House.[2]

The other noteworthy building that represents the best of Nicaraguan architecture is the Rubén Darío National Theater, built in Managua in 1969. When the terrible 1972 earthquake shook the capital and flattened most of the city, the theater did not succumb. The building has maintained its style and original design and is the most important theater in the country and also, perhaps, in Central America. Its solemn exterior is the precise affirmation of its visual richness and interior technical perfection. It houses 1,200 seats that are distributed on three balconies.[3]

NICARAGUAN RELIGIOUS ARCHITECTURE

To speak about Nicaraguan religious architecture means addressing the entire Catholic cultural heritage of Spain and the buildings that accompanied the religious doctrine that forms such an important part of people's personal lives in Nicaragua. The Catholic churches represent a center of community faith shared by the majority of the population of Nicaragua. This architecture is present throughout the entire country except the Caribbean coast. For this reason, it is best to review some cities individually and mention the most important churches in each of them. Later in the chapter, the Moravian religious architecture of the Atlantic side of Nicaragua is examined.

Leon

León has 16 churches, the greatest number of any city in Nicaragua, in addition to the Real Basílica de Nuestra Señora de la Asunción, known more commonly as the Cathedral of León. The latter is an undeniable tourist attraction, with architectural examples whose styles range from the baroque to the neoclassical.

The Cathedral of León

The construction of the cathedral began 260 years ago. Taking into account that its first stone was put into place in 1747, the entire building process was completed in 30 years. It is the most important building in Nicaragua and one of the jewels of Ibero-American architecture. Naturally, it is an important symbol that Nicaraguans speak of with great pride.[4] The cathedral can be appreciated from the central plaza of the city. To enter it is to know part of the nation's sociocultural history. In its interior are the remains of the universally acclaimed Nicaraguan poet Rubén Darío (1867–1916), whose marble tomb is guarded by a distraught lion in tears. It is said that when the construction of the church began, many wealthy families of the era bought spaces in the subterranean areas so that they could be buried in tombs there. That money was used for some of the construction costs and for maintenance. The cathedral, finally, was a product of numerous prelates who modified its form and style as time passed.

From the rooftop, there is perhaps the best panorama of León, including views of many of the other churches. The cathedral's towers are united by a central body supported by four columns. In its interior are several main decorative elements: the pulpit, the bishop's throne, and the tabernacle with its bronze baldachin and silver *frontal*. Treasures in the cathedral include the rococo monstrance covered with diamonds, the tabernacle whose altar is made of gold and silver and is decorated with precious stones, and the chorus from Córdoba, which is used in the rituals of the ancient liturgy. Other personalities who are buried in the cathedral include the poets Salomón de la Selva (1893–1958) and Alfonso Cortés (1893–1969), one of the founding fathers of Nicaraguan independence Miguel de Larreynaga (1772–1847), the

The Cathedral of León with the fountain in Jerez Park in the foreground. © Wilmor López. Used by permission.

nineteenth-century physician Luis H. Debayle, and the master composer of Nicaragua's national anthem José de la Cruz Mena (1874–1907).

La Recolección

The construction of this church began in 1786. Next to it, La Recolección School was built in 1880, under the direction of a French religious order that belonged to the Congregation of San Vicente de Paul. It is an emblematic Mexican baroque-style monument composed of four separated spaces and five vertical strips formed by the columns carved in garlands with medallions in relief that symbolize the Passion of Christ. Its façade is considered the most important part of the structure, as it is the only one carved in masonry and decorated with religious symbols.[5]

San Francisco

The original church was established in 1639 by Fray Pedro de Zúñiga. The church has undergone many changes, which explains why few original elements remain. San Francisco has an eclectic mix of architectural styles in its altar covering, as well as its colonial baroque interior. From the original construction, one can still see the wall of the façade, with its aligned buttresses parallel to the axis of the vertical spaces formed by the columns at the head of the church. Noteworthy in its interior are the altar-pieces of San Antonio and Nuestra Señora del Perdón, which date from the eighteenth century, in addition to the wood structure of the ceiling, especially the eaves on the south side of the church.[6]

Nuestra Señora de la Merced

This church, one of Leon's oldest, was built in 1762 under the direction of master Guatemalan builder Pascual Somarriba. Its decorative theme is the redemption of the captives, highlighting candles and shackles. Above the main entrance are small guardian angels.

The main altar was designed by León's master builder Ayestas and presides over the central nave. There is a precious chamber on the altar in which the powerful image of Nuestra Señora de la Merced is venerated. The Virgin is clothed in a dress finely embroidered with gold thread. Her crown is of gold with a magnificent handmade finish. It is said that, at the beginning of the nineteenth century, the main altar caught fire and a black slave broke the chamber's glass to save the image. Holding it in his bloody arms, he saved it from perishing in the flames. The main altar and the chamber that holds the Patron Saint of León, the Virgen de Mercedes, were erected by Bishop Fray Nicolás García Jérez.[7]

Sutiaba Church

The Sutiaba Church is located in the indigenous plaza of the same name. It has a peculiar atrium surrounded by walls. On the western side are the remains of the palace of the *cacique* Adiac, the last indigenous chief of Sutiaba. After the Cathedral of León, this church is considered the most important monument in the city. Construction began in 1698 and ended in 1710. Over time, it suffered some deterioration and, in 1804, was restored through government funding. With its half-orange cupola and the box-shaped vault to cover square and rectangular spaces, this church is considered an architectural link between the primitive colonial period (1600–1620) and the baroque period itself (1700–1800). One can also observe medieval and romantic traits, Renaissance decorative style in the breaking up of space, as well as baroque qualities in terms of the verticality of the façade and the cornice and columns. This church is an example of popular colonial art.[8]

In the interior, the altar-pieces carved from wood are excellent examples of indigenous artwork. They combine European religious conceptions with indigenous symbolic systems, as seen, for example, in the metal adornment of two coiled serpents that are drinking from a cup (an indigenous symbol that conveys the sacred sense of fleeting time), seeking to calm their anguish in the living waters of the eternal. Likewise, the ceiling is decorated by the impressive face of a sun that dominates the center of the church, which represents the respect the indigenous people had for that celestial body. This work was ordered by Fray Bartolomé de las Casas (1484–1566), the most important defender of the rights of indigenous people who suffered the abuse of Spanish colonial rule.

Other examples of Leon's religious architecture can be found in the remaining 12 churches: San Pedro, El Calvario, Nuestra Señora de Dolores, San Nicolás de Tolentino, Zaragoza, San José, San Isidro, San Felipe, Guadalupe, San Juan de Dios, San Juan Bautista, and San Sebastián.

Granada

Cathedral of Granada

The Cathedral of Granada on the east side of the city's central park is an impressive structure. Its construction dates from 1583, although it was rebuilt after it was destroyed by fire in 1856, the year that the infamous U.S. mercenary William Walker burned down the city as he retreated with his troops. Its current design was planned by the Italian architect Andrés Zapata and finally finished in 1915. Its style is neoclassical, with a simple façade and four chapels in its interior.[9]

La Merced

This church was originally built in 1534 and, since then, many changes have been made to increase the size of the church and improve it. Its main tower was destroyed in a pirate attack in 1535, and it was reconstructed in 1862. The last architectural changes to the church were made in 1950. Its façade is baroque in style.[10] The tower of La Merced is famous as the meeting place of the young *vanguardistas* Pablo Antonio Cuadra, Joaquín Pasos, and others, who began to make their lasting mark on Nicaraguan literature in the late 1920s and early 1930s.

Guadalupe

This church is located in the eastern part of Granada on the Calle de la Calzada. Its construction is registered in 1626 by Fray Benito Baltodano. It was occupied by William Walker for 18 days in the mid-nineteenth century as one of his last bastions, resulting in a great deal of damage. The church was finally rebuilt in 1965.[11]

Granada's Independence Plaza with the historic Cathedral of Granada in the background. © Wilmor López. Used by permission.

Xalteva

Xalteva refers to the indigenous barrio that once was located in the area where the church was built. It is in the western part of Granada on the Calle Real. It was built during the colonial period, although originally it was a military fort given its strategic position. During the National War of 1890, its façade and much of its interior were destroyed. Later, it was damaged by an earthquake and subsequently rebuilt from 1895–1898. Its final reconstruction occurred in 1921.[12]

San Francisco

This church, a beautiful blue building, is located only a few blocks from Granada's central park, and was built shortly after Granada was established. Initially, its walls and roof were made of wood. Its architecture is solidly romantic. In 1885, the church was almost completely modified, and these changes were finally completed in 1939.[13]

Matagalpa

This city, located in the mountainous, coffee-growing region of northern Nicaragua, has some important architectural monuments worthy of mention.[14]

Cathedral of San Pedro

The cathedral was begun in 1874 by the congregation of Jesuits who asked for help from residents, rich and poor alike. The division of labor for this project also provides insights into the building techniques that have had a great influence on Nicaraguan architecture. The wealthy residents of Matagalpa provided materials such as lime ash, sand, bricks, stone, wood, egg whites, beasts of burden, and carts to transport the materials. The poor residents provided free labor, doing all the work as masons, stonecutters, and *mozos alpinistas* (the people who did the grueling work of carrying the boxes with the mixture of sand, earth, and egg whites to the highest places of the construction site). For the more specialized tasks, for example, working on sculptures and cornices, skilled workers from León and Granada were hired. The stone that was used to erect the thick walls was transported in ox carts from a quarry that was located in an ancient settlement of Sumo Indians called Guanaca. The Jesuits taught the people who made roof tiles how to make bricks of baked mud, although they were larger and thicker than normal. These are the kind of bricks that were used in the construction of the cupola. By 1887, the primary structure of walls, cupolas, and towers was complete. The church was opened to the public on January 1, 1895. The cathedral is the most beautiful building in Matagalpa. In its interior are beautiful examples of filigree, inlaid designs, and sculptures of high and low relief.

In addition to the Cathedral of San Pedro, the baroque style of the San José de Laborio church and San Nicolás de Selva Negra chapel is worth noting.

Masaya

Masaya was declared Cultural Patrimony of Nicaragua in 1989 because this city and its environs have important historical and archeological monuments. It is also called the city of flowers and the cradle of Nicaraguan folklore.[15]

Parroquia San Jerónimo

San Jerónimo was built in 1928 and has an eclectic style. In 2000, it suffered serious damage from an earthquake that shook the city. For the people of Masaya, this place is the heart of all religious celebrations.[16]

Nuestra Señora de la Asunción

This church has a Renaissance style with a baroque vernacular influence and dates from 1750. One of its characteristics is the presence of a bell tower, a typical colonial element.[17]

El Calvario

After the 2000 earthquake, El Calvario was rebuilt and completely remodeled. It is best known for its images of Jesus of Nazareth and the grotesque image of Jestas, the thief who was also crucified.[18]

San Juan Bautista

The construction of this church dates from the late colonial period in 1848, and its prototype is vernacular architecture.[19]

San Sebastián

Built in 1935 by the priest Francisco Robleto with an eclectic style, this example of religious architecture was donated to the Salesian order.

Managua

In 1750, the residents of Managua lived on parcels of land near the churches of San Sebastián, Santiago, San Mateo, and San Miguel. Over the course of time, Managua has had three cathedrals: the Iglesia Parroquial de Santiago, the Santiago Apóstol Cathedral (which was destroyed by the 1972 earthquake), and the new Metropolitan Cathedral of the Purísima Concepción, which was inaugurated in 1993. Managua became the seat of executive power in Nicaragua, as well as its capital, on February 5, 1852. In 1963, Managua was considered an important Latin American city with a well-developed urban center. The 1972 earthquake, however, changed all this, totally devastating the city: 90 percent of its buildings were affected and 54,000 homes destroyed. After more than three decades, there are still some areas of rubble as a reminder of that tragedy.[20]

Santiago Apóstol Cathedral

This cathedral symbolizes the introduction of modernity in Nicaraguan architecture in that twentieth-century materials such as iron and cement were used in the construction process. This was somewhat new in a developing country that was so dependent on international aid. At that time, the majority of the buildings throughout the country were constructed of wood and adobe. Work on the cathedral began in 1927. In 1931, it underwent its first test by surviving an earthquake with its iron skeletal structure intact. The rest

Hammocks made in Masaya on display in
Managua's Plaza of the Revolution during Saturday events organized by the Nicaraguan Institute
of Culture. In the background is Managua's historic cathedral, which was left a shell by the 1972
earthquake that devastated the Nicaraguan capital.
© Wilmor López. Used by permission.

of Managua's buildings were destroyed. This provided hope that future construction efforts in Nicaragua would be able to withstand natural disasters. The
cathedral became a symbol of the reconstruction of the country and of a
neoclassical and premodern current that coincided with an era of liberal ideals.
The cathedral has a classical Greek-style pediment that is a visual representation
of Santiago on horseback, killing Moors. At the same time, however, it highlights Christian architecture. The 1972 earthquake destroyed this cathedral,
one of the most important structures in Nicaragua, erasing an intimate human
space of baptisms, confirmations, communions, weddings, and funerals.[21]

Metropolitan Cathedral of the Purísima Concepción

After the geological disasters and the isolation that Nicaragua experienced,
a new cathedral dedicated to La Purísima was born in 1993, with the fervent

support of those who worship there. Its roof is a baroque assemblage that represents an intriguingly original monument to unity by means of the small cupola-lanterns that contrast with a tropical rhythm of curves. The most surprising thing about this impressive building is that it is one of the few churches in the Americas with a north-south, rather than east-west axis. Catholic churches are generally oriented toward the west to indicate the land where Christ was born. That position is focused on the main altar where Christ descends and renews his sacrifice as redeemer for followers of Catholicism. The Metropolitan Cathedral was designed by Mexican architect Ricardo Legarreta, and its construction was financed by the U.S. entrepreneur Thomas Monahan, who owns Domino's Pizza and who contributed $3.5 million of the $4.5 million total cost. This is the most modern and recent example of religious architecture in Latin America, although its design has generated severe criticism because of similarities to the structure of mosques, which, according to these critics, distance the church from Roman Catholicism. The cathedral has eight bells, which belonged to the destroyed cathedral that it replaced, and each has its own name: Trinidad, Miguel, Jacobo, Concepción, Carmen, Socorro, Guadalupe, and Fátima.[22]

Boaco

Boaco is a peculiar and enchanting city that was founded on a broken topography that has given it the nickname "Two-Story City," as it has two levels, upper Boaco and lower Boaco. Each has its colorful houses, avenues and churches, with a neoclassical architecture such as the Iglesia de Santiago and the Iglesia de Nuestra Señora del Perpetuo Socorro. The latter has an eclectic mix of Gothic and Russian architectural styles.[23]

Estelí

Located in Nicaragua's cooler northern region, Estelí is the city of the Cathedral of Nuestra Señora del Rosario de Estelí. To understand its architecture, it is important to remember that it was built in stages involving five priests and different blueprints and building crews. The façade was built first in keeping with a special plan and builder from Estelí. The self-taught builder, Wenceslao González Meza, was given complete freedom to create the design. Even though he was not an architect and had never taken academic courses, he planned his architectural design correctly. Years after this part was finished, the main body and head of the church were continued in keeping with other blueprints and with other builders from Managua. For this reason, the church reflects two completely different architectural styles, neoclassical and modern. The project took 25 years to complete and was finished in 1962, the year that the Diocese of Estelí was created, and Monsignor Clemente Carranza y López was named its first bishop.[24]

Rivas

The city of Rivas is blessed not only with the beautiful beaches along the shore of Lake Nicaragua, but also with the stunning Iglesia Parroquial de San Pedro, which is a source of great pride for the residents of Rivas. The church was begun by Jesuits in 1874. With its baroque style and covering an entire city block, it is considered the third most beautiful church in the country. Another church with a great deal of history is San Francisco. The date of its construction is not entirely clear, with some people believing that it began in 1860 and others in 1844. The bell tower is placed as if on a balcony and located in the center of the church. It has two bells, one dated 1867 and the other 1890. The church has indigenous designs on its façade—a plumed serpent and the perfect face of an indigenous person wearing a feather and looking southeast, which is where the great indigenous leader Nicaragua was said to have died of melancholy. The columns of the church are made of royal oak. Its interior has many beautiful images. The frescoes on the ceiling, just above the main altar, were painted by the Austrian artist Juan Fuchs Hall.[25]

Jinotega

Jinotega is called the city of fog because of its cool climate and houses and roads filled with mist at dawn and dusk. The San Juan Cathedral, built in 1805, with important remodeling in 1882, 1952, and 1958, is an important example of Nicaragua's religious architecture. It is best known for its religious paintings brought from Spain. It was designated a cathedral in 1983.[26]

THE CARIBBEAN COAST

The architecture of Nicaragua's Atlantic region is part of the country's culture and national identity. It possesses a diverse architecture that has survived through time despite different catastrophes. The richness and value of a culture lie in the diversity of its components and origins. The population of Nicaragua, as a result of unique geographical and climatic factors, is multiethnic, multilingual, and multicultural, with sources from three continents: America, Africa, and Europe. This reality also influences the architecture of the region. There is a predominance of English architecture on the Caribbean coast, which also manifests itself in the Moravian church constructed in the city of Bluefields, which takes its name from its founder, Abraham Blauveldt, a Dutch buccaneer who settled there in 1621. Reflecting a nineteenth-century Victorian style, the Moravian church in Bluefields was built of precious wood from 1907–1909 with English-influenced doors and arched windows. This church, unfortunately, was completely destroyed down to its foundation by Hurricane Joan in 1988. In its place, another church has been built under the direction of Nicaraguan architect Daniel González with many formal similarities, including a tower in the central axis of the façade, although the walls are made of cement, not wood. In this way, at the citizens' request, the Bluefields church kept many of the main characteristics of the previous church that was destroyed.[27]

COLONIAL ARCHITECTURE

The two cities that best represent Nicaraguan colonial architecture are León (located in the western part of the country with beaches on the Pacific Ocean) and Granada (situated elegantly on the shores of Lake Nicaragua, or Cocibolca as it is sometimes called). In urban terms, the cities have a certain resemblance as a result of the architectural concepts that came from the Spaniards and were imposed by them on the indigenous population. It was mandated by law to build in certain ways, using squares, for example, and these methods were incorporated throughout Nicaraguan towns and villages, immediately creating a different way of dividing space than was reflected by indigenous forms of architecture, which was more linear with dispersed and separate constructions. For several reasons, the confluence of Spanish techniques and indigenous systems gave birth to a kind of hybrid architecture. Over the centuries, each city with its own climate, soil, geographical location, as well as political, social and economic situations, consolidated and developed its unique mix of architectural styles.

León

When the city of León was first established, it was built on the shores of Lake Xolotlán on land that belonged to the Imabite indigenous group. At the beginning of the seventeenth century, however, the residents, who feared an imminent eruption of the Momotombo volcano, decided to leave old León and seek a safer place. Consequently, they moved to the site of Sutiaba, where the city is still located. León has managed to conserve its old architecture, which consists of single-story houses with roof tiles, high ceilings, and a house structure surrounding a patio or garden that produces a welcome coolness, as the city's climate is hot during most of the year. What follows is a brief architectural description of particularly noteworthy houses in León.[28]

Don Juan de Dios Vanegas House

This house is situated on the Calle Real (which joins downtown León with the indigenous part of Sutiaba) near the El Calvario church. Don Juan de Dios Vanegas, the original owner was a celebrated historian, lawyer, and writer from León. It is a colonial structure with a simple façade and a balcony protruding from it that was built later in the twentieth century as an extension of the hallway floor. It has elements that are characteristic of colonial architecture such as depressed arches, windows with supports and inset seats, a main square, and tooled eaves.

Derbyshire House

This gigantic house, whose construction was registered at the end of the eighteenth and beginning of the nineteenth century on the Calle Real, is located on the corner opposite the San Francisco church and the El Convento Hotel. It is named after the important physician Juan Derbyshire, who was a leading figure in the modernization of culture and Creole customs of colonial León, and was one of the first citizens to drive the newly invented Ford automobiles on the stone streets of the city. The house is roofed with tiles above crossbeams. Its walls are high and of thick adobe covered with mortar. It keeps the traditional position of the main corner salon, with the main patio and the back patio framed by corridors with arches. Currently it forms part of the Ortiz-Gurdián Art Center.[29]

Casa de Salud Debayle

This house is located in the El Sagrario barrio near the central market. It was built in 1814 as a bank called The Golden Ball. Later it was remodeled to be the first private clinic in Central America and functioned under the supervision of Dr. Luis H. Debayle. It is a unique building with many colonial architectural details, for example, two stories, with a running exterior balcony and a mezzanine of wood with a typical corner pillar. Internally, each area maintains a traditional distribution based on an ample patio with corridors that are repeated on the second floor. Currently, it is the property of the mayor's office and is used as a cultural extension of the National Autonomous University of León, where a wide variety of artistic and cultural activities take place.

Casa Cural de Sutiaba

This building was constructed from 1743–1752 and has a primitive colonial architecture, which differs from the baroque period during which it was built. It is located on the southern side of the Sutiaba Plaza on the corner opposite the indigenous church. The house and the adobe wall of its patio occupy the entire length of the street, which serves as an element of circulation between the immense corridor of three stairways situated parallel to the street and the plaza.

Other buildings of interest in León include La Casa de los Lacayo, La Casa de los Gurdián, La Casa de Alfonso Cortés, Colegio Tridentino San Ramón, Colegio La Asunción, Museo-Archivo Rubén Darío, Casa de Protocolo de la Universidad Nacional Autónoma de Nicaragua UNAN-León, Teatro Municipal José de la Cruz Mena, and the Hotel El Convento.

Granada

Homes in Granada typically are characterized by exuberant interiors, ceilings made of tongue-and-groove boards, ornate molding, attached garages, and decorative paintings on ceilings and walls. There are also printed mosaics with references to Italy, large, cool semidark bedrooms ventilated by interior gardens with tropical plants and stone decorations, such as old, centrally situated ceramic fountains. Corridors filled with light surround a central patio.

To understand Granada's architecture, it is necessary to review some history regarding the looting and burning of the entire city by the nineteenth-century U.S. mercenary William Walker. After this devastation in 1856, homes could not be recognized, even by their owners when they were able to return. Post-fire Granada grew slowly. Bridges were built so that the city could expand beyond the rivers that border it. A new architecture replaced structures built of sugarcane with adobe houses. This technique for construction became increasingly popular, resulting in beautiful two-story houses with clean facades. The buildings with corridors that faced the plaza had a neoclassical look that hid their colonial antiquity. The growth of Granada, in general, has been a series of outward displacements.[30]

The predominant style of architecture corresponds to the beginning of the twentieth century, as many modern styles (as well as economic and cultural influences) were imported from the United States and Spain. One might say that the idea of buildings serving human values changed to that of being commercially viable. This activity gave rise to large construction companies financed with money from the public and private sectors.

In addition to the buildings described in this section, other important examples of Granada's architectural style include Estación del Ferrocarril, Palacio de las Comunicaciones, Hotel Alhambra, Hotel La Gran Francia, El Convento San Francisco, and Casa de la Familia Cuadra.

Fuerte La Pólvora

From the site of this fortress built in 1748 to protect munitions, house troops, and serve as a prison, there are beautiful views of Lake Nicaragua and the Mombacho volcano. Its walls and towers remain intact, close to an old cannon.

El Palacio Municipal

On its façade, this important building, with its two stories and double interior patios, has the symbolic coat of arms of the city of Granada that was a gift from Spain.

El Palacio Episcopal

This colonial-style building was built at the end of the nineteenth century for military purposes. In 1897, an explosion destroyed it. Rebuilt in 1913 by the Cardenal family, it was donated to the archbishop of Granada as a residence in 1920.

Casa de los Leones

Built in 1809 in front of the Plaza de los Leones, the house's colonial style fits well with the construction of other nearby buildings Previously called the Casa Cadenas, it is now known as the Casa de los Tres Mundos, and regularly sponsors a wide variety of cultural events.

Masaya

The colonial remnant most representative of Masaya is its market. The conquistadors designed the urban shape of the village, building large houses with corridors for the most important families. This design established the physical conditions between *mestizos* and the indigenous population. Over time, there were ever more complex Indo-Latino relationships that resulted in *mestizaje*. The rise of this commercial class necessitated the creation of a place to carry out commerce. In 1888, the contract to build the market was signed, and the market was inaugurated in 1891. Its urban location follows the colonial practice of establishing commerce in the plazas. The market was built in the same place where an old *tiangue* (indigenous market) was located. It is square-shaped and has stone walls with a vaguely romantic architectural style. During years of war, the market was often converted into a fortress, for the strength of its stone construction and the height of its walls made it resistant to attacks. In 1966, its interior was destroyed by fire, but it was soon rebuilt. During the insurrection of 1979, the building was bombarded by planes of the Somoza dictatorship. It was subsequently rebuilt in the 1980s

A variety of crafts made of wood created by Francisco Ticay. There is an abundance of talented Nicaraguan craftspeople. © Wilmor López. Used by permission.

and reinaugurated. It is now more than 100 years old and remains an important commercial center and architectural monument.[31]

ENGLISH ARCHITECTURE OF THE CARIBBEAN COAST

In terms of their architectural expression, Nicaragua's Caribbean population draws on nineteenth-century Anglo-American influences. It is a prefabricated architecture, purchased in pieces to be assembled in Nicaragua at the beginning of the twentieth century. This architecture came primarily from New Orleans and Baltimore, cities that, at the time, had strong commercial ties with the Nicaraguan Caribbean as a result of the interest in trade for rubber, gold, precious woods, and fruit. Throughout the twentieth century, established maritime routes allowed owners of plantations and other wealthy people to purchase architecture in the form of prefabricated pieces (some with decorative details) to build homes and community buildings. The materials consisted of wooden panels that required assembly. The roofs of these structures were sharply angled and composed of small waterproof wooden shingles. The style was a kind of Victorian "ginger bread" house with flat, decorated wooden panels. Currently, the architecture reflects the racial mixture of the region and its colorful historical past, including an English colonial style, huts from the Antilles, and New Orleans-style plantations. Most of the houses in the other areas of the Nicaraguan Caribbean (Autonomous Region of the North Atlantic) are made of wood on top of *tambos* (foundations) that protect the dwellings from the constant rain in that part of the country.[32]

Rural Architecture

The rural zones of Nicaragua are characterized by the simple dwellings for *campesinos,* or farmers who work the land. These constructions are ranchos with thatched palm roofs, dwellings similar to the indigenous homes of ancient times. Inside, the dwellings have *taburetes* (round or square wooden seats with a covering made of cowhide or deerskin) or *patas de gallina* (simple three-legged chairs), *molenderos* (grinding stones), calabash gourds for glasses, large ceramic jars called *tinajas, tapescos* (beds made by tying together the branches of a guácimo tree or woven palm branches in the Department of Masaya), ceramic jugs, woodstoves called *tenamastes, tinajeros* (places for

A traditional kitchen belonging to the Alvarado family in El Cuá, department of Jinotega. It is made of adobe and is always kept clean, with the wood-burning stove lit. © Wilmor López. Used by permission.

A gourd handcarved by Doña Evangelina Loaisiga who is from Pueblo Nuevo in the department of Rivas. © Wilmor López. Used by permission.

keeping the *tinajas* filled with water and other substances), and a branch called a *garabato* whose many little branches serve as a rack for hanging the gourd cups. Not too many years ago, the walls of these houses were generally made of the long, tough stems of *jalacate* plants tied together to form panels and walls. This custom persists in the more remote areas of the country. They are dwellings in perfect harmony with their environment.

Slowly but surely, however, these dwellings made of vegetal materials have been replaced by lumber, stone, and ceramic tiles. Because it is so important for Nicaraguans to preserve their cultural identity by means of a national architecture, special efforts have been made in recent years to ensure that aboriginal construction techniques are not lost. The most important of these projects is the Museum of Indigenous Dwellings, located on the Masaya-Catarina highway and founded by Carlos Centeno, coordinator of the Association of Artists from Monimbó. The project was financed in part by The Ohio State University. The trees most commonly used in the building of these dwellings include *gauchipilín, laurel, palo de acacias, talchocote, zonzonate,* and *caña de castilla* tied together using parts of banana and *guácimo* trees or vines.

Another construction in the rural zones closest to the cities are mixed dwellings—brick (sometimes cement bricks) on the lower part and wood on the upper part. The roof might be made of tiles or zinc sheets over a wooden frame. The houses in the countryside with their land are farms owned by people who live in urban zones and managed by trusted families. These farms produce a wide variety of fruit, vegetables, and grains. The general custom is to visit the farms on the weekends as a way of interacting socially and sharing with family and friends.

On the Atlantic coast, houses are made of wood with zinc roofs or wooden shingles. In the indigenous communities in this zone, the houses are often made of bamboo with thatched roofs, although some have walls made of adobe.[33]

Housing

In 2001, there was a housing shortage in Nicaragua on the order of 1 million homes. As a response to this crisis, a law was passed in 2003 to make funds available to begin to rectify a problem that has affected a large portion of the Nicaraguan population. Over the next two years, the Institute of Urban and Rural Dwellings constructed 18,000 homes. The type of house that was built belongs to a style classified as Popular Dwelling Series B, which consists of a simple design on lots of 80–120 square meters, with no more than 60 square meters of living space. These basic homes that can be increased in size by their owners are made of wood and cinder blocks. The first constructions of this type were made after the 1972 earthquake and have all the basic services and infrastructure.[34]

Although there is a wide variety of housing options for the very poor, as well as the very rich, it is important to point out that there continues to be a serious lack of affordable housing for many Nicaraguans. This has led to a phenomenon called *asentamientos espontáneos,* which are groups of people who invade available land spontaneously and illegally and then build simple one- or two-room dwellings out of scraps of lumber, cardboard, plastic, and metal on this occupied space. The living conditions, of course, in terms of infrastructure, are atrocious. There is no drainage or sewer system, nor is garbage collected. This phenomenon is most prevalent in the capital city Managua, where there are approximately 300 of these *asentamientos,* in which 50,000 families are living.[35]

Nicaragua has received a large amount of international aid for housing. Many of these projects are unofficial, or *clandestinos,* which are efforts that occur based on post-1985 visits to Nicaragua by generous internationalists who want to help. The Dutch government and the United Nations also have supported housing projects in Nicaragua's central region. Several non-governmental organizations (NGOs) and Christian religious groups have supported the construction of homes in different zones as well. In general,

A straw dwelling with a roof that nearly touches the ground in an area called Aser-radores in the department of Chinandega. © Wilmor López. Used by permission.

international aid for housing is given in the form of small, private donations that are, nevertheless, very significant. The most serious limitations that will affect any future housing program in Nicaragua are economic crises coupled with increases in population. During the war in the 1980s, the violence and economic sanctions of the United States against Nicaragua made it unrealistic to think that the Nicaraguan government would be able to carry out significant housing programs, especially in the cities. It certainly could not undertake these efforts at the level that the people demanded. One of the most serious problems that Nicaragua faced was the increase in the number of people gathering in small urban areas, pressuring the government for a better infrastructure and more services, even though these people were barely contributing in terms of producing for the national economy. The continual appearance of *asentamientos espontáneos* in Managua and other urban areas deepened the problem on a daily basis. One particular issue that characterizes the work with *campesino* groups is their level of expectation given their special needs and concerns. One group of architects and U.S. planners who were acting in solidarity with Nicaragua has been building houses in northern Nicaragua for *campesinos* since 1985. The organization is financed with donations from people in the United States. It is estimated that the houses constructed by this group are perhaps half the price of the model houses that the Nicaraguan construction companies build.[36]

It is well known that the poorest members of Nicaraguan society have been excluded from the benefits that the urbanization process has generated. There were changes to the laws during the 1980s and, furthermore, there has been an increased level of people's trade unions. This has increased the participation of NGOs within the communities as they seek to find ways to improve the living conditions for those with the fewest resources in Nicaragua. These organizations have offered legal, financial, and technical support when it has been necessary for the marginal classes to negotiate with government authorities regarding the issue of land available for building houses. The most critical situation in terms of a lack of housing for the poor is affecting the inhabitants in the Departments of Madriz, Nueva Segovia, the Autonomous Regions of the North and South Atlantic, Matagalpa, and Jinotega. It is abundantly clear that the most impoverished zones are those where the war was waged in the 1980s. And it is in these areas that the most inadequate housing is built from rubbish. The current challenge is to do everything possible to reduce the housing shortage in Nicaragua, now estimated to be 300,000–400,000 homes. All candidates in the 2006 presidential elections made this a top priority in their campaigns. Agreements recently have been reached between the government and private construction companies to begin to meet this high demand with 25,000 new houses per year.

NOTES

1. Norbert-Bertrand Barbe. "Arquitectura nicaragüense," *El Nuevo Diario, Nuevo Amanecer Cultural* (March 17, 2007): n.p.

2. Maryórit Guerrero. "106 años de historia archivada," *La Prensa* (July 11, 2002): n.p.

3. Anielka Rodríguez. "Tres décadas y media del teatro Rubén Darío," *El Nuevo Diario* (March 9, 2004): n.p.

4. Julio Valle-Castillo. *La Catedral de León de Nicaragua.* Managua: IMPRIMATUR, 2001, pp. 17–37.

5. Manuela Sacasa. *Historia de las iglesias de León.* León: Asociación Amigos del Teatro, 2006, pp. 3–11.

6. Ibid.

7. Ibid.

8. Personal Interview, Edgardo Buitrago, León, November 23, 2006.

9. *Historia de Granada.* Granada: Alcaldía de Granada, n.d.

10. Ibid.

11. Ibid.

12. Ibid.

13. Ibid.

14. Celso Martínez Orozco. "Jesuitas Construyeron Parroquia," *La Prensa* (January 9, 2000): n.p.

15. "Decreta a Masaya Patrimonio Cultural de la Nación, N° 61 aprobada el 21 de agosto de 1989," *La Gaceta* 190 (October 9, 1989): n.p.

16. Ulises Huete-Loredo. "Masaya: terremotos y reliquias," *La Prensa* (July 6, 2003): n.p.

17. Huete-Laredo.

18. Miguel Flores. "Restauración de la Asunción casi lista," *La Prensa* (October 3, 2002): n.p.

19. Huete-Laredo.

20. Alcaldía de Managua. *Historia de Managua*. Managua: Alcaldía de Managua, n.d., pp. 9–18, 45–53.

21. Porfirio García Romano. "Catedral de Santiago: símbolo del S. XX," *El Nuevo Diario* (June 6, 1999): n.p.

22. Norbert-Bertrand Barbe. "Nueva Catedral," *El Nuevo Diario, Nuevo Amanecer Cultural* (December 23, 2006): n.p.

23. Auxiliadora Martínez. "Un tour por la ciudad de dos pisos," *La Prensa* (March 9, 2006): n.p.

24. Personal interview with the historian Orient Bolívar Juárez, Estelí, May 12, 2006.

25. Mireya Pravia. "Parroquia San Pedro patrimonio cultural," *La Prensa* (October 1, 2005): n.p.

26. Personal interview with Silvia González and Simeón Jarquín Blandón, Managua, May 16, 2006.

27. Porfirio García Romano. "Iglesia Morava: símbolo de nuestra nicaraguanidad," *El Nuevo Diario* (June 13, 1999): n.p.

28. Personal interview with Silvia Morales, Director Archivo Diocesano de León, León, January 25, 2007.

29. Personal interview with Yolanda Padilla de Jirón, León, January 4, 2007.

30. Jorge Eduardo Arellano. "La primavera de Granada," *La Prensa Literaria* (December 18, 2004): n.p.

31. Edgar Herrera Z. *Construcciones Municipales de Nicaragua en los Períodos Neoclásico y Moderno*. Available at www.manfut.org/masaya/mercado.html-36k.

32. Porfirio García Romano. "Iglesia Morava símbolo de nuestra nicaraguanidad," *El Nuevo Diario* (June 13, 1999): n.p.

33. Auxiliadora Rosales. "Nuestra vivienda indígena," *Revista, La Prensa* (June 27, 2004): n.p.

34. Moisés Castillo Zeas. "Déficit Habitacional es de 500 mil viviendas," *El Nuevo Diario* (July 24, 2001): n.p.

35. Centro Nicaragüense de Derechos Humanos (CENIDH). *Derechos humanos en Nicaragua: informe anual 2003, derecho de propiedad en Nicaragua*. Managua: La Prensa, 2004, pp. 144–152.

36. Equipo Envío. "Vivienda: algunos pequeños grandes pasos," *Revista Envío* 84 (June 1988): n.p.

Appendix: Calendar of Important Religious and Traditional Festivals in Nicaragua

January 6   Feast of the Epiphany in Masaya.

February 8   Virgin of San Marcos in San Marcos, Carazo.

March 16   Feast of the Assumption in Masaya.

Passion Sunday in March   Pilgrimage of St. Lazarus, taking of the costumed dogs to the Magdalena church in Masaya.

April 22   Day of San Jorge in Rivas, which ends with a parade of horses.

April 30   Day of the Cross in Jinotega.

May 1   Festival of Mayo Ya (May Pole) in Bluefields, a fertility festival that lasts for the 31 nights of May.

June 22   The Virgen de Cuapa in Cuapa, Chontales, where the apparition of the Virgin in this place is celebrated.

July 16   Day of the Virgen del Carmen in Estelí and San Juan del Sur, Rivas. In Rivas, the sailors have a procession with the Virgin at sea. This virgin is considered the patron saint of sailors.

July 17   Day of St. Anne in Chinandega.

August 1 and 4   Celebrations to Santo Domingo de Guzmán in Managua.

August 14   Celebration of the Gritería Chiquita in León, a smaller version of the festival of La Purísima that occurs in December.

August 27   Festival of the Crab on Corn Island, Day of Emancipation of the Slaves.

September 24 Celebration of the Virgen de Merced, patron saint of León.

September 30 Fiesta de San Jerónimo in Bluefields, León, Masaya, Bonanza, and Rosita (in the North Atlantic region). In León, the image of the saint emerges from Sutiaba and moves to the Cathedral accompanied by the dances of the Toro Huaco. In Masaya, this is the most colorful of all the patron saint festivals, with dances by negras (black women), diablos (devils), *torovenados,* and *aguisotes.*

October 8 Celebration of the Virgen del Rosario, patron saint of Estelí.[1]

November 4 San Carlos Borromeo in San Carlos, Río San Juan.

November 12–17 San Diego de Alcalá in Altagracia, Island of Ometepe. This is celebrated with the Dance of the Zompopos (leaf-cutting ants), which is an integral part of the folkloric heritage of Rivas.

November 22 Virgen del Hato in Chinandega.

An image of the Virgin de la Dolorosa and the woman who is the Virgin's caretaker in the church in Dolores, a small town in the department of Carazo. © Wilmor López. Used by permission.

A cockfight in the city of Estelí. The people in the crowd grow increasingly animated as they watch the small gladiators and bet more and more money. © Wilmor López. Used by permission.

December 6   Purísima Concepción de El Viejo, Chinandega.

December 7   La Gritería in honor of the Purísima Concepción de María throughout the entire country.

December 8   Immaculate Conception of Mary, procession of the virgin in Masaya.

December 20–24   Festivals throughout the country to celebrate the birth of Jesus, or Niño-Dios (Child-God).

December 31   Celebrations to bid farewell to the old year throughout Nicaragua.

NOTE

1. During the majority of these religious celebrations, while all the women are in church observing the Catholic rituals, most of the men gather in improvised structures for cockfighting, where they wager on the outcome of these *peleas de gallos*.

Bibliography

Agüero, Arnulfo. "El Güegüense: ícono de Nicaragua," *La Prensa Literaria* (December 3, 2005): pp. 1–3.

Anduray Palma, Plutarco. *Algunos ingredientes del folklore nicaragüense.* Chinandega, Nicaragua: Impresos Modernos, n.d.

Arellano, Jorge Eduardo. *La pintura en Nicaragua, antecedentes, desarrollo contemporáneo.* Managua: Banco Central de Nicaragua, n.d.

———. *Historia de la pintura nicaragüense.* Managua: CIRA, 1990.

———. *Entre la tradición y la modernidad: El movimiento nicaragüense de vanguardia.* San José, Costa Rica: Libro Libre, 1995.

———. *Literatura nicaragüense.* Managua: Distribuidora Cultural, 1997.

———. "¿Por qué el béisbol es nuestro deporte rey?" *Lengua* (Revista de la Academia Nicaragüense de la Lengua) 28 (February 2004): pp. 141–144.

———. "Inicios del periodismo en Nicaragua (1830–1884)," *La Prensa* (March, 2004): 10B.

———. "El Güegüense, patrimonio de la humanidad," *Boletín Nicaragüense de Bibliografía y Documentación* 129 (October–December 2005): n.p.

Argüello-Lacayo, José. *Un pobre de Jesús: El poeta de las palabras evangelizadas.* Managua: Hispamer, 2000.

Ayón, Tomás. *Historia de Nicaragua.* Vol. 1. León, Nicaragua: Banco Nicaragüense, 1993.

Barbe, Norbert-Bertrand. "Nueva Catedral," *El Nuevo Diario, Nuevo Amanecer Cultural* (December 23, 2006): n.p.

———. "Arquitectura nicaragüense," *El Nuevo Diario,Nuevo Amanecer Cultural* (March 17, 2007): n.p.

Beverly, John, and Marc Zimmerman, eds. *Literature and Politics in the Central American Revolutions.* Austin: University of Texas Press, 1990.

Blandón, Erick. "El torovenado, lugar para la diferencia en un espacio no letrado," in Marc Zimmerman and Gabriela Baeza Ventura, eds. *Estudios culturales centroamericanos en el nuevo milenio.* Houston: LACASA, 2007, pp. 204–218.

Booth, John A. and Thomas W. Walker, eds. *Understanding Central America.* Boulder: Westview, 1993.

Brentlinger, John. *The Best of What We Are: Reflections on the Nicaraguan Revolution.* Amherst: University of Massachusetts Press, 1995.

Brown, Timothy C. *The Real Contra War: Highlander Peasant Resistance in Nicaragua.* Norman: University of Oklahoma Press, 2001.

Brüssel, Juanita M. *Isnaya: Manual de plantas medicinales para el promotor de medicina preventiva y salud comunitaria.* Estelí, Nicaragua: Fundación Centro Nacional de la Medicina Popular Tradicional, 1998.

Cabestrero, Teófilo. *Ministros de Dios.* Managua: Ministerio de Cultura, 1983.

Castillo-Zeas, Moisés. "Déficit Habitacional es de 500 mil viviendas," *El Nuevo Diario* (July 24, 2001): n.p.

Castro, Vanessa, and Gary Prevost, eds. *The 1990 Elections in Nicaragua and Their Aftermath.* Lanham, MD: Rowman and Littlefield, 1992.

Centeno, Rebecca. "Preguntas pendientes a la descentralización: ¿Está conduciendo hacia la igualdad de género?" *Encuentro* 76 (2007): pp. 67–86.

Centro Nicaragüense de Derechos Humanos (CENIDH). *Derechos humanos en Nicaragua: informe anual 2003, derecho de propiedad en Nicaragua.* Managua: La Prensa, 2004.

Chamorro Cole, Alejandro. *145 años de historia política en Nicaragua.* Managua: n.p., 1967.

Coe, Sophie D. *Las primeras cocinas de América.* Mexico City: Fondo de Cultura Económica, 2004.

Colburn, Forrest D. *Managing the Commanding Heights: Nicaragua's State Enterprises.* Berkeley: University of California Press, 1990.

CONPES. *Acción ciudadana para el próximo quinquenio.* Managua: CONPES, 2007.

Coronel Urtecho, José. *Pol-la d'ananta katanta paranta.* León, Nicaragua: UNAN, 1970.

———. *Elogio de la cocina nicaragüense.* San José, Costa Rica: EDUCA, 1977.

———. *Rápido tránsito (al ritmo de Norteamérica).* Managua: Nueva Nicaragua, 1985.

———. *Prosa reunida.* Managua: Nueva Nicaragua, 1985.

———. *Reflexiones sobre la historia de Nicaragua (de la colonia a la independencia).* Managua: Fundación Vida, 2001.

Cortés, Alfonso. *Antología poética.* Edited by Francisco Arellano Oviedo. Managua: PAVSA, 2004.

Cuadra, Pablo Antonio, ed. *El Güegüense.* Managua: Cuadernos del Taller San Lucas, 1942.

———. "Prólogo," in Joaquín Matilló Vila. *Ometepe: isla de círculos y espirales.* Managua: Centro de Investigaciones Rupestres, 1973.

———. *Ensayos I. (El nicaragüense, América o El tercer hombre, Otro rapto de Europa).* Managua: Fundación Vida, 2003.

———. *Crítica de arte.* Managua: Fundación Uno, 2005.

———. *Seven Trees against the Dying Light.* Translated by Greg Simon and Steven F. White. Evanston, IL: Northwestern University Press, 2007.

Cuadra, Pablo Antonio, and Francisco Pérez Estrada. *Muestrario del folklore nicaragüense.* Managua: Fundación Uno, 2004.

Cuadra Downing, Orlando, ed. *La voz sostenida: antología del pensamiento nicaragüense.* Introduction by Nicasio Urbina. Managua: PAVSA, 2007.

Darío, Rubén. *Selected Poetry and Prose.* Edited and with an introduction by Ilán Stavans, translated by Andrew Hurley, Greg Simon, and Steven F. White. New York: Penguin, 2005.

Dawes, Greg. *Aesthetics and Revolution: Nicaraguan Poetry 1979–1990.* Minneapolis: University of Minnesota Press, 1993.

Dennis, Philip Adams. *The Miskitu People of Awastara.* Austin: University of Texas Press, 2004.

Devés Valdés, Eduardo, and Alfredo Lobato, eds. *Nicaragua: ideas siglo xx.* Managua: UNAN and Academia de Geografía de Historia de Nicaragua, 2005.

Dodson, Michael and Laura Nuzzi O'Shaughnessy. *Nicaragua's Other Revolution: Religious Faith and Political Struggle.* Chapel Hill: University of North Carolina Press, 1990.

Duarte, Vilma. "Vamos a la sopa del cangrejo," in *Almanaque escuela para todos.* Managua: n.p., 2004.

Educación para la conservación de las plantas medicinales. Managua: TRAMIL, 2001.

Enríquez, Laura J. *Agrarian Reform and Class Consciousness in Nicaragua.* Gainesville: University Press of Florida, 1997.

Entre la agresión y la cooperación: la economía nicaragüense y la cooperación externa en el periodo 1979–1989. Managua: Instituto de Investigación, Capacitación y Asesoría Económica (INICAE), n.d.

Equipo Envío. "Vivienda: algunos pequeños grandes pasos," *Revista Envío* 84 (June 1988): n.p.

Espinosa González, Isolda. *Perfil del género de la economía nicaragüense en el nuevo contexto de la apertura comercial.* Managua: UNIFEM, 2004.

Field, Les W. *The Grimace of Macho Ratón: Artisans, Identity and Nation in Late-Twentieth Century Western Nicaragua.* Durham, NC: Duke University Press, 1999.

Flores, Miguel. "Restauración de la Asunción casi lista," *La Prensa* (October 3, 2002): n.p.

Floripe Fajardo, Alejandro. *Plantas que curan.* 3 vols. Estelí, Nicaragua: CECALLI, 2000.

Fonseca C., Enma. *La purísima en Nicaragua* (2nd revised edition). Managua: Impresiones y Troqueles, 2004.

Fowler, William R. Jr. *The Cultural Evolution of Ancient Nahua Civilizations: The Pipil-Nicarao of Central America.* Norman and London: University of Oklahoma Press, 1989.

Frühling, Pierre, Miguel González, and Hans Petter Buvollen. *Etnicidad y nación: El desarrollo de la autonomía de la Costa Atlántica de Nicaragua, 1987–2007.* Guatemala: F&G Editores, 2007.

Fundación DEMUCA. *Estudios sobre la aplicación de políticas públicas de género en los gobiernos de Centroamérica y República Dominicana.* San José, Costa Rica: DEMUCA, 2006.

García-Romano, Porfirio. "Catedral de Santiago: símbolo del S. XX," *El Nuevo Diario* (June 6, 1999): n.p.

———. "Iglesia Morava: símbolo de nuestra nicaraguanidad," *El Nuevo Diario* (June 13, 1999): n.p.

Gobat, Michel. *Confronting the American Dream: Nicaragua under U.S. Imperial Rule.* Durham, NC: Duke University Press, 2005.

Gordon, Edmund Tayloe. *Disporate Diasporas: Identity and Politics in an African Nicaraguan Community.* Austin: University of Texas Press, 1998.

Guerrero, Maryórit. "106 años de historia archivada," *La Prensa* (July 11, 2002): n.p.

Gutman, Roy. *Banana Diplomacy: The Making of American Policy in Nicaragua, 1981–1987.* New York: Simon and Schuster, 1988.

Hale, Charles R. *Resistance and Contradiction: Miskitu Indians and the Nicaraguan State, 1894–1987.* Stanford, CA: Stanford University Press, 1994.

Herrera Z., Edgar. *Construcciones Municipales de Nicaragua en los Períodos Neoclásico y Moderno.* León: Universidad Nacional Autónoma de Nicaragua, n.d.

"Homenaje a la Costa Caribe de Nicaragua," *Anide* 12 (May–August 2006): pp. 5–14.

Huete-Loredo, Ulises. "Masaya: terremotos y reliquias," *La Prensa* (July 6, 2003): n.p.

Hurtado, Isolda. *Diagnóstico del arte contemporáneo en Nicaragua.* Managua: Gráfica Editores, 2002.

Idiáguez, José. *El culto a los ancestros en la cosmovisión religiosa de los Garífunas de Nicaragua.* Managua: Instituto Histórico Centroamericano, 1994.

Incer, Jaime. *Geografía dinámica de Nicaragua.* Managua: Hispamer, 2000.

Incer Barquero, Jaime, ed. *Descubrimiento, conquista y exploración de Nicaragua.* Managua: Fundación VIDA, 2002.

Jones, Adam. *Beyond the Barricades: Nicaragua and the Struggle for the Sandinista Press, 1979–1998.* Athens: Ohio University Center for International Studies, Ohio University Press, 2002.

Lacayo, Sofía. *Patria: Contemporary Nicaraguan Painting.* Durham, NC: Duke University Press, 1995.

Llana, Sara Miller. "Evangelicals Flex Growing Clout in Nicaragua's Election," *Christian Science Monitor* (November 2, 2006): 1, 5.

López, Irene. *Indias, inditas, negras y gitanas: los bailes de marimba en el pacífico nicaragüense.* Managua: Instituto de Historia de Nicaragua y Centroamérica, Universidad Centroamericana, 2007.

Luciak, Ilja A. *The Sandinista Legacy: Lessons from a Political Economy in Transition.* Gainesville: University Press of Florida, 1995.

Kraudy Medina, Pablo. *Historia social de las ideas en Nicaragua: el pensamiento de la conquista.* Managua: Banco Central de Nicaragua, 2001.

Kruckewitt, Joan. The *Death of Ben Linder: The Story of a North American in Nicaragua.* New York: Seven Stories Press, 1999.

Kunzle, David. *The Murals of Revolutionary Nicaragua, 1979–1992.* Berkeley: University of California Press, 1995.

Madariaga, Hilda Rosa. "Más de 600 estudiantes en concierto didáctico," *La Prensa* (Managua) (June 2001): 2C.

Mántica, Carlos. *Introducción al habla nicaragüense.* Managua: Hispamer, 1997.

Martínez, Auxiliadora. "Un tour por la ciudad de dos pisos," *La Prensa* (March 9, 2006): n.p.

Martínez, Carlos, and Oscar Cantarero. "Staccato celebra 9 años," *El Nuevo Diario* (Variedades) (Managua) (October 2001): n.p.

Martínez, M., Luis Eduardo. "La Feria del Maíz." *La Prensa* (Revista) (August 28, 2002): p. 10B.

Martínez Cuenca, Alejandro. *Sandinista Economics in Practice: An Insider's Critical Reflections.* Boston: South End Press, 1992.

Martínez-Orozco, Celso. "Jesuitas Construyeron Parroquia," *La Prensa* (January 9, 2000): n.p.

Méndez, Jennifer Bickham. *From the Revolution to the Maquiladoras: Gender, Labor, and Globalization in Nicaragua.* Durham, NC: Duke University Press, 2005.

Moser, René. *Adorable Nicaragua.* n.p.: Edition del Roisse, n.d.

Navarro-Génie, Marco Aurelio. *Augusto "César" Sandino: Messiah of Light and Truth.* Syracuse, NY: Syracuse University Press, 2002.

Pau-Llosa, Ricardo. "Landscape and Temporality in Central American and Caribbean Painting." http://pau-llosa.com/Gallery/1984Landscapes3.html.

Pérez Estrada, Francisco. *Teatro folklore nicaragüense.* Managua: Nuevos Horizontes, 1946.

Pérez-Ramírez, Oswaldo. *Naturaleza y salud: naturismo centroamericano.* Managua: n.p., 2006.

Pintura contemporánea de Nicaragua. Managua: Unión Nacional de Artistas Plásticos (UNAP), n.d.

Prado, Gustavo A. *Leyendas coloniales.* Managua: Editorial Católica, 1951.

Pravia, Mireya. "Parroquia San Pedro patrimonio cultural," *La Prensa* (October 1, 2005): n.p.

Ramírez Mercado, Sergio. *El Alba de Oro, la historia viva de Nicaragua.* México: Siglo Veintiuno, 1983.

———. "Literatura nicaragüense," in *Enciclopedia de Nicaragua.* Barcelona: Océano, 2002.

Randall, Margaret. *Sandino's Daughters: Testimonies of Nicaraguan Women in Struggle.* Vancouver, BC: New Star Books, 1981.

———. *Sandino's Daughters Revisited: Feminism in Nicaragua.* New Brunswick, NJ: Rutgers University Press, 1994.

Reyes Monterrey, José. *Apuntes básicos para el estudio general de Nicaragua.* León, Nicaragua: UNAN—León, 1989.

Rivas-Sotelo, Adelaida. "*El Güegüense:* hito de la tradición dramática del mestizaje, sones y corridos," *La Prensa* (special supplement) (November 29, 2006).

Rodríguez, Anielka. "Tres décadas y media del teatro Rubén Darío," *El Nuevo Diario* (March 9, 2004): n.p.

Rodríguez Silva, Isidro. "Grupo de Cámara Kinteto: en la formación de instructors nacionales de la APC," *Nuevo Amanecer Cultural* (Managua) (January 2001): 5.

———. "El trabajo teatral de Nixtayolero (entrevista al director Valentín Castillo)," *Nuevo Amanecer Cultural* (June 23, 2001): n.p.

Rosales, Auxiliadora. "Picardía titiresca," *La Prensa* (Revista) (June 14, 2001): 3C.

———. "Nuestra vivienda indígena," *Revista, La Prensa* (June 27, 2004): n.p.

Ryan, Phil. *The Fall and Rise of the Market in Sandinista Nicaragua.* Montreal and Buffalo: McGill-Queen's University Press, 1995.

Saavedra, Mario A. *Compendio nicaragüense de plantas medicinales.* Taipei: Forward Enterprise, 2000.

Sabia, Debra. *Contradiction and Conflict: The Popular Church in Nicaragua.* Tuscaloosa: University of Alabama Press, 1997.

Sacasa, Manuela. *Historia de las iglesias de León.* León: Asociación Amigos del Teatro, 2006.

Salas Estrada, Juan B. *Árboles de Nicaragua.* Managua: IRENA, 1993.

Silva, Fernando. *La lengua de Nicaragua: pequeño diccionario analítico.* Managua: Academia Nicaragüense de la Lengua, 1999.

Solís, Pedro Xavier. *El movimiento de vanguardia de Nicaragua: análisis y antología.* Managua: Fundación Vida, 2001.

Spalding, Rose J. *Capitalists and Revolution in Nicaragua: Opposition and Accommodation, 1979–1993.* Chapel Hill: University of North Carolina Press, 1994.

Stevens, W. D., Carmen Ulloa Ulloa, Amy Pool, and Olga Martha Montiel, eds. *Flora de Nicaragua* (3 volumes). St. Louis: Missouri Botanical Garden Press, 2001.

Tibol, Raquel. "El rigoroso proyecto estético de Alejandro Aróstegui," *La Prensa Literaria* (July 12, 2003): pp. 1–3.

"Un poco de historia de la danza en Nicaragua," *Nuevo Amanecer Cultural* (April 29, 2000): n.p.

Valle-Castillo, Julio, ed. *La Catedral de León de Nicaragua.* Managua: IMPRIMA-TUR, 2001, pp. 17–37.

———. *El siglo de la poesía en Nicaragua.* Managua: PAVSA, 2005.

———. *Artes visuales de Nicaragua en el siglo xx/Nicaraguan Visual Arts in the Twentieth Century.* Managua: BANPRO, 2006.

Vargas, Oscar-René. *Elecciones 2006, la otra Nicaragua posible.* Managua: Centro de Estudios de la Realidad de Nicaragua (CEREN), 2006.

Walker, Thomas W. *Nicaragua: The Land of Sandino.* Boulder, CO: Westview, 1991.

———, ed. *Reagan versus the Sandinistas: The Undeclared War on Nicaragua.* Boulder, CO: Westview, 1987.

———, ed. *Revolution and Counterrevolution in Nicaragua.* Boulder, CO: Westview, 1991.

Whisnant, David E. *Rascally Signs in Sacred Places: The Politics of Culture in Nicaragua.* Chapel Hill and London: University of North Carolina Press, 1995.

White, Steven F., ed. and trans. *Poets of Nicaragua (1918–1979).* Greensboro, NC: Unicorn Press, 1982.

———. *Culture and Politics in Nicaragua: Testimonies of Poets and Writers.* New York: Lumen 1986.

———. *Modern Nicaraguan Poetry: Dialogues with France and the United States.* London/Toronto: Associated University Presses, 1993.

———. *El mundo más que humano en la poesía de Pablo Antonio Cuadra: un estudio ecocrítico.* Managua: Asociación Pablo Antonio Cuadra, 2002.

Zambrana Fonseca, Armando. *El ojo del mestizo, o la herencia cultural.* Managua: PAVSA, 2002.

Zepeda Henríquéz, Eduardo. *Mitología nicaragüense.* Managua: Academia de Geografía e Historia de Nicaragua, 2003.

Zúñiga, Edgar. *Historia eclesiástica de Nicaragua.* Managua: Hispamer, 1996.

Index

About the Authors

STEVEN F. WHITE is Professor of Spanish at St. Lawrence University in Canton, New York. He is a Corresponding Member of the Nicaraguan Academy of the Language.

ESTHELA CALDERÓN is the General Coordinator of the Municipal Theater of the city of León, Nicaragua. She is also the Secretary General of the Nicaraguan Association of Women Writers (ANIDE).

Recent Titles in
Culture and Customs of Latin America and the Caribbean